D1086777

Early Social–Emotional Development

Early Social–Emotional Development

Your Guide to Promoting Children's Positive Behavior

by

Nicole M. Edwards, Ph.D.
Rowan University
Glassboro, New Jersey

·P A U L·H·
BROOKES
PUBLISHING C<u>O</u> ®

Baltimore • London • Sydney

par | teach
+
372.21
Edw
Main

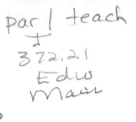

Paul H. Brookes Publishing Co.
Post Office Box 10624
Baltimore, Maryland 21285-0624
USA

www.brookespublishing.com

Copyright © 2018 by Paul H. Brookes Publishing Co., Inc.

"Paul H. Brookes Publishing Co." is a registered trademark of
Paul H. Brookes Publishing Co., Inc.

Typeset by Progressive Publishing Services, York, Pennsylvania.
Manufactured in the United States of America by
Sheridan Books, Inc., Chelsea, Michigan.

Cover image © iStockphoto.com/luckyraccoon.
Clip art © iStockphoto.com.

The individuals described in this book are composites or real people whose situations are masked and are based on the author's experiences. In all instances, names and identifying details have been changed to protect confidentiality.

Purchasers of *Early Social-Emotional Development: Your Guide to Promoting Children's Positive Behavior* are granted permission to download, print, and photocopy the online companion materials provided with this text for educational purposes. These materials may not be reproduced to generate revenue for any program or individual. Photocopies may only be made from an original book. *Unauthorized use beyond this privilege may be prosecutable under federal law.* You will see the copyright protection notice at the bottom of each photocopiable page.

CHILDREN'S DEPARTMENT
Falmouth Public Library
300 Main Street
Falmouth, MA 02540

Library of Congress Cataloging-in-Publication Data

Names: Edwards, Nicole Megan, author.
Title: Early social-emotional development: your guide to promoting children's positive behavior/by Nicole Megan Edwards.
Description: Baltimore, Maryland: Paul H. Brookes Publishing Co., 2018. | Includes bibliographical references and index.
Identifiers: LCCN 2017051004 (print) | LCCN 2018005148 (ebook) | ISBN 9781681252704 (epub) | ISBN 9781681252698 (pdf) | ISBN 9781681251929 (paperback)
Subjects: LCSH: Early childhood education—Psychological aspects. | Child development. | Developmental psychology. | Social interaction in children. | Emotions in children. | BISAC: EDUCATION/Preschool & Kindergarten. | FAMILY & RELATIONSHIPS/Life Stages/ Infants & Toddlers.
Classification: LCC LB1139.23 (ebook) | LCC LB1139.23 .E38 2018 (print) | DDC 372.21—dc23
LC record available at https://lccn.loc.gov/2017051004

British Library Cataloguing in Publication data are available from the British Library.

2022   2021   2020   2019   2018

10   9   8   7   6   5   4   3   2   1

Contents

About the Author

Nicole M. Edwards, Ph.D., Assistant Professor of Special Education, James Hall College of Education, Department of Interdisciplinary and Inclusive Education, Rowan University, Glassboro, NJ 08028

Dr. Nicole Megan Edwards is Assistant Professor of Special Education at Rowan University and previously worked at Georgia State University as Associate Director of a statewide early intervention professional development initiative. She began her career as a center- and home-based early intervention provider in New York City, working with infants and toddlers with special needs and their families. She earned her M.Ed. in early childhood special education from New York University. She earned her Ph.D. in special education from University of Maryland, College Park. She became a faculty member at Rowan University in 2013 and was awarded tenure with promotion to Associate Professor, effective September 2018. Dr. Edwards teaches several courses, including Positive Behavior Support Systems.

Dr. Edwards is a member of the Division for Early Childhood (DEC) and Teacher Education Division (TED) of the Council for Exceptional Children (CEC), the National Association for the Education of Young Children (NAEYC), ZERO TO THREE, and the American Educational Research Association (AERA). She is an annual conference proposal reviewer for DEC and AERA, reviews for *Early Education and Development* and *Journal of Early Intervention,* serves on the editorial board for *TEACHING Exceptional Children,* serves as co-leader of the DEC's Early Intervention Special Interest Group, and disseminates research at professional conferences and in peer-reviewed journals.

Dr. Edwards' research interests include improving access to and quality of early intervention and early childhood/early childhood special education (across birth–5 settings), family–provider collaboration and capacity building, the perceived role of caregivers and providers in early emotional development, and roadblocks to implementing positive behavior interventions and supports. She lives with her husband and two sons in Pennsylvania.

Foreword

I am delighted to offer prefatory and centering remarks about *Early Social-Emotional Development: Your Guide to Promoting Children's Positive Behavior* by Nicole M. Edwards. My long career has focused on the development of young children's emotional competence, so I will situate thoughts and comments within this crucial phenomenon. (For more details, see Denham & Bassett, in press.)

Dr. Edwards' volume is unique in its support of educators and parents—melding concern for young children's emotional development with the positive behavior interventions and supports framework for dealing with sometimes challenging behaviors. Notably, this unique support includes 1) giving clear and numerous examples; 2) supporting readers with reflection questions and online material; and finally—so importantly!—3) showcasing the voices of caregivers, parents, and early childhood educators as they work through these vital issues for the betterment of children. This volume should be on the bookshelf of everyone who cares about and nurtures young children.

It is my task to highlight the critical nature of emotional development and its support by the adults in children's lives. Historically, emotions were long considered mere by-products of more significant cognitive and motor processes. However, in this volume Dr. Edwards disabuses us of this outdated notion, putting emotional development at the forefront of young children's potential strengths and obvious needs while emphasizing how it fits within all domains of development. Thus, emotions are important and are at the center of the system of care that Dr. Edwards proposes.

Preschoolers are learning more than ABCs. They are learning how to express and regulate all their myriad feelings and how to understand their own and others' emotions. They are acquiring *emotional competence*: the ability to express a variety of emotions purposefully and fully, regulate emotional expressiveness and experiences when necessary, and understand the emotions of self and others (Denham, 1998). These skills develop dramatically during early childhood and help preschoolers to succeed at key developmental tasks of this period—engaging positively with their physical and social environment; forming and maintaining relationships with other children and adults; and dealing with emotions in demanding group contexts where they are required to sit still, attend, and follow directions.

These new skills appear just in time, because emotions are ever-present in early childhood classrooms. Learning alongside and in collaboration with teachers and peers, young children can utilize their emotional competencies to facilitate learning. Expressing healthy emotions and regulating them, and understanding the emotions of self and others, are skills that work together to grease the cogs of school success—including children's overall adjustment to the classroom, their learning behaviors, their preacademic outcomes like understanding letters and numbers, and the growth of their later academic competence (Denham, Brown, & Domitrovich, 2010). Children with combined deficits in emotional competence are especially likely to suffer cascading difficulties. They are more often rejected by peers, develop less supportive relationships with teachers, participate in and enjoy school less, achieve at lower levels, and are at risk for later struggles in school.

Thankfully, educators and parents are becoming ever more aware of the importance of emotional competence. For example, when discussing training and technical assistance, Head Start personnel and parents cite emotional-behavioral issues among their top areas of need (e.g., Buscemi, Bennett, Thomas, & Deluca, 1996). Teachers view children's readiness to learn and teachability as marked by positive emotional expressiveness, the ability to regulate emotions and behaviors, and other emotional competence–related social strengths. Emotional competence also is being recognized within educational policy, particularly in state early childhood legislation and emerging national legislation (CASEL, 2016). This book is a vital aid to help these initiatives come alive; Dr. Edwards integrates a system of response to challenging behavior and support for positive behavior, along with considerations of communication, collaboration, and reflection among the adults so important to young children. The integration of classroom techniques and ways adults can cooperate makes this volume special.

Thinking about how adults can promote emotional competence is a key focus of this book. Emotional competence does not develop in a vacuum. In the social world of preschoolers, both parents and teachers/caregivers loom large as socializers, and both are likely to provide children experiences that promote or deter the development of emotional competence. Parents' socialization of emotion—their modeling of genuine, appropriate emotional expressiveness; supportive reactions to children's emotions, and teaching about emotions—contributes much to their children's emotional competence (Denham, Bassett, & Wyatt, 2014; Eisenberg, Cumberland, & Spinrad, 1998). Their generally positive emotional expression (with "safe" expression of negative emotions), encouraging reactions to children's emotions, and openness to and expertise in talking about emotions all help their preschool-age children to become emotionally competent.

Teachers' socialization of emotional competence should also promote social-emotional and even academic success in school. As I've already noted, preschool is rich in emotional experiences; all children, either directly during interaction or indirectly via observation, are experiencing teachers' socialization of emotion. Teachers' vital contribution to children's emotional competence may differ from parents' because they spend less time with children and attend to groups of children in an instructive role. Even so, teachers are key players in preschoolers' emotional development (Denham, Bassett, & Zinsser, 2012).

We know that many early childhood teachers are already intuitively aware of the importance of their own emotions, as well as children's, to learning and well-being, and they closely attend to these issues in the classroom. The ways teachers deal with their own emotional lives—perceiving and understanding the emotions of self and others, using emotions to facilitate cognition and action, and managing them—undoubtedly contribute to their socialization of emotion. Nonetheless, preservice teachers report little training on developing students' emotional competence or managing their own internal feelings and external displays of emotion (Buettner, Hur, Jeon, & Andrews, 2016); relatively few schools of education are prepared to train teachers on these matters (Marlow & Inman, 2002). Encouraging research is, however, emerging to suggest that emotional competence concepts can be successfully infused in an undergraduate course on curriculum and instruction.

To promote emotional competence, for example, teacher training could focus on helping teachers to be willing to show emotions, remain emotionally positive in the classroom despite challenges, and modulate understandable negative emotions. Furthermore, it could focus on ways of helping teachers value their supportive role concerning children's emotions and give them specific strategies to use in reacting to children's more difficult emotions, as well as showing them how to use emotion talk most advantageously. All of these concerns point to the value of a volume like this one, which mentions *all* of these possible areas for teacher development—particularly with the strengths of supporting material and the breadth of topics explored. Dr. Edwards has crafted a well-researched, theoretically supported, *practical* guidebook to encourage, advocate for, and foster young children's emotional development by giving adults the tools to be effective socializers of emotion.

Susanne Denham, Ph.D.
University Professor Emerita
Department of Psychology
George Mason University
Editor, Early Education and Development

REFERENCES

Buettner, C. K., Hur, E. H., Jeon, L., & Andrews, D. W. (2016). What are we teaching the teachers? Child development curricula in US higher education. *Child and Youth Care Forum, 45*, 155–175.

Buscemi, L., Bennett, T., Thomas, D., & Deluca, D. A. (1996). Head Start: Challenges and training needs. *Journal of Early Intervention, 20*, 1–13. doi:10.1177/105381519602000101

Collaborative for Academic and Social-Emotional Learning (CASEL). (2016). *Federal policy.* Retrieved from http://www.casel.org/federal-policy-and-legislation

Denham, S. A. (1998). *Emotional development in young children.* New York, NY: Guilford Press.

Denham, S. A., & Bassett, H. H. (in press). Implications of preschoolers emotional competence in the classroom. In K. Keefer, D. Saklofske, & J. Parker (Eds.), *The handbook of emotional intelligence in education.* New York, NY: Springer.

Denham, S. A., Bassett, H. H., & Wyatt, T. (2014). The socialization of emotional competence. In J. E. Grusec & P. D. Hastings (Eds.), *Handbook of socialization: Theory and research* (2nd ed.; pp. 590–613). New York, NY: Guilford Press.

Denham, S. A., Bassett, H. H., & Zinsser, K. (2012). Early childhood teachers as socializers of young children's emotional competence. *Early Childhood Education Journal, 40,* 137–143. doi:10.1007/s10643-012-0504-2

Denham, S. A., Brown, C. A., & Domitrovich, C. E. (2010). "Plays nice with others": Social-emotional learning and academic success. *Early Education and Development, 21,* 652–680. doi:10.108 0/10409289.2010.497450

Eisenberg, N., Cumberland, A., & Spinrad, T. L. (1998). Parental socialization of emotion. *Psychological Inquiry, 9,* 241–273.

Marlow, L., & Inman, D. (2002, November). *Prosocial literacy? Are educators being prepared to teach social and emotional competence?* Paper presented at the Annual Meeting of the National Council of Teachers of English, Atlanta, GA.

Preface

Thank you for your interest in this book! This is intended to be an informative, practical, evidence-based resource for those who are employed in an early childhood or early childhood special education setting (ECE/ECSE; ages birth–5) as teachers, therapists, or administrators; for preservice students or faculty members in an ECE/ECSE program; and for anyone who is passionate about better understanding and promoting adaptive behavior and meaningful family–provider partnerships to support early social-emotional development.

It is widely acknowledged that there is pervasive concern with children's challenging displays of emotions and behavior across home- and center-based settings. Early childhood practitioners, including child care workers and early intervention service providers, vary in their level of comfort in addressing these concerns and in the resources available to them, which may influence their willingness to broach this topic or explore intervention options with families. This book provides a timely and substantive narrative to enable home- and center-based professionals to reflect deeply on the role of providers in supporting emerging social-emotional growth in the first 5 years of life. Readers will enhance their awareness of, and appreciation for, contributing roles among key players; broaden their repertoire for a sampling of recommended strategies to use before, during, and/or after challenging emotional displays and behaviors; and feel more confident in discussing recommendations with others to provide a stronger foundation for every child.

A note about language: Throughout this book, the term *challenging* is used to describe emotional displays and behaviors that are not the most effective ways of managing one's own emotions or interacting with others. In other words, "challenging" behaviors contrast with the healthy, adaptive behaviors and responses that educators aim to foster in young children. They are the behaviors some educators (or families) might label as "problem" or "difficult" behaviors or "acting out." This book uses the term "challenging" to describe these behaviors in a way that does not judge or label the child. When a child exhibits one of these behaviors—for example, screaming because he is upset, or pulling another child's hair because that child took a toy away from her—the *teacher* is challenged to help the child learn a more adaptive way of coping with the situation. It is not the child who is challenging (or a problem or difficult). It is the behavior.

No matter what term you use, however, parents or other caregivers might respond defensively if they think their child is being labeled. Be sensitive to this possibility. It is wise to make sure you stay in regular contact with the families of all children in your care, forging a positive relationship right from the beginning. Having this strong relationship in place early on will help ensure that if you do communicate with parents about their child's challenging behavior, they will be receptive to your concerns and will understand that you are not judging them or their child. Work to establish good, ongoing communication with parents, and when challenging behaviors need to be discussed, focus on the challenging *behavior*, not on labeling the child. This will help ensure that parents and other caregivers are your partners in teaching their child adaptive social-emotional behaviors.

SPECIFIC FEATURES

The following are specific features to be aware of as you read this book:

- Its focus on ways in which adults contribute to early social-emotional development and adaptive behavior across birth–5 settings (home based and center based)
- Its emphasis on shared accountability, including collaboration between providers and families
- Its usefulness as a resource to provide a range of evidence-based strategies, broken down into practical, generalizable examples and descriptions for widespread application
- Its user-friendly, evidence-based narrative, related in a conversational tone using nontechnical jargon
- Its embedded opportunities for meaningful reflection (e.g., real-world vignettes, guiding questions, sample forms, and authentic quotes)
- Online companion materials for each chapter; the Online Resources sections direct the reader to additional resources to learn more about the topics discussed

The following vignettes are included to illustrate concepts and strategies discussed.

Chapter 1

- Not Seeing Mommy Behind the Curtain: Understanding Infant Development

Chapter 2

- Special Treat: Team Consistency Yields Results
- Handling Frustration at Playtime: Emotion Coaching in Action
- Saying Good-Bye (Part 1): Anticipating Challenging Situations
- Saying Good-Bye (Part 2): Validating and Addressing Children's Emotions
- Learning to Like the Sand Table: Building on a Child's Strengths

Chapter 3

- You Have Given Me a New Child: The Importance of Positive, Proactive Approaches
- She's Not Making Progress: The Importance of Patience

Chapter 4

- Wanting a New Song on the Radio (Part 1): A Teaching Opportunity
- Wanting a New Song on the Radio (Part 2): Using Redirection
- Posting an Emotion Chart at Eye Level: Helping Children Express Emotion Nonverbally

Chapter 5

- Why Is He Drawing All Over the Table? The Value of Peer Coaching
- Varying Part C Early Intervention Service Models: Effects on Team Communication
- Two Ways to Respond: How Disposition and Training Affect Responses

Chapter 6
- Sharing Concerns via E-mail: The Importance of Communicating Concerns Promptly
- Seeing Is Believing: Learning to Embrace Setting Limits

Chapter 7
- Mommy Should Have Stayed Calm: Supporting Mindful Parenting
- The Other Teacher Ignores His Crying: Addressing Differences in Interaction Style
- A Supervisor Lends a Helping Hand: Supporting Providers

WHY DO I WANT TO WORK WITH YOUNG CHILDREN AND THEIR FAMILIES?

Have you ever felt like you were part of something much larger than yourself? Think about people who are drawn to early childhood education or early childhood special education. Maybe they have always enjoyed working with children and/or helping others. Perhaps they strive to have the biggest possible impact, not only on a developing child but on the entire family unit, or it is possible they began working in this field years ago and have not yet figured out if this is truly a career or merely a job. Discovering one's niche may unfold through a wide array of hands-on opportunities.

I majored in psychology with a certification in elementary education, and completed undergraduate and graduate coursework in early childhood special education. I was also influenced by numerous hands-on volunteer experiences, including those in a pediatric oncology unit, an adult hospice, and a group home for those with profound intellectual disability. Such opportunities, in addition to serving as a home- and center-based early intervention provider in New York City, heightened my awareness of contextual factors that influence development and reinforced my passion for empowering others. At the same time, I noted a frustrating disconnect between what was discussed in lecture and what I observed in the field. I grew increasingly concerned by teaching practices within early childhood settings that did not seem to consistently reflect evidence-based recommendations on the importance of shared accountability in emerging emotional development. Similar to others, I sought inspiration from those professors and mentors who not only shared content but also specific ways in which theory and ideals informed actual real-life scenarios. I value authenticity and meaningful application of content and have written this book through multiple lenses.

- *Caregiver:* I am a proud mother to two incredible boys, both of whom were in their first 5 years of life and enrolled in birth–5 center-based settings when much of this text was written. My husband and I embrace and use the recommendations noted in this book. Real-life examples and direct quotes from my family are embedded in this text.
- *Provider:* I enjoyed working as an urban early intervention special education teacher in New York City (center- and home-based settings). Multiple vignettes are incorporated based on authentic experiences with families, children, and providers.
- *Supervisor:* I was an associate project director on a statewide initiative in Georgia providing ongoing professional development to early intervention providers and service coordinators. I have also supervised early childhood special education teacher candidates in field placements in Maryland and New Jersey.

- *Researcher:* I publish research findings in peer-reviewed journals. My research interests include family–provider collaboration and empowerment (birth–5), shared role in emotional development and earlier referrals for young children with special needs, and obstacles to implementing positive behavior interventions and supports. Via focus groups, observation, expert reviewed surveys, and preexisting measures, I enjoy collecting and analyzing data from diverse key players, including primary caregivers, preservice teacher candidates, and early childhood/early intervention providers and administrators.

- *College professor:* I have taught multiple courses, including the following: Methods for Teaching Infants and Toddlers With Disabilities, Early Childhood Special Education Blended Field Seminar, Human Exceptionality, and Positive Behavior Support Systems for Students With Exceptional Learning Needs. I also learn from and share research findings with families, service providers, administrators, teacher educators, and researchers at professional conferences.

Acknowledgments

To my parents, Amy and Len; family members; and friends: Thank you for your love and support.

To the many inspiring mentors I have had during my academic training and in the field: Thank you for sharing your knowledge and fueling my passion to investigate and improve the quality of service delivery across birth–5 settings.

To birth–5 professionals I have had the privilege to meet as students, workshop attendees, study participants, and key players in my sons' early education: Thank you for all that you do to support young children and their families. I hope this serves as a valuable resource!

*Dedicated with love and gratitude to my husband, Adam,
and our sons, Jacob and Sean*

I

Overview

Early Social–Emotional Development and Intervention

1

The Impact of Early Social-Emotional Development

For early childhood educators and service providers to understand young children's behavior, and to provide appropriate intervention when needed, it is crucial first to understand not only their emotional development, but also their progress across other domains. Chapter 1 will provide an overview of early growth and learning across developmental domains from birth–5, with particular emphasis on the components of emotional development in young children with and without special needs. As you read, you'll come to understand how emotional development fits into the larger picture of growth across domains.

Emotional development is associated with adaptive or challenging behavior as well as a child's social and academic outcomes and family outcomes. All of these aspects of a child's life are interrelated. Understanding and articulating the links among them, and the links among different developmental domains, will help you be more effective in supporting young children's emerging emotional development.

DEVELOPMENTAL DOMAINS IN EARLY CHILDHOOD

For those who work in the fields of early childhood education or early childhood special education, it is essential to recognize and be able to comfortably discuss and support various *developmental domains*—that is, areas in which young children learn and develop. Particularly in the first 5 years of life, there is exciting and remarkable growth across multiple domains (Harms, Clifford, & Cryer, 2014; Kim, 2011; Phillips & Shonkoff, 2000), including the following:

- *Fine motor skills:* Using one's hands and/or pincer grasp (thumb and pointer finger) to engage in activities such as picking up a crayon, holding a toy, or pushing a button

- *Gross motor skills:* Using one's arms and/or legs to engage in activities such as crawling, standing, running, or throwing a ball

- *Expressive language skills:* Verbally communicating needs, wants, feelings, or information such as "Daddy, up!" "I see brother," or "Can I have more milk please?"

- *Receptive language skills:* Responding to others' one-step or multistep requests to do such things as picking up a toy, holding someone's hand, or helping with getting dressed

- *Cognitive development:* Engaging in activities that demonstrate an emerging ability to problem-solve, remember, or manipulate increasingly complex toys or objects; examples may include identifying a cause–effect relationship, matching or classifying objects by one or more attribute, or making predictions about what will happen to a character in a story

- *Adaptive development:* Activities of daily living (ADLs), or ADL skills; this term refers to one's emerging ability to complete everyday tasks like putting on a coat, combing one's hair, or brushing one's teeth

- *Social-emotional development:* One's emerging ability to effectively label, express, and regulate emotions, and to interact meaningfully with others by engaging in activities such as sharing, taking turns, delaying gratification, and smoothly making transitions between tasks.

As noted in available research literature about development in early childhood, it is important to remember that "[s]kills are not traits set in stone at birth and determined solely by genes. They can be fostered. Cognitive and noncognitive skills change with age and with instruction. Interventions to improve skills are effective to different degrees for different skills at different ages" (Kautz, Heckman, Diris, Ter Weel, & Borghans, 2014, p. 2).

The Role of Play in Early Development

In early childhood, development in each domain is fostered by play. Scholars have long acknowledged play as one important vehicle for understanding and supporting early child development (Eisert & Lamorey, 1996; Lifter, Mason, & Barton, 2011). As an example, think about which developmental areas or domains are involved when children play with blocks, as depicted in Figure 1.1. This activity potentially requires both fine motor skills, such as the ability to manipulate and stack blocks of varying size and shape, and gross motor skills, such as the ability to stand or bear weight while playing, walk across a row of blocks like a balance beam, or perhaps toss blocks into a nearby

Figure 1.1. Children playing with blocks. Think about which developmental domains are potentially involved when a child engages in this activity.

container. Depending on the specific type of play, it might also call upon the child's cognitive skills—for example, organizing different towers by block color or shape, counting the number of blocks in each tower, and problem solving. Moreover, during play, the child is likely to communicate with others. An educator examining the child's development in the language domain would consider not only the child's expressive language skills—the string of sounds, utterances, or words the child uses; sentences like "Me block" or "Look, I do it myself!"—but also his or her receptive language skills. Receptive language encompasses skills such as the ability to follow a one-step direction, such as "Take this block" or comply with a two-step direction, such as "Can you pick up that block and put it on the table?" In addition, the activity might call upon the child's adaptive skills—that is, skills involved in completing ADLs. For instance, following the teacher's lead to clean up at the end of the activity is an adaptive skill; so is the ability to complete everyday tasks that are part of the classroom routine, such as hanging up one's coat, using the bathroom, and washing one's hands.

Lastly, observing block play provides an educator with a great snapshot of the domain which is the primary focus of this book: the child's social-emotional skills. For example, when playtime begins, the teacher might look at any of the following:

- The child's ability to calmly make the transition to playing with blocks when playing begins, and, later, to cleaning up the blocks when playtime is over
- The child's willingness to share/take turns with others
- The child's emotional response when a tower falls or when waiting for a desired block

You might have already noticed a certain degree of overlap across developmental domains. For example, refer to Figure 1.2 and consider how a child demonstrates cognitive, receptive language, and social-emotional skills (in response to your request and toward a peer) when calmly following a request to share a specific type of block, the light-colored triangle block, with a peer named Amy. The child uses receptive language skills to understand what you are asking him or her to do. The child uses cognitive skills to identify the block that has two specific properties (light color, triangular shape) and to distinguish it from other blocks that have a different color or shape. Finally, the child uses social-emotional skills to complete the request.

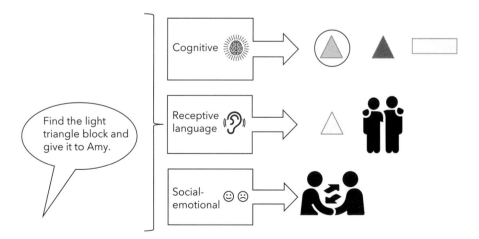

Figure 1.2. One verbal request may involve a child demonstrating skills across multiple developmental domains.

For example, patience and persistence might be needed to find the block and find Amy. If the child wants the light-colored block for him- or herself, giving it to another child instead also involves social-emotional skills, such as delaying gratification and sharing.

Developmental Milestones Within Each Domain

In reading the previous example, you might already have formed some ideas of how a typical child might manage transitions, sharing with others, and so forth, depending on his or her age. In the field of early childhood education, performance expectations for each age group—infants, toddlers, preschoolers, and children in prekindergarten and kindergarten—are influenced by what researchers, pediatricians, program administrators, and practitioners know about typical *developmental milestones*. That is, there tends to be a time during which most children of a particular age are expected to master or gain proficiency in certain skills across domains. For instance, think about when children typically begin to 1) smile and visually fixate on faces, 2) sit up independently, 3) crawl, 4) show hesitation around strangers, 5) bang two objects together, 6) point to show someone what they want, 7) run, 8) say two- to four-word sentences, 9) follow directions with two or three steps, 10) understand "same" and "different," or 11) tell the difference between real and make-believe. Table 1.1 summarizes a sampling of milestones within each developmental domain. (For more information, see the resources listed in the online companion materials for this chapter.)

As you read the following vignette about 6-month-old Nathanial, consider what you know about cognitive development in infants. Think about what might explain Nathanial's emotional response to the situation described.

Table 1.1. Sampling of typical milestones across developmental domains

	6 months	2 years	4 years
Fine motor	Transfers objects from one hand to the other	Copies straight lines and circles	Uses scissors
Gross motor	Begins sitting without support	Begins running	Begins to stand on one foot
Expressive language	Makes sounds to show emotions	Uses two- to four-word sentences	Enjoys telling stories
Receptive language	Responds to own name	Points to pictures when they are named	Follows three-part commands
Cognitive	Explores by putting things in mouth	Begins sorting by shape and color	Understands the difference between "same" and "different"
Adaptive	Begins to hold bottle independently	Follows directions to put away familiar items	Can pour and mash
Social-emotional	Knows familiar faces	Shows defiance by doing what he or she is told not to do	Prefers playing with others rather than alone

Not Seeing Mommy Behind the Curtain: Understanding Infant Development

Emily has just finished feeding, burping, and changing her 6-month-old baby boy, Nathanial. She wraps him in a soft blanket and places him securely in one of his favorite places, a rocker that allows him to gently bounce as he wiggles and listens to lullaby music. Emily says, "Hi, sweet boy. Mommy loves you!" and smiles at him as she gets ready for her shower and turns on the water. She hopes to quickly take a shower before he starts to cry. Showers used to be a calm place to recharge, but Emily now finds them to be a source of heightened stress. As anticipated, as soon as Emily closes the shower curtain, Nathanial begins to scream. Emily tries singing to Nathanial as she lathers and washes her hair, but his screams grow louder. When the soap is washed off her face, Emily pulls back the curtain to assure Nathanial she is still there. Nathanial instantly stops crying and smiles in his rocker. Emily closes the curtain to continue her shower, but Nathanial resumes screaming. Once again, he settles down when the curtain is opened. Emily feels harried as she quickly finishes showering with the curtain half open.

Some readers may have had a similar experience with a young child. In this vignette, Emily felt a bit stressed, but she was not alarmed, because she had taken time to review helpful web sites on child development. She understood that babies do not typically establish object permanence until nearly 9 months of age. At 6 months, baby Nathanial actually thinks Mommy is no longer there when she is hidden by the shower curtain. Screaming at him to stop crying or ignoring his cries would *not* have helped Nathanial's emotional development. Notice how his mother's sensitivity to where he was developmentally aided both mother and baby in this situation. Being reassured that his trusted caregiver was still there greatly helped Nathanial, and Emily could be comforted by the fact that this phase would likely only last a few more months. (For more detailed information on developmental milestones in various domains, see Gerber, Wilks, & Erdie-Lalena, 2010, for motor milestones; see Hoff, 2006, or the Communication Matrix web site at https://communicationmatrix.org/ for language milestones; see Wilks, Gerber, & Erdie-Lalena, 2010, for cognitive milestones; see Denham, Wyatt, Bassett, Echeverria, & Knox, 2009, or Saami, 1999, for social-emotional milestones.)

The Wide Range of Developmental Variability

Educators should be familiar with the typical progression of skills and developmental milestones to establish realistic baseline expectations for what is likely to occur at different ages. At the same time, individual differences in strengths, needs, and experiences must be considered. Rather than having a one-size-fits-all approach to working with and supporting children and families, skilled providers are aware that, within the range of what is considered developmentally typical, there is a great deal of variability. For example, if you search on various web sites that provide information about early language development, you will see that the typical age for babies to say their first true word can range from 10 to 14 months, with more than 75% of children saying their first word before the age of 12 months (Schneider, Yurovsky, & Frank, 2015). As noted by Neitzel (2011, p. 25),

Many young children will focus on mastering one particular skill before moving on to others. For example, an infant might spend much of his time learning how to crawl and have little interest in babbling. Another child, on the other hand, might be more interested in learning how to talk. Typically developing children will quickly catch up in the areas they have neglected once they have mastered a particular skill of interest; however, children who experience true developmental delays will continue to experience difficulties.

Skilled providers show enhanced sensitivity to this wide variability by *tailoring* their approach and information-sharing on children's emerging development whenever possible.

Furthermore, a child's chronological age may not necessarily neatly align with the same child's developmental age across domains (Frank & Esbensen, 2015). Suppose Billy is chronologically 18 months old. Billy may be at the level of a typical 18 month old in motor skills (age-appropriate), but at the level of a typical 12 month old in expressive language and social-emotional skills (below age level). Educators may also work with a child who is developing in the same overall progression as typically developing peers but at a slower pace across all developmental domains (Berglund, Eriksson, & Johansson, 2001). Other children may display *splinter skills,* meaning they skip over some skills within an expected progression of developmental milestones (e.g., going from sitting to walking, without ever crawling). As noted by Gomez Paloma, D'Anna, and Agrillo (2013, p. 1),

> [Instead of] the stereotyped idea of fixed phases [it is] important to underline that apart from the neurological development of the child, there can also be psycho-motor, mechanical and environmental factors, for example their previous experiences, motivations, external stimulations and various other aspects that can change from person to person.

No matter what type of educational setting you work in, be prepared to encounter a wide range of developmental variation. Educators in center-based, inclusive settings will likely work with children with and without delays or disabilities, and those who are at risk for being diagnosed with disabilities. Educators and therapists in home-based settings can share advice with families on how siblings or playmates with and without disabilities can successfully and meaningfully engage in the same activities in the natural environment with the right accommodations. Even in a self-contained setting, where all students have diagnosed special needs, there will be notable variation in children's strengths, interests, temperament, experiences, and level of functioning across domains.

Recommended Practices for
Supporting Development Across Domains

Although the remainder of this book focuses on understanding roles in supporting the emotional development of young children with and without disabilities, other sources (e.g., Barton & Smith, 2015; Salazar, 2012; Sandall & Schwartz, 2008; Turnbull, Turnbull, Wehmeyer, & Shogren, 2013; Wood, 2015) focus on inclusive practices and ways to meaningfully embed service plan goals into naturally occurring routines and activities. One such source is the Division for Early Childhood's (DEC's) 2014 document on evidence-based recommended practices for all learners.

DEC Recommended Practices   The publication *DEC Recommended Practices in Early Intervention/Early Childhood Special Education* (2014) addresses eight areas: leadership, assessment, environment, family, instruction, interaction, teaming and collaboration, and transition. The following subsections explore each practice area.

Leadership   The DEC notes that "Leaders have a professional responsibility to use all the mechanisms within their control to create the conditions needed to support practitioners . . ." (p. 6). For example, the third recommended practice in this area (L3) is that "Leaders develop and implement policies, structures, and practices that promote shared decision making with practitioners and families" (p. 6).

Assessment   The DEC defines *assessment* as "[T]he process of gathering information to make decisions" (p. 8). Regarding assessment, one DEC Recommended Practice (A2) is that "Practitioners work as a team with the family and other professionals to gather assessment information" (p. 8).

Environment   The DEC explains that "Environmental practices refer to aspects of the space, materials (toys, books, etc.), equipment, routines, and activities that practitioners and families can intentionally alter to support each child's learning across developmental domains" (p. 9). For example, the fourth recommended practice pertaining to environment (E4) is that "Practitioners work with families and other adults to identify each child's needs for assistive technology to promote access to and participation in learning experiences" (p. 9).

Family   The DEC describes goals in the family area as

> Ongoing activities that (1) promote the active participation of families in decision-making related to their child (e.g., assessment, planning, intervention); (2) lead to the development of a service plan (e.g., a set of goals for the family and child and the services and supports to achieve those goals); or (3) support families in achieving the goals they hold for their child and the other family members" (p. 10).

For example, the fifth DEC Recommended Practice in the family area (F5) is that "Practitioners support family functioning, promote family confidence and competence, and strengthen family-child relationships by acting in ways that recognize and build on family strengths and capacities" (p. 10).

Instruction   The DEC defines *instructional practices* as "intentional and systematic strategies to inform what to teach, when to teach, how to evaluate the effects of teaching, and how to support and evaluate the quality of instructional practices implemented by others" (p. 12). For example, the fifth recommended instructional practice (INS5) is that "Practitioners embed instruction within and across routines, activities, and environments to provide contextually relevant learning opportunities" (p. 12).

Interaction   The DEC notes that "Sensitive and responsive interactional practices are the foundation for promoting the development of a child's language and cognitive and emotional competence" (p. 14). For example, the first recommended instructional practice (INT1) is that "Practitioners promote the child's social-emotional development by observing, interpreting, and responding contingently to the range of the child's emotional expressions" (p. 14).

Teaming and Collaboration   The DEC explains that "Teaming and collaboration practices are those that promote and sustain collaborative adult partnerships, relationships, and ongoing interactions to ensure that programs and services achieve desired child and family outcomes and goals" (p. 15). For example, the second Teaming and Collaboration DEC Recommended Practice (TC2) is that "Practitioners and families work together as a team to systematically and regularly exchange expertise, knowledge, and information to build team capacity and jointly solve problems, plan, and implement interventions" (p. 15).

Transition   *Transition* is defined by the DEC as "the events, activities, and processes associated with key changes between environments or programs during the early childhood years and the practices that support the adjustment of the child and family to the new setting" (p. 16). For example, the second recommended practice for transition (TR2) is that "Practitioners use a variety of planned and timely strategies with the child and family before, during, and after the transition to support successful adjustment and positive outcomes for both the child and family" (p. 16).

Other Applications Related to Recommended Practices   The DEC Recommended Practices document is available through the DEC web site (see the related entry in this book's reference list for details). You may wish to consult that publication for additional examples and ideas related to any previously discussed specific area. Readers are also strongly encouraged to visit the DEC web site and review the video explanations provided for each practice. A link to these explanations is provided in the Chapter 1 online companion materials.

As previously noted, the eight practices described by the DEC (2014) are applicable to all learners in early childhood settings. In addition, universal design for learning (UDL) supports diverse learners by providing multiple ways for children to represent, express, and engage in learning. One DEC Recommended Practice (E2) refers directly to UDL: "Practitioners consider Universal Design for Learning Principles to create accessible environments" (p. 9). The DEC Recommended Practices document highlights specific examples relevant to young children, such as ensuring sufficient space for children to access all areas and activities and meaningfully embedding learning opportunities across all settings in the child's daily routine (e.g., classroom, playground, dinner and bath time at home). A number of useful articles also address UDL in early education (e.g., see Stockall, Dennis, & Miller, 2012).

Finally, it is important to keep in mind, consistently, the wide range of variability in young children's development within different domains—not only in working directly with children, but also in your interactions with and recommendations for families. For specific recommendations, see the Collaborating With Families discussion in this chapter about fostering development across domains.

Collaborating With Families: Fostering Development Across Domains

For children not meeting typical developmental milestones, educators must avoid being too quick to label or to assume a diagnosis for a child. Instead, educators play a critical role in:

- Helping fellow providers and family members collect and reflect on objective, detailed information about which strategies are working/not working across settings to support the child, and gaining clarity as to specific concerns during certain times or parts of the day, and the frequency/duration of concerns.

- Encouraging the family to follow up with a developmental pediatrician or developmental neurologist (both of whom have an advanced specialization in development). For example, educators might say something like, "We have noticed concerns with [domain or area of development] during [these times of the day]. For example, [objectively describe a specific situation, what the child did, and how the provider responded]. I think sharing these concerns with a doctor could be very helpful."

- Connecting the family with relevant and timely educational resources. This may include giving families of children under the age of 3 information on the state Part C Early Intervention (EI) referral number so that a free developmental assessment can take place and to see if the child may be eligible for services. (Note that the Early Childhood Technical Assistance Center web site at http://www.ectacenter. org/contact/ptccoord.asp lists the Part C EI coordinators in each state.) Or, if the child is over age 3, this may include sharing contact information for the local district referral number for preschool special education.

- Linking the family with broader supports, such as local or national parent-to-parent support networks, sib shops to support and provide fun activities for the sibling of a brother or sister with a disability, respite or planned/emergency care for a child or adult with disabilities, local play groups, or online information to learn more about a particular disability (Edwards, 2012; Hanson, Lynch, & Poulsen, 2013; Turnbull, Turnbull, Erwin, Soodak, & Shogren, 2015).

To enhance your understanding of early screening, see also the supplemental exercise at the end of this chapter.

EARLY SOCIAL-EMOTIONAL DEVELOPMENT: AN OVERVIEW

Early childhood is a critical period in social-emotional development. As noted in the research literature, "The early years of life present a unique opportunity to lay the foundation for healthy development [with] [r]esearch on early childhood [underscoring] the impact of the first five years of a child's life on his/her social-emotional development" (Cooper, Masi, & Vick, 2009, p. 3). We will begin by focusing primarily on the emotional aspects of social-emotional development.

When discussing *emotions* in early childhood, what comes to mind? Some readers may think of a child's various feelings, such as feeling happy, sad, tired, or angry. Others may envision certain times during the day when a child may react negatively or positively to various situations—for example, crying, or feeling sad, when someone knocks down a block tower; smiling, or feeling happy, when the child gets to play with his pet at the end of the day. Sometimes, as in situations like these, it might be easy to anticipate what a typically developing child will feel. Other times, however, as Figure 1.3 demonstrates, what a child is likely to feel may be less clear. One child might be excited to arrive at school in the morning; another might be grumpy; still another might be anxious—and, of course, the same child might have a different emotional response on different days.

External behaviors, including expressive communication, may indicate what emotions a child is experiencing. Consider the photos in Figure 1.4 of the young boy in his high chair at mealtime. What emotions seem to be displayed by this child? Look closely at his nonverbal cues and body language. Ask yourself, "What do I think he is trying to say?" That is, imagine if you could put words to what you are seeing.

His crying and banging on the tray in the first photo may suggest feelings of anger or frustration that he had to wait for his food (e.g., "I don't like to wait! I want

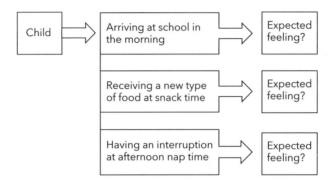

Figure 1.3. Each child may feel differently about, and react differently to, a range of predictable routines and unexpected situations.

my food!"). At the same time, even though he does not yet have the ability to express himself using multiword sentences, his visibly calmer expression and body language in the second photo suggest he felt happy once his food arrived (e.g., "I love getting my food! I am so relieved!").

A Complex, Interconnected Emotional System

It is important for educators to recognize and appreciate that emotions are more than just simply feeling happy, sad, tired, and so on. *Emotion* is a term (or construct) that represents something that is quite complex and multifaceted. There is even some debate in the literature about its definition (Russell, 2012). As noted by Izard (2013, pp. 3–4), "emotions constitute the primary motivational system for human beings" and so the definition of emotion must account for the following:

- The conscious feeling of emotion
- Processes that take place in the brain or nervous system
- The observable, expressive pattern of emotion, particularly in the face

It can also be helpful for educators to view emotions as *processes* that help generate, sustain, or interrupt the connection between a person and his or her environment (Campos, Campos, & Barrett, 1989). In fact, there is an interconnected emotional

Figure 1.4. Ask yourself, "What do I think this child is trying to say in both photos?"

system in our brains that is constantly changing, with *feelings* (i.e., the inner mental states of emotion) helping to monitor and influence these changes (Hoeksma, Oosterlaan, & Schipper, 2004). As explained by Cummings, Davies, and Campbell (2002), there is a *continuous reorganization* of emotional competencies. As the child gains preliminary skills across domains, this promotes evolving adaptation to environmental stimuli, which in turn sets the stage for mastering new skills. Given that earlier skill attainment informs later development, "an early disturbance in functioning may ultimately cause much larger disturbances to appear later on" (Stein, Leventhal, & Trabasso, 2013, p. 363). Better understanding changes in brain development may help explain why emotions appear so variable during childhood (Goldsmith & Davidson, 2004). The "continuous reorganization" of emotional competencies is influenced by ongoing growth across the earlier mentioned domains. In the first 2 years of life, young children exhibit fundamental or *primary emotions* (characterized in part by universal facial expressions). Emerging in the first year of life (at or shortly after birth through 12 months of age), these primary emotions include fear, joy, anger, sadness, disgust, and surprise (Lewis & Michalson, 1983; Lewis, Sullivan, Stranger, & Weiss, 1989).

When children are between 3 and 9 months old, they typically undergo a distinct shift in response to their own emotions, going from automatic/reflexive patterns (e.g., sucking their finger) to more intentional and voluntary responses (Cummings et al., 2002; Goldsmith & Davidson, 2004). The child's developing motor, cognitive, and visual abilities contribute to this shift. Growth across domains, for example, enables a child to turn his or her head away from something upsetting or toward something calming, reach or grasp for a soothing toy or person, distinguish facial features, and make sense of simple emotions expressed by others (Dunsmore & Karn, 2001).

Young children then become more goal-directed in navigating social contexts. This is in part due to growth in motor skills and development of the frontal lobes of the brain (e.g., becoming increasingly able to move away and/or redirect attention from adverse stimuli). Children begin to more readily check in with caregivers, a process called *social referencing*, when faced with new situations or people. According to Campos, Sorce, Emde, and Svejda (2013, p. 57), social referencing refers to "the active search by a person for emotional information from another person, and the subsequent use of that emotion to help appraise an uncertain situation." This goal-directed ability may also include devising plans to get adult support and using play/exploration to divert attention, or look away, from negative stimuli. As children make these advances in cognition and develop greater awareness of their social world (including social rules/scripts), they commonly begin to exhibit *secondary emotions*—usually toward the middle of the second year of life. These secondary emotions include embarrassment, empathy, and envy, followed by pride, shame, and guilt (Lewis & Michalson, 1983; Lewis, Sullivan, Stranger, & Weiss, 1989). (See also the Encyclopedia on Early Child Development article "Emotions: Synthesis" available at http://www.child-encyclopedia.com/emotions/synthesis.)

In the older preschool years, children continue to grow in self-awareness and in their emerging understanding of which things in the environment may trigger stress. A child gradually builds his or her repertoire for ways to cope or respond to stressors. A wide repertoire of coping behaviors supports healthy emotional development, whereas a limited repertoire may be less helpful. For example, suppose a child masters the option of looking away when faced with something stressful. Consider various situations in which this is not likely to be useful or effective. Rather than rely on one approach, children may likely experience long-term success if they are explicitly taught, and subsequently able to select from, an array of constructive strategies to use at different times, depending on the demands of the situation (Gilliom, Shaw, Beck, Schonberg, & Lukon, 2002). Teachers and families should help guide and reinforce use of a range of techniques at appropriate times. These techniques may include the following:

- Redirecting attention by focusing on a toy
- Redirecting attention by looking away (averting eye contact)
- Trying to remove the source of stress
- Walking to another part of the room
- Seeking comfort from a trusted caregiver (a technique possibly used less often by older children)

Emerging Competencies in Social-Emotional Development

You probably noticed earlier that social development and emotional development are merged as a single domain: social-emotional development. To understand development in this domain, it is necessary to examine both aspects closely: emotional competence and affective social competence.

Emotional Competence   *Emotional competence* falls under the larger umbrella of social-emotional development (Dunsmore & Karn, 2001). It can be broken down further into three components: emotion knowledge, emotion expression, and emotion regulation (Denham et al., 2003). Examples of each of these are depicted in Figure 1.5.

Emotion knowledge involves an emerging ability to infer or identify basic emotions from facial expressions or situations, use proper emotion language, and learn to identify others' emotions that may differ from one's own in the same situation (e.g., feeling happy versus upset when going fast on a swing). *Emotion expression* refers to ways in which children display their emotions behaviorally. This includes showing appropriate *affect,* or emotional response, during social interactions (e.g., not smiling

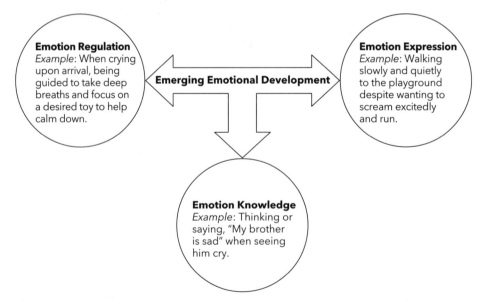

Figure 1.5.   Three components of emerging emotional development.

when a friend gets hurt on the playground), or holding back (suppressing) or activating expression of positive or negative emotion depending on the situation (e.g., Dennis & Hajcak, 2009). *Emotion regulation* has to do with children's emerging ability to self-soothe and control or inhibit impulses.

Affective Social Competence Readers may have already suspected or noticed from their own practice that the components of emotional development described may overlap during certain situations or events—and that they overlap with a child's development of social skills. Social competence and emotional competence are closely related; both involve awareness of *affect* or emotional state in oneself and others. These abilities can be termed *affective social competence*. Building on a model for affective social competence (Denham, 2006; Halberstadt, Denham, & Dunsmore, 2001), children must:

- Learn to be attuned to their own and other people's affect or emotions
- Make sense of ever-changing social situations or contexts
- Show emerging competences in managing and regulating emotions

It is helpful for early childhood providers to remember that there is continuous growth in the three components of emotional development, and social situations provide rich opportunities to teach and improve existing skills. Consider how emotional and social competence are intertwined in the following scenario.

Suppose Kyle is upset with his prekindergarten teacher for removing the box of crayons from the table before he is finished with his drawing. What would be a negative way for Kyle to respond? What would be a more positive way for Kyle to respond? If Kyle expresses his negative emotions by yelling and/or throwing himself on the ground, this will not be well-received by his teacher. Instead, gaining *emotion regulation* skills can help realign his emotion system along a more favorable path (Hoeksma et al., 2004). That is, when Kyle gains these skills, his emotion system is able to change its course to help him feel less angry and to avoid experiencing a negative consequence for yelling or throwing himself on the ground. Emerging growth within his emotion system can help him make a more appropriate choice by using words, a picture cue, or another means of communication to calmly let the teacher know he was not finished with his drawing and to ask for more crayons. Chapters 2, 3, and 4 will highlight specific ways in which teachers and caregivers contribute to this early growth and learning.

Think about a young child you have known (e.g., on your caseload, in your classroom, or from a more personal connection in your family or neighborhood). Can this child:

- Self-soothe?
- Understand/label different emotions experienced by the child and others?
- Redirect attention away from something he or she finds upsetting?
- Resist the urge to jump up and down excitedly in the middle of a quiet activity (e.g., storytime) when hearing exciting news?
- Transition or switch between activities or parts of the home/school routine with minor reluctance?
- Calmly manage personal disappointment?
- Not show lengthy, excessive positive or negative emotions that lead to negative behavior or inappropriate social interactions?

These abilities are all part of learning emotion regulation (Chang, Schwartz, Dodge, & McBride-Chang, 2003; Contrerras, Kerns, Weimer, Gentzler, & Tomich, 2000; Fitzgerald, McKelvey, Schiffmen, & Montañez, 2006).

The child you were considering may not yet be able to do some or all of these tasks. If a typically developing preschool child is not able to do what is described in the bulleted list most of the time, this child *may* be experiencing some degree of emotion dysregulation (Cole, Michel, & Teti, 1994). Specific strategies to provide tailored supports for children experiencing emotion dysregulation are outlined in subsequent chapters.

Embracing and Accounting for Individual Variation

Developmental changes in how children talk about, express, and regulate emotions have to do in part with changes in the brain. This is true both in terms of general developmental changes children undergo—for example, prefrontal cortex not fully developing until later in development for all children—and changes an individual child undergoes, such as expressing oneself or responding in different ways to the same situation or context (Goldsmith & Davidson, 2004). Some of the variation in children's emotional responses and development can be accounted for by differences in gender, by the presence or absence of different kinds of disabilities, and by differences in executive functioning.

Gender Differences Based on common stereotypes about boys and girls, and/or personal, anecdotal examples of some boys and girls, readers may suspect that boys tend to display more externalizing emotions (e.g., anger) and girls tend to exhibit more internalizing emotions (e.g., sadness, anxiety). A meta-analysis of 166 studies (Chaplin & Aldao, 2013) suggested these and other significant but *notably small* gender differences in male and female children's emotional expression. These authors also emphasized variation in gender differences as a result of age (e.g., toddler/preschool age, middle childhood, adolescence) and context (e.g., with parents, with an unfamiliar adult, with peers, or alone). More specifically, they found more pronounced gender differences in displaying positive emotions as children get older (e.g., increasingly more positive emotions among girls). Interestingly, boys may exhibit greater externalizing emotions in early and middle childhood (compared to girls), but fewer externalizing emotions than girls in adolescence. It is important to keep in mind how such differences may be influenced by ways in which male and female children are socialized (e.g., sociocultural expectations) (Brody, 1985; McClure, 2000). For example, in a study of 60 4 to 6 year olds, fathers attended more to preschool daughters' submissive emotion (compared to sons') and responded more to early school age sons' disharmonious emotion (compared to daughters') (Chaplin, Cole, & Zahn-Waxler, 2005). At the same time, children may show less evidence of gender differences when they are with their parents, with more pronounced differences in positive emotions when they are with unfamiliar adults and in externalizing emotions when they are interacting with peers (Chaplin & Aldao, 2013).

Potential Differences Arising From Disabilities The presence or absence of certain kinds of disabilities can also affect emotional expression. For example, infants with visual impairment have been found to display a more limited range of facial expressions and less responsiveness compared to typically developing infants (Troster & Brambring, 1992). Young children (ages 2.5–5 years) with hearing impairment, even when receiving a cochlear implant, were shown by Wiefferink and colleagues (2013) to score lower on verbal and nonverbal measures of emotion understanding, compared with typically developing children. Furthermore, high-functioning individuals with autism spectrum disorder (ASD) may vary in their sensitivity to and production of emotional expressions compared to others (Macdonald et al., 1989). Similarly, a laboratory study compared reactions of three groups of children (i.e., children with ASD, intellectual disability, and those without disabilities) to varying emotions displayed by adults. Findings indicated that, compared with the other groups, children with ASD paid less attention to adults' emotional responses and were more engaged in toy play when adults pretended to be hurt (Sigman, Kasari, Kwon, & Yirmiya, 1992). Moreover, compared with children with hearing impairment, those who have both hearing impairment and ASD may demonstrate delays in emotion recognition during sign language processing (Denmark, Atkinson, Campbell, & Swettenham, 2014).

There is emerging research on treatments to enhance social interaction across individuals with disabilities. For example, a medical trial with only seven treated participants (including adolescents and young adults with ASD) suggested improvement in emotion recognition (e.g., while looking at faces clearly displaying strong emotions) when participants were given a certain medication over a 10-month period to activate brain regions involved in social and emotional perception (see Hadjikhani et al., 2015). Chapters 3 and 4 will present evidence-based educational and developmental strategies, and suggestions early childhood educational staff can use to support emotional development in young children. (For a comprehensive discussion of how emotional development is affected across a wide range of disabilities, see Lewis & Sullivan, 2014.)

Differences in Executive Functioning

Differences in executive functioning (an aspect of cognitive development) can also affect emotional expression. Executive functioning in early childhood comprises several emerging, teachable skills. This aspect of development is increasingly receiving attention in the research literature (Schore, 2015; Ursache, Blair, Stifter, & Voegtline, 2013). It includes four specific areas:

- Focus (staying engaged in the task at hand)
- Working memory (remembering specific rules and directions during the task)
- Cognitive flexibility (adjusting to ever-changing demands or contexts)
- Inhibitory control (resisting the desire to behave in a way that may not be appropriate in that particular setting)

These skills help a child keep track of information, avoid distractions, and adjust to changing situations. Variation in executive functioning may help account for some differences in emotion regulation or expression across same-age peers (Hoeksma et al., 2004). For example, if a child is not yet proficient in remembering specific directions (executive functioning), the child may have difficulty adjusting to a change in the scheduled routine and/or resisting temptation to act silly during a listening/quiet activity (emotional regulation and expression).

Other Factors Affecting Differences in Emotional Expression

Finally, several additional factors may help account for differences in emotional development and expression. For instance, innate, biological considerations such as genetic factors or the child's temperament contribute to some variability in emotional development. Temperament, for example, comprises multiple components, including emotional intensity, activity level, frustration tolerance, reaction to new people, and reaction to change. As Keogh (2003) explained, "thinking in temperament terms does not excuse a child's unacceptable behavior, but does provide direction for responding to it." Researchers suggest a noteworthy interconnection between emotion reactivity and emotion regulation in infants, and early executive functioning (Ursache et al., 2013). More specifically, in a large low-income, rural sample, Ursache and colleagues found that children with high levels of emotional reactivity and poor emotion regulation had difficulties with executive function. In contrast, children with high levels of emotional reactivity and high levels of emotion regulation had high levels of executive function. Interestingly, participating infants with high emotional reactivity and high emotion regulation were more likely to have caregivers who displayed positive, supportive interactions when observed one-on-one with their child. (We'll talk more about what these positive interactions may include in subsequent chapters.)

As stated earlier, it is important for educators to track variability in where children are developmentally and generate tailored plans for next steps in social-emotional growth. This information can then become an informative baseline, or starting point, from which to improve each child's foundation of emotional competencies. Chapters 2–4 will provide a more in-depth discussion of teachers' role and specific strategies teachers can use.

Emotions and Behavior

Practitioners may find it difficult or nearly impossible to look solely at emotions without also thinking about the child's behavior. Certain concerning behaviors might be described by terms such as *negative, problematic, challenging, inappropriate,* or *maladaptive*. For consistency, the term *challenging* will be used throughout this book to refer to behaviors that are cause for concern. (Elaboration on a word of caution when using this term can be found in this book's Preface.) *Adaptive* will be used to refer to those behaviors that are associated with positive social and emotional outcomes, and that educators can foster in children to best support early emotional development.

Leading scholars view challenging behavior in early childhood as a "serious impediment to social-emotional development" (Dunlap et al., 2006). Estimates suggest 10%–20% of preschoolers display challenging behavior (National Scientific Council on the Developing Child, 2008; Powell, Fixsen, & Dunlap, 2003), with some estimates as high as 25% of young children (Raver & Knitzer, 2002). Challenging behavior can be *internalizing* (e.g., social withdrawal, extreme shyness) and/or *externalizing* (e.g., physical aggression, defiance) (Edwards, 2012), and oftentimes, the two co-occur (Bayer, Hiscock, Ukoumunne, Price, & Wake, 2008). See Table 1.2 for additional examples of both types of challenging behaviors.

Table 1.2. Challenging internalizing and externalizing behaviors

Challenging, internalizing behaviors	Challenging, externalizing behaviors
Sliding under table to avoid answering the teacher or therapist during snack	Screaming, "No!" in response to the teacher or therapist's request during snack
Crying when not being chosen to be line leader	Knocking over a chair when not chosen to be line leader
Going to the opposite side of the room to avoid sand play with peers	Pushing peers and throwing sand toys during small-group sand play

Challenging behaviors that are prolonged, or exhibited for several weeks or months, may suggest an existing limitation in the ability to regulate emotions (Spinrad et al., 2007). Such behaviors are often detectable in the early years in both home- and center-based contexts. Some readers might ask, "Won't concerning behaviors just go away on their own because the children are so young?" Unfortunately, the literature suggests this is not typically the case. Challenging behaviors that persist into the preschool years are likely to *continue through adulthood* in the absence of intervention (Alink et al., 2006; Kimonis et al., 2006).

EARLY SOCIAL-EMOTIONAL DEVELOPMENT AND LATER OUTCOMES

Throughout this chapter, the focus has been on emerging emotional competencies in the first 5 years of life. Indeed, individuals do not become proficient or fully capable in certain emotional skills until late adolescence or adulthood (Zimmermann & Iwanski, 2014). Some readers may initially question the extent to which it matters whether young children display basic emotional skills and early adaptive behavior. Does emotional competence in the early years really matter in the long run?

The short answer is, yes! Early emotional development is of critical importance. As noted previously, if children who exhibit challenging behaviors do not receive appropriate interventions, these behaviors persist. Moreover, emotion dysregulation and challenging behaviors have been associated with negative short- and long-term social and academic outcomes for children (Benedict, Horner, & Squires, 2007; Denham, 2006; Peth-Pierce, 2000; Smith, Lochman, & Daunic, 2005). These impact a child's life at school and, later, in the broader community, as well as impacting family life at home.

Social and Academic Outcomes at School

Readers have likely heard of the concept of *school readiness,* which influences social and academic success. Being "ready" for school is influenced by one's emotion knowledge, emotion self-regulation, social competence, and family/school involvement (Denham, Bassett, Brown, Way, & Steed, 2015; Webster-Stratton, Reid, & Stoolmiller, 2008). Readers may not be surprised that a child's emotional expression and regulation can influence teachers' perceptions of school readiness (Denham, 2006) and reported school adjustment (Herndon, Bailey, Shewark, Denham, & Bassett, 2013; Wilson, Fernandes-Ruchards, Aarskog, Osborn, & Capetillo, 2007). Expressiveness, regulation, and emotion knowledge predict preliteracy performance (alphabet knowledge and print and phonological awareness) when controlling for gender, age, maternal education, and attentional abilities (Curby, Brown, Bassett, & Denham, 2015). Social competence and school success are also linked (Raver & Knitzer, 2002).

Thus, developing emotional competence is an essential developmental task in the early childhood years with notable implications for academic and social development (Rodriguez et al., 2005). As noted by Wagner and Davis (2006, p. 227), children with concerning behavior coupled with limited social skills may:

- Demand teachers' attention
- Interfere with instruction
- Experience strained social relationships
- Negatively impact the learning environment for all students

Furthermore, for children who display emotional and behavior concerns, the national expulsion rate is alarmingly high. More specifically, children are expelled from preschool at a rate 3.2 times higher than the *combined* rate for all students in kindergarten through twelfth grade, with higher rates for older preschoolers and African Americans, and with boys being 4.5 times more likely to be expelled than girls (Gilliam, 2005). To address the high expulsion rate, some researchers have investigated a promising state-specific initiative to increase the number of early childhood mental health consultants and improve providers' use of evidence-based practices to address and minimize challenging behavior (Vinh, Strain, Davidon, & Smith, 2016).

A child's early emotional and social competence and tendency toward adaptive or challenging behavior have long-term significance throughout the school years and beyond. There is a connection between emerging emotional competence during early development and long-term growth during middle and late childhood (Izard, Trentacosta, King, & Mostow, 2004). Early behavior concerns have been linked to poor school performance and grade retention (Denham, 2006), and aggressiveness has been shown to account for a large proportion of special education referrals (Smith, Lochman, & Daunic, 2005).

Family Outcomes

In addition to resulting in adverse child outcomes, emotion dysregulation can negatively influence the family unit. Negative long-term outcomes are certainly not the case for every child and family experiencing challenging behavior on the child's part. Outcomes depend on various considerations, such as the presence or absence of a significant disability, the duration and severity of the child's behavior, additional stressors in the family's life, and the quality of existing systems of support. With this in mind, research has suggested that brothers and sisters of children with developmental concerns may possibly feel resentful when restrictions are placed on family activities, embarrassed by certain behaviors, or upset that they may receive less parental attention (Gray, 2002; Howlin, 1988). At the same time, siblings of children with developmental concerns might have higher levels of social competence, with negative outcomes depending on other risk factors in the home (Macks & Reeve, 2007). Furthermore, parents of children with challenging behavior may experience diminished confidence in childrearing abilities, depression, feelings of isolation and stigmatization, increased caregiver stress, marital discord (negative interactions with their spouse), and/or poor family–provider communication (Dadds, Sanders, Behrens, & James, 1987; Levac, McCay, Merka, & Reddon-D'Arcy, 2008; Shaw, Connell, Dishion, Wilson, & Gardner, 2009; Webster-Stratton, 2015).

Long-Term Child Outcomes and Their Broader Impact

For young children with and without special needs, emotional competence over time influences the quality of interactions with others (Wilson et al., 2007). Moreover, long-term child outcomes ultimately have an impact upon the broader community. A study that tracked children from early childhood to late adolescence suggested that "among children with early externalizing behavior problems, increased risk for later antisocial behavior or mood dysfunction may be identifiable in early childhood based on levels of overt aggression and emotion dysregulation" (Okado & Bierman, 2015, p. 735). Adolescents with emotional and behavioral disorders (EBD) experience one of the highest rates of school dropout of any disability category (Cullinan & Sabornie, 2004). Furthermore, kindergarten social competence has been linked to negative young adult outcomes beyond education, affecting employment, criminal activity, substance abuse, and mental health (Jones, Greenberg, & Crowley, 2015).

The association with long-term outcomes may be even more enduring for those with more severe challenging behavior and those exposed to numerous risk factors (Benedict, Horner, & Squires, 2007). There may also be greater concern for those with special needs because cognitive and/or language delays may coincide with emotional and behavioral difficulties (Nungesser & Watkins, 2005).

Mental health needs of young children and adults, including issues that arise from emotion dysregulation, have resulted in widespread public health concerns (Bayer et al., 2008). There remains a shortage of mental health professionals; pervasive stigma about having a mental disorder; and a need for earlier, more proactive interventions (Patel, Flisher, Hetrick, & McGorry, 2007). As noted by the World Health Organization (2001, p. xiii), "Sectors other than health, such as education, labour, welfare, and law, and nongovernmental organizations should be involved in improving the mental health of communities."

The Role of Early Childhood Educators and Service Providers

It may seem daunting to consider the potential long-term impact of emotional dysregulation and challenging behaviors upon children, their families, and their communities. Rather than having a grim outlook, however, it is important for educators and service providers to recognize the great potential for what we can do to help young children and families. Coaching others and explicitly teaching skills in a meaningful, supportive, and developmentally appropriate manner will help promote more adaptive behavioral displays of emotion and contribute to positive developmental outcomes.

Building on this chapter's overview of early emotional development, subsequent chapters will empower readers to appreciate their pivotal role in collaborating with all families to facilitate a strong foundation for adaptive emotions and behavior in the first 5 years of life.

QUESTIONS FOR REFLECTION

1. Review the developmental domains introduced at the beginning of this chapter. Can you think of another skill emerging in early childhood that might fit within each domain? List at least one skill or activity that exemplifies learning in each domain. Then, add an example of a skill or activity that is an example of overlap across domains.

2. Suppose you work with a child who is not meeting some of the typical developmental milestones. What are some ways you can approach this?

3. List three things you can do to address the needs of those with and without disabilities in your classroom.

4. Review the term *continuous reorganization*. What does this term mean to you? Do you see this as positive or negative? Think of the emotional competencies you have today, compared to what you recall having when you were a teenager.

5. What problems might emerge if a child is only taught one way to respond to frustration? Can that child successfully cope with adversity? Why or why not?

6. Recall that this chapter discussed three components of emotional development. Read the behaviors described in the following bulleted list. Which component of emotional development does each represent? Would you classify each behavior as adaptive or challenging? Why?

    •   A child calmly counts "1 . . . 2 . . . 3 . . . 4 . . . 5" and says, "I'm ready to make nice," when asked to "calm his body" after pushing another child.

    •   A child runs over and knocks down blocks when told he cannot go outside.

    •   A child tells you, "I am making a picture for Sam because he looks sad."

7. Have you noticed differences in emotional responses among children with and without disabilities? What specifically have you observed (or what would you anticipate) to be different?

8. Think about a child you know who engages in challenging behavior. How are the child's parents and siblings affected by his or her emotions and behavior? What are this family's strengths? What concerns or needs do family members have related to their child's behavior?

SUPPLEMENTAL EXERCISE:
DEEPENING UNDERSTANDING OF DEVELOPMENTAL MILESTONES

Review Table 1.1's list of developmental milestones in early childhood. You may also wish to view an online developmental milestone checklist, such as the one provided by the Centers for Disease Control and Prevention (available in English, Spanish, and Vietnamese; go to the Checklists section of https://www.cdc.gov/ncbddd/actearly/ freematerials.html) or the one provided by the Child Development Institute (http:// childdevelopmentinfo.com/child-development/normaldevelopment).

Next, choose two age groups (e.g., 2-year-olds and 4-year-olds). Use the information provided in this chapter, along with the information in any supplemental resources you consult, to compare the two. For the first age group, identify one example of where most children are expected to be within *each* of the listed domains (e.g., "In the Cognitive domain, this age group should be able to _____."). Do the same thing for the other selected age group, across each of the listed domains (e.g., "In the Cognitive domain, this age group should be able to _____."). What noteworthy differences did you find? What insights can you gather through this comparison?

ONLINE RESOURCES

See the online companion materials for Chapter 1, available at www.brookes publishing.com/edwards/materials to learn more about the following topics:

•   Disabilities: Emotional Responses and Screening

•   Executive Function

•   Expulsion

•   Developmental Milestones

•   Recommended Practices

•   Temperament

•   Universal Design for Learning

2

Environmental
Influences and the Educator's Role

As part of your work with young children, you will want to be prepared to proactively support social-emotional development as well as address and minimize challenging emotions and behavior. Be aware that, in addition to innate or inborn factors, such as temperament and executive functioning, environmental factors can greatly influence social-emotional development (Fitzgerald, McKelvey, Schiffman, & Montañez, 2006; Hastings et al., 2008). Therefore, it is important to be able to pinpoint environmental considerations, including negative risk factors and the role different key players have in a child's early social-emotional development. Thorough preparation involves learning to recognize early learning standards on proactively addressing challenging emotions and behavior. Chapter 2 will explore these topics in depth, focusing on how providers' increased knowledge and continual reflection can improve child outcomes, provider–family collaboration, and self-efficacy. Clarity on these topics can improve your sense of self-efficacy as an educator, your ability to collaborate, and, ultimately, child outcomes for the children with whom you work.

CHILDREN'S NATURAL ENVIRONMENTS:
GUIDING THEORIES AND POTENTIAL RISK FACTORS

What are some typical, everyday settings in which a young child may interact with others, play, and spend quality time? Readers might think of a child's home, child care, the local grocery store, the community playground, or even the zoo. Do any other places come to mind? Such locations are commonly part of many children's *natural environments*; natural environments include places where all children, with and without disabilities, participate in the ordinary activities of daily life.

Consider, for a moment, the wealth of teachable moments afforded to children within such locales to practice emerging skills across each of the developmental domains discussed in Chapter 1: gross and fine motor skills, receptive and expressive language, cognitive development, adaptive development, and social-emotional development. In fact, there are clear, positive benefits to practitioners using everyday activities within these environments as sources of learning opportunities. For example,

Select a common activity within each of these four environments (e.g., meal time in the home setting, circle time in the child care setting), and identify at least one thing a child can learn across each area of development:

- Gross motor skills
- Fine motor skills
- Expressive language
- Receptive language
- Cognition
- Adaptive development/self-help (activities of daily living)
- Social-emotional development

Figure 2.1.   Sampling of everyday natural environments in which a child lives and learns.

when a child visits the local grocery store, he or she may meaningfully use expressive language to ask that a desired item be purchased, such as the child's favorite cereal. Review Figure 2.1, which is informed by literature on the importance of working with children and families in familiar settings in which they live (e.g., Dunst, Bruder, Trivette, & Hamby, 2006). Consider other opportunities for development afforded by each of the natural environments shown.

Guiding Theory: Bronfenbrenner's Bioecological Systems Theory

When highlighting the importance of environmental influences on child development, it is useful to consider not only what research suggests, but also theoretical frameworks that inform or guide our thinking. Such frameworks acknowledge an underlying way of looking at or understanding various events, ideas, or phenomena.

Suppose you are at a restaurant and see two brothers at a nearby table, both under the age of 6, pushing and yelling at each other. An adult woman sitting with them, reading her menu, does not react or respond to their behavior. In this case, what might be your theoretical lens? That is, what thoughts come to mind about why the behavior episode is happening? If you were a practitioner working with this family, what are a few questions you would want to ask?

Even if you do not know the name of any particular theory to apply to this scenario, the questions you would be inclined to ask about it—or ask in response to behavior episodes that arise in your work environment—can reveal a lot about the lens through which you view emotions and behavior. For example, were you more concerned about what happened right before the pushing, or were you more curious about family dynamics and modeling in other settings, or did you perhaps wonder about both? Although discussing a wide array of diverse, insightful theories (e.g., behavioral, social learning, psychodynamic, biological, developmental) is beyond the scope of this book, interested readers are encouraged to explore a sampling of behavior-related theoretical frameworks through the links provided in the online companion materials for this chapter. (See also Ayers, Clarke, & Murray, 2015 for a practical guide to multiple perspectives on behavior.)

Certainly, there are strengths and valuable insights associated with each framework. None is "more correct" than any other. If we are committed to understanding the lens through which we each view behavior, we can more readily reach common ground with diverse key adults in a child's life—especially as we seek to partner with these adults. For example, if Teacher Amira is strongly aligned with Skinner's behaviorist approach and Teacher Brianna highly values Vygotsky's social learning theory, they might be prone to seeing a behavior episode—such as a child throwing blocks—in a different way. That is, Teacher Amira may be more concerned with what happened before and/or after the behavior episode (e.g., cause–effect). Teacher Brianna, on the other hand, may focus more attention on whether the child is learning to throw things when frustrated by imitating what a family member may do at home, another child in the classroom, or even something observed on TV.

When looking at where educators fit within the larger context of the child's life, it can be especially helpful to consider Bronfenbrenner's (2001) *bioecological systems theory* (an extension of his original framework, known as *ecological systems theory*). This theory suggests there are multiple levels of direct and indirect influence on a developing child. An example of a direct influence might be a teacher helping a child learn the alphabet song and recognize letters in his or her name. An indirect influence might be a company policy restricting additional paid leave for a primary caregiver to be with a sick child. This theory acknowledges reciprocal, bidirectional relationships between children and key players in the *microsystem,* or immediate natural environment (Bronfenbrenner & Morris, 2006). Examples might include the relationships depicted in Figure 2.2.

What each individual says or does may influence the other in a positive and/or negative manner. If an adult is driving in a car with a screaming infant, for example, imagine how challenging it can be to stay calm.

Bronfenbrenner's theory identifies five layers of environmental influence:

1. The *microsystem,* defined as "a place where people can readily engage in face-to-face interaction" (Bronfenbrenner, 1979, p. 22). Family interactions are part of this system.

2. The *mesosystem,* defined as "the interrelations among two or more settings in which the developing person actively participates" (Bronfenbrenner, 1979, p. 25). Caregiver–provider interactions are part of this system.

3. The *exosystem,* defined as "one or more settings that do not involve the developing person as an active participant, but in which events occur that affect, or are affected by, what happens in the setting containing the developing person" (Bronfenbrenner, 1979, p. 25). The sick leave policy at the caregiver's job is an example of an exosystem factor that influences a child's environment.

Figure 2.2. Typical relationships within a child's microsystem.

4. The *macrosystem,* defined as "consistencies, in the form and content of lower-order systems that exist, or could exist, at the level of subculture or culture as a whole, along with any belief systems or ideology underlying such consistencies" (Bronfenbrenner, 1979, p. 26). For example, the macrosystem encompasses societal views on early intervention, mental health, and/or disability.

5. The *chronosystem,* defined as "the influence on the person's development of changes (and continuities) over time in the environments in which the person is living" (Bronfenbrenner, 1986, p. 724). For instance, the chronosystem includes transitions such as a family relocating across states or changing from home-based to center-based service delivery.

See Neal & Neal, 2013, for an interesting alternative to the nested model that considers a more overlapping, networked view of these systems.

Other theorists agree that children develop within social systems (Lewis & Feiring, 1981; Ramsden & Hubbard, 2002). It is important to consider how the quality of interactions *across systems* or environments, in what Bronfenbrenner terms the *mesosystem,* can positively or negatively influence the child and family unit. Figure 2.3 depicts examples of possible interactions at this level.

Environmental Considerations: Risk Factors

Caregivers and providers may not fully realize their role in emerging emotional development and the link between emotions, behavior, and social and academic outcomes (Graziano, Reavis, Keane, & Calkins, 2007). Before discussing positive, practical ways in which adults can meaningfully provide emotional socialization, let's first acknowledge confounding or multiple risk factors in the environment that may negatively influence a developing child.

Child Abuse and Neglect   Have you ever worked with a young child who experienced neglect or abuse? Perhaps you or someone you know suspected that a child was experiencing this and has made a mandatory report; perhaps you have worked with a child whose history includes substantiated neglect or abuse. Abuse may be physical, sexual, and/or emotional. (See the online companion materials for this chapter for a link to more information.) Sadly, abuse is highly prevalent among young children. More than four children die daily as a result of child abuse, and nearly 70% of such children are under the age of 4 (ChildHelp, 2015; Dingwall, Eekelaar, & Murray, 2014).

Experiencing abuse and/or neglect can significantly affect a child's social-emotional development. There are many potential adverse effects, with outcomes

Figure 2.3.   Typical relationships within a child's mesosystem.

likely dependent on numerous considerations. Available research literature (e.g., Dube & Rishi, 2017; Folger et al., 2017; Iwaniec, Larkin, & Higgins, 2006; Kendall-Tackett, Williams, & Finkelhor, 1993) suggests a range of possible factors, such as the type of abuse, its timing, its severity, and its duration, as well as the supports available to the child and family.

Physical abuse, for example, has been associated with strained, negative peer interactions (Salzinger, Feldman, Hammer, & Rosario, 1993). Furthermore, as explained by Shackman and Pollak (2014, p. 1021), "physical maltreatment leads to inappropriate regulation of both negative affect and aggression, which likely place maltreated children at increased risk for the development and maintenance of externalizing behavior disorders."

Emotional abuse, particularly in early development, can permanently affect a child's brain, with negative consequences in terms of social, behavioral, and cognitive development (Campbell & Hibbard, 2014). More specifically, symptoms may include later social withdrawal, lower academic achievement, and defiance (Erickson & Egeland, 2002). It is important for readers to keep in mind that even a handful of incidences of verbal abuse per year can harm a developing child (English, Thompson, White, & Wilson, 2015).

Outcomes following sexual abuse may include posttraumatic stress disorder, challenging behaviors, sexualized behaviors, and lower self-esteem; however, "no one symptom characterizes a majority of sexually abused children. Some symptoms are specific to certain ages, and approximately one-third of victims have no symptoms" (Kendall-Tackett, Williams, & Finkelhor, 1993, p. 164). In a retrospective review of 501 children (ages 8–17 years), researchers looked at possible symptoms such as difficulty with school, weight, sleep, sadness, and self-harm; 83% of the children had at least one trauma symptom, with outcomes influenced by the child's age and by the severity of the abuse (Melville, Kellogg, Perez, & Lukefahr, 2014). Early occurrence of child neglect can negatively affect cognitive and social-emotional development, with the child experiencing more difficulty academically, fewer peer interactions, and more internalizing behavior problems (Hildyard & Wolfe, 2002). Adults' inconsistent use of sensitive, responsive care when interacting with a young child (or the lack of such care) negatively impacts the developing brain (Garner et al., 2012). It may contribute to deficits in cognition, executive functioning, and the body's stress response.

Finally, bear in mind that substantiated abuse or neglect may result in a child's being removed from the family home, temporarily or permanently, and being placed in foster care. Youth in foster care are at risk for poor developmental outcomes, challenging behavior, and increased mental health problems (Harden, 2004; Harman, Childs, & Kelleher, 2000; Vig, Chinitz, & Shulman, 2005).

In an ideal world, providers would proactively empower families *before* any abuse occurs. (See online companion materials for this chapter for guidance.) But this is not always possible. Therefore, giving providers and families useful information on negative outcomes associated with abuse, their shared role in emotional development, and direct intervention strategies, as well as connecting families with holistic, tailored family-centered psychosocial supports, is especially vital after substantiated abuse or neglect, foster care, and/or attempted reunification (i.e., return of children to biological caregivers after abuse).

Concerted effort is needed to ensure safe and lasting reunification with caregivers, and better support of the developing child (Wulczyn, 2004). Furthermore, primary caregivers who personally experienced childhood trauma may need even more support and coaching from diverse service providers to consistently provide their young child with responsive, empathic interactions (Briggs et al., 2014; Folger et al., 2017).

Toxic Stress   There is growing literature on the negative impact of toxic stress on brain development. According to leading experts in this field of research, "persistent health disparities associated with poverty, discrimination, or maltreatment could be reduced by the alleviation of toxic stress in children" (Harris, Marques, Oh, Bucci, & Cloutier, 2017; Johnson, Riley, Granger, & Riis, 2013; Shonkoff et al., 2012, e232). Shonkoff and colleagues further note that toxic stress results from "strong, frequent, or prolonged activation of the body's stress response systems in the absence of the buffering protection of a supportive, adult relationship" (e237). Multiple stressors can induce this dangerous stress response, including child abuse, neglect, parental substance abuse, and/or caregiver depression. Such early stressors may contribute to actual changes in different regions of the developing brain, with potentially permanent effects. On a positive note, trusted adults' positive expressiveness and responsiveness may buffer or protect young children from the negative impact of varying environmental stressors (Raver & Spagnola, 2002).

Consider families with whom you have interacted and the types of stressors they have experienced. Although children and their families may certainly experience multiple stressors regardless of socioeconomic status or income level, literature suggests significantly greater "cumulative environmental risk exposure" for children from low-income households, compared with children from middle-income households (Evans & Marcynyszyn, 2004, p. 1942). There is a reported association, for example, between living in poverty and preschoolers' decreased emotion knowledge (Denham, Bassett, Brown, Way, & Steed, 2015). At the same time, we should consider within-group variability in attributes such as low-income parents' receptiveness to behavior support (Edwards, 2014b) and self-expressiveness (Edwards, 2014b) that can influence the developing child.

Punitive Responses   Young children have limited, emerging self-regulation capabilities. They need ongoing, meaningful exposure to fundamental socialization practices, including direct modeling of self-regulation skills during times of distress and nonpunitive responses from adults when they display challenging emotions (Eisenberg & Fabes, 1994; Eisenberg, Fabes, Carlo, & Karbon, 1992; Ramsden & Hubbard, 2002; Spinrad et al., 2007). Unfortunately, too many children do not have exposure to supportive, nonpunitive responses across settings. Webster-Stratton (1990) observed that when parents experience heightened stressors, this tends to result in more punitive, critical parenting. This researcher noted these stressors may include unemployment, low income and socioeconomic status, marital discord, divorce, child stressors, and poor family interactions. (The impact of such stressors may be heightened or diminished depending on the extent of other considerations, such as the parent's psychological well-being or social support system.) Children with challenging behavior may also likely elicit coercive, controlling, and negative adult responses (see Scaramella & Leve, 2004). Martorell and Bugental (2006) noted that mothers with increased feelings of powerlessness (e.g., lack of perceived control or marital support) exhibited greater use of harsh control practices, including spanking, on their infants and toddlers with a difficult temperament. Other researchers have also found that low perceived control is associated with caregivers' use of negative affect when responding to a child's challenging behaviors (Bugental, Blue, & Cruzcosa, 1989). Furthermore, a sample of children exposed to high neighborhood violence was 1.9 times more likely to be spanked, compared to children from a low-neighborhood-violence group (Fitzgerald et al., 2006).

Birth–5 service providers also play a key role in emotional development (Denham, Bassett, & Zinsser, 2012) and should avoid using punitive responses to challenging emotions and behavior. As stated in the Division of Early Childhood's (DEC's) Recommended Practices, providers are encouraged to "promote the child's social-emotional development by observing, interpreting, and responding contingently to the range of the child's emotional expressions" (DEC, 2014, p. 14, INT1). Providers can promote social-emotional competence in part by managing their emotions and relationships with others as well as being reflective and aware of social situations (Collaborative for Academic Social and Emotional Learning, 2014; Jennings, 2015; Zins, Weissberg, Wang, & Walberg, 2004). Unfortunately, preservice teachers report little training on how to facilitate young children's emotional competence, or how to manage their own feelings and displays of emotion (Denham, Bassett, & Zinsser, 2012; Garner, 2010; Marlow & Inman, 2002; Poulou, 2005).

As the author of this book, I am hopeful that more birth–5 service providers will commit to enhancing their skills repertoire and consistently modeling use of non-punitive, supportive interactions with children. This is especially urgent given that public schools across 19 states in the United States still allow the use of corporal punishment, affecting over 160,000 children each year (Gershoff & Font, 2016; Gershoff, Purtell, & Holas, 2015; Wheeler & Richey, 2014) and there is international concern with teachers' reliance on punitive, corporal punishment (e.g., Malak, Sharma, & Deppeler, 2015). According to Nese and McIntosh (2016, p. 175),

> [A] ubiquitous response to unwanted behavior is exclusionary discipline practices, including time-out, office discipline referrals, and suspensions. However, extensive research has demonstrated that these practices are associated with negative outcomes, including increased likelihood of further unwanted behavior, decreased achievement, and racial/ethnic discipline disparities.

Other researchers agree teachers may rely too heavily on time-out, even when it is ineffective in reducing behavior problems (Ryan, Sanders, Katsiyannis, & Yell, 2007).

Coercion Theory

To review, multiple factors may contribute to adults' responding in a punitive way when children exhibit challenging behaviors: Adult family members may be experiencing stressors that affect how they respond to children, and educators may not have received adequate training in how to respond effectively to young children's challenging behaviors. To further inform understanding on why coercive, punitive responses might be so widespread and persistent, consider the *coercion theory* framework (Patterson, 1982). This framework suggests a process of mutual reinforcement between the adult and child. Some readers may have heard the expression, "negative attention is still attention." That is, caregivers may actually reinforce children's challenging behaviors, which provoke caregiver negativity, and so on, as shown in Figure 2.4.

For example, suppose a child and her father sit side-by-side during a bus ride home at the end of a hot summer day, following an afternoon at the park. They are calm at first, with the father focused on his phone, not saying anything as his daughter quietly

Figure 2.4. Theoretical link between child misbehavior and punitive responses from adults, as described in coercion theory.

looks out the window. The child soon becomes visibly bored. Her father, who is tired after playing at the park all afternoon, tells her to be quiet when she asks questions. The child playfully begins to kick her legs under the seat and sing. Her father sternly whispers, "Stop it, I said! Quiet!" The child is now getting desired attention from her dad, albeit negative attention, and continues kicking her feet and making up songs. Her father's frustration increases and he raises his voice to yell. The child begins to cry. Her father sighs heavily, and alternates between ignoring her and telling her to stop. Their negative exchange continues for the remainder of the bus ride. As they near their stop, the father insists the child will have her favorite toy taken away when they get home. Can you think of another example of this kind of encounter, in which emotions escalate on both sides as the child and adult mutually reinforce one another's behavior?

An adult's anger and hostility are often intensified as the "coercive cycle" escalates (Snyder, Edwards, McGraw, Kilgore, & Holten, 1993). This pattern of relating to adults can begin in early infancy (Patterson, 2002) and carry over into interactions with others across settings (Smith et al., 2014).

Consider the likely impact of this negativity on the developing child. When trusted adults regularly use negative expressiveness and ineffective modeling of ways to regulate and express emotions, early development is adversely shaped by this exposure. When my elder son was 5 years old, he overheard a conversation about how some adults use harsh discipline with their children. He asked clarifying questions and then remarked, "I don't think that's nice to even hit, because it just isn't nice. Because then their child will hit their kids." Indeed, scholars have argued that, although it is not inevitable, being maltreated may enhance the risk of later becoming abusive (Kaufman & Zigler, 1989). Main and Goldwyn (1984, p. 203) similarly found that, "a mother's apparent experience of her own mother as rejecting is systematically related to her rejection of her own infant."

In addition to the potential long-term impact on the child's development, harsh discipline and negativity can be confusing and upsetting to the child in the short term. Imagine how confusing it can be for a young child to reconcile or make sense of harsh statements made by the most influential people in their lives, such as the following:

- "Stop yelling! We do not yell inside!"
- "Who threw that? Come on, it's already June 1st!"
- "He's acting like a baby. I can't understand him when he cries!"

- "I'm so tired of this! This is the last time I take you shopping!"
- "Go in that classroom or you're losing toys. . . . You're upsetting me. Get in there!"
- "You're going to sit in [the director's] office if you do that again!"

In addition to contributing to a harsh, non-nurturing climate, such remarks do nothing to validate children's feelings or actually teach children what they can say or do instead to get their needs met in a more appropriate manner.

On a positive note, researchers are increasingly investigating possible protective factors that can be embedded in a family-centered intervention to break the "intergenerational cycle of harsh parenting" (Schofield, Conger, & Conger, 2016, p. 1). Examples include improving intergenerational and romantic partner communication and enhancing self-control.

The Ineffectiveness of Rapid Suppression Approaches

It is very common for students in kindergarten through twelfth grade to face one or more disciplinary actions each school year (Curran, 2016; Verdugo, 2002), and this can occur even at the preschool level. In what ways do you suspect K–12 schools typically respond when disciplinary action is needed? It is concerning that there are schools in the United States that still use traditional, punitive disciplinary practices (Moreno & Seguira-Herrera, 2014). More specifically, available research literature refers to disciplinary responses such as yelling, hitting, overuse/misuse of time-out, expulsions, suspensions, or loss of privileges as *rapid suppression approaches,* meaning that these approaches are efforts to quickly eliminate or stop challenging behavior (e.g., Moreno & Gaytán, 2013; Noguera, 2003; Wheeler & Richey, 2010). It is likely that most if not all readers have experienced at least one of these responses to their own behavior during childhood. Even though they likely sound familiar and are widely used, consider how they do not actually teach children new skills or promote long-term success. More specifically, researchers such as Durand (1990) and Wheeler & Richey (2010) emphasize several key problems with rapid suppression approaches to challenging behaviors:

- These approaches repeatedly fail over time to promote lasting behavior change.
- They are reactive in response to a problem.
- They fail to teach alternate replacement behaviors.

This raises an important question: If these approaches don't really help, why do we continue to use them?

The use of rapid suppression approaches may persist even when adults know these approaches are not having the desired effect on behavior. In a study I conducted with mothers of children in an urban Head Start program that examined their perceived role in early emotional development, several mothers acknowledged the ineffectiveness of these rapid suppression approaches in their own interactions with their children. For example, one mother remarked, "I get frustrated—I keep beatin' 'um. It's a waste of time, not getting nowhere. Next day the same thing . . ." Another commented on how her responses had changed over time with increased parenting experience: "My firstborn son, 19 years old, he was spanked and it never got anywhere . . . enraged me even more—just a huge battle! With my [preschool child], I'm older, know what to expect. We talk more . . . or I make her go to bed early" (Edwards, 2010; see also Edwards, 2012, which examines mothers who have one child compared to mothers with two or more children). Other researchers similarly elucidate the internal dialogue and potential conflict caregivers may feel when reflecting on whether to use spanking (e.g., Kim & Hong, 2007; LeCuyer, Christensen, Kearney, & Kitzman, 2011).

Adult negativity and poor modeling, exemplified by the use of the rapid suppression approaches described earlier, may lead to strained adult–child interactions as well as negative child outcomes, including:

- Lower emotion understanding (e.g., Denham, Zoller, & Couchoud, 1994)

- Decreased proficiency in confronting emotional situations (e.g., Fabes et al., 1999)

- Less effective coping with negative emotions across settings (e.g., Eisenberg & Fabes, 1994; Gottman, Katz, & Hooven, 1996)

- Increased likelihood of externalizing behaviors or conduct problems (e.g., Spinrad et al., 2007; Webster-Stratton, 1990)

Fortunately, as an ECE or ECSE professional, you are well positioned to provide interventions that best support emerging emotional competencies and increase the likelihood of long-term positive outcomes. The remainder of this chapter will explore general principles and practices to keep in mind for early intervention; specific strategies will be discussed in subsequent chapters.

BASIC PRINCIPLES OF EARLY INTERVENTION

At this point, you might be wondering, "What do early learning standards say about recommended teaching practices?" To pinpoint and address environmental factors that influence emotional development (Hoeksma, Oosterlaan, & Schipper, 2004), the available research literature stresses the need to enhance teachers' capacity for using more *prevention-oriented, proactive approaches* (DEC, 2014; Fox et al., 2010). As noted by Gardner, Shaw, Dishion, Burton, and Supplee (2007, p. 398), "even within a brief and multifaceted preventive intervention, change in proactive parenting skills contributes modestly but significantly to change in child problem behavior." This principle will be discussed in greater depth in subsequent chapters of this book. For now, just be aware of the importance of thoughtfully putting recommended strategies into place from the first time you interact with the child and family, so as to minimize or prevent potential problems. Such strategies include positive, responsive interactions; clear expectations; and engaging, developmentally appropriate instruction. Prevention-oriented, proactive approaches also rest on another key principle: Educators should closely observe the child and collect data on what is working and not working to inform intervention efforts *as soon as* a concern arises, rather than ignoring prolonged concerns and reactively attempting to respond after challenging emotions and behavior escalate. To reinforce this point, think of personal examples of the following circumstances:

- Think of something you have done or put in place to prevent or reduce the chance of something else happening. Examples include labeling all toy bins with a word and picture to promote less confusion and more independence when children put things away during clean up; or taking folic acid during pregnancy to reduce the chance of a baby having neural tube defects (Milunsky et al., 1989).

- Now, consider a time you have responded right away to a situation instead of waiting for things to get worse. Examples might include noticing a few water droplets on the floor from a suspected leak and immediately calling for someone to take a look at the roof; or receiving a note about a child's misbehavior in another setting and following up with the parent and/or fellow provider that same day.

The first two examples show how a preventive approach can reduce the likelihood of a specific problem occurring; the third and fourth examples illustrate the importance of being proactive when a problem does occur.

Connection to Early Learning Standards

Perhaps some of the most underutilized resources available to providers are the evidence-based position statements and recommended practices outlined in guiding organizations' early learning standards. Why are these important? Leading experts in early childhood and early childhood special education provide useful information via standards, codes of ethics, and position statements that align with theory and decades of evidence-based research.

For example, the following list is a sampling from Paragraph 3 of the Council for Exceptional Children's (CEC's) practice standards in the category of Teaching and Assessment. (This document was approved in October 2011 and is available on the CEC web site through the page titled "Professional Standards and Practice Policies and Positions.") Note that in the standards cited in the following list, *evidence-based* refers to recommended strategies or practices that are validated or supported by rigorous, empirical qualitative, quantitative, single-subject, and/or mixed methods research; for example, evidence-based practices or strategies will be found in peer-reviewed journals (Horner et al., 2005; Shavelson & Towne, 2002). *Positive behavior supports* refers to a multi-tiered, evidence-based framework for supporting diverse learners, discussed in depth in Chapter 3. Take a moment to review these CEC practice standards:

- *Standard 4:* Create safe, effective, and culturally responsive learning environments which contribute to fulfillment of needs, stimulation of learning, and realization of positive self-concepts.
- *Standard 7:* Only use behavior change practices that are evidence-based, appropriate to their preparation, and which respect the culture, dignity, and basic human rights of individuals with exceptionalities.
- *Standard 8:* Support the use of positive behavior supports and conform to local policies relating to the application of disciplinary methods and behavior change procedures, except when the policies require their participation in corporal punishment.
- *Standard 9:* Refrain from using aversive techniques unless the target of the behavior change is vital, repeated trials of more positive and less restrictive methods have failed, and only after appropriate consultation with parents and appropriate agency officials.
- *Standard 10:* Do not engage in the corporal punishment of individuals with exceptionalities.
- *Standard 11:* Report instances of unprofessional or unethical practice to the appropriate supervisor.

Reflect on the extent to which you follow these standards. How can reviewing professional standards help you and your fellow child care and home-based providers? You can use these standards in several ways to improve the quality of care provided in your setting. For example, perhaps some readers do not agree with or feel adequately supported by certain colleagues or supervisors in their immediate agency, program, or center. How might you respond, for example, if another provider does not see anything wrong with using aversive techniques such as yelling to get children to comply with requests? In this case, it can be helpful to situate or align the rationale for your concern or desired practice with the corresponding standard in one of the guiding professional organizations. Perhaps the provider or supervisor could share CEC Practice Standards 8 and 9. This may empower and unify stakeholders to engage in thoughtful dialogue on recommended practices, and provide credibility to reinforce concerns.

Reviewing professional standards can provide guidance in responding to novel situations and promote reflective practice by encouraging you to consider the extent to which your practices align with what the standards recommend. To explore professional standards further, visit the web sites of guiding professional organizations such as Division for Early Childhood, Council for Exceptional Children, and National Association for the Education of Young Children.

Proactive Supports From Educators and Families

As an educator, you are positioned to provide proactive supports to the children in your care, following standards for professional practice as described earlier in the chapter. You can also encourage families to provide these supports. Supportive and positive caregiving behavior correlates or is associated with greater emotion regulation for highly reactive infants (Gergely & Watson, 1999; Ursache, Blair, Stifter, & Voegtline, 2013). Furthermore, maternal sensitivity on the first day of kindergarten has been linked to social competence and school performance in eighth grade when controlling for maternal education, ethnicity, estimated child IQ, and child's gender (Morrison, Rimm-Kauffman, & Pianta, 2003). The literature tends to highlight mother–child connections; however, researchers agree (Dunsmore & Karn, 2001; Fitzgerald, McKelvey, Schiffman, & Montanez, 2006; Ramsden & Hubbard, 2002; Spinrad et al., 2007) that *all* key players in children's everyday natural environments have meaningful, ongoing opportunities to

- Contribute to a positive or negative emotional climate,
- Effectively or ineffectively model varying behavioral displays of emotion, and
- Be supportive or dismissive of children's negative emotions.

Consider the opportunities family members might have during an outing to a restaurant, as described in the following vignette.

Special Treat: Team Consistency Yields Results

Billy, who is about to turn 3, is a child with a mild sensory processing disorder who receives early intervention (EI) services in the home where he lives with his mom, Kelly, and his dad, Alex. His EI service provider, Sarita, has worked closely with the family for the past 6 months. One day, as a special treat, Sarita and Alex decide to take Billy to a restaurant for lunch. A man and woman watch them intermittently from a nearby booth. Billy sits calmly and copies Sarita and Alex's modeling to order while looking at the waitress, asking, "May I have grilled cheese with applesauce?"

This is progress. The last time Billy had visited a restaurant with his parents, 8 months ago, he was visibly upset when waiting for his food to arrive. So today, before getting out of the car, Sarita reminds Billy that they will have to wait a little while before their food comes. She asks Billy if he would prefer to color or play "I Spy" while they wait, as Sarita has noticed that Billy finds both of these activities relaxing and can more easily maintain calm while engaging in either one. Billy nods and asks to color.

Once they order their food, Alex keeps Billy's attention focused on sharing crayons to draw on a piece of paper. When their food arrives, Billy is reminded that he needs to stay in his seat until the meal is finished. Billy talks with his dad and Sarita during lunch, sometimes needing help choosing the right words. Alex periodically tells Billy, "I love the way you're sitting. You're doing a great job!"

As the nearby couple stands to leave, the woman approaches their table. "Excuse me," she says, smiling, "I just want to say how impressed I am by your son. He sat so calmly throughout the whole meal, and my husband and I enjoyed watching him. You are a wonderful father." Alex thanks the woman and asks Billy to thank her as well. Billy mumbles a sweet "thank you" while happily taking a spoonful of ice cream from his sundae.

Alex and Sarita both appreciate having an unfamiliar person take time from her day to offer such a nice compliment. They smile, though, thinking of the constant "behind the scenes" work reinforcing Billy's good behavior before the experience that prompted this couple's observation. As they drive back to the house with Billy falling asleep in the back seat, Alex and Sarita talk about the ongoing guidance, reinforcement, and consistency in responses that Billy has received from his parents, grandparents, babysitter, child care professionals, and EI provider to help him get his needs met and display good emotion regulation across different people, situations, and settings. It has truly been a team effort.

Let's look at the specific role of early childhood teachers and service providers and therapists in home- and center-based settings. They certainly should be included as key players, with an essential role in socializing children to learn to identify and cope with a range of emotions (Davis et al., 2015; Dunsmore & Karn, 2001; Hyson & Lee, 1996). In center-based settings, for example, child care can place unique demands on a child's ability to regulate emotions (Denham, 2006). Specific demands might include:

- Interacting/sharing with same-age peers
- Waiting turns; delaying gratification
- Negotiating or handling peer conflict for the first time
- Possibly having to learn different cultural expectations/norms at home and at child care
- Being expected to display greater independence than what may be the norm in the child's home
- Not being with trusted primary caregiver(s) for an extended period each day
- Potentially facing abrupt separations from the primary caregiver during arrival
- Frequent transitioning across activities and routines
- Experiencing changes in staff from morning to afternoon
- Adjusting to change in noise volume and stimulation
- Possibly experiencing inconsistent responses from child care providers

Scholars increasingly acknowledge "theoretical and practical benefits [to] focusing on early childhood teacher socialization of emotions" (Denham, Bassett, & Zinsser, 2012, p. 137). Notwithstanding the importance of embracing variability in emotion discourse within and across cultural groups (Harris, 2000; Hooven, Gottman, & Katz, 1995), children's emotional literacy and emotion regulation are enhanced when children are exposed to trusted adults' use of *emotion coaching*; that is, "responding supportively, verbally labeling emotions, using empathy, and teaching children to understand and regulate their emotions" (Wilson, Havighurst, & Harley, 2012, p. 57). Emotion coaching comprises both responsiveness and direct instruction with regard to emotion expression and experience (Gottman, Katz, & Hooven, 1996). This process necessitates being aware of children's emotions, accepting children's emotions, and providing appropriate instruction on managing emotions (Ramsden & Hubbard, 2002). Emotion coaching enhances child sensitivity to others' emotional cues and minimizes aggressive behavior (Garner, Dunsmore, & Southam-Gerrow, 2008). Matching of emotion and distracting attention from an emotionally challenging situation links with early adaptive emotion regulation (Garner, 2006).

What might emotion coaching look like in practice? Consider the following vignette as an example.

Handling Frustration at Playtime: Emotion Coaching in Action

Glen, an occupational therapist, enjoys working with 2-year-old Sue and her mother, Vanessa, twice a week in Vanessa's apartment. Glen is helping Sue with fine motor skills, such as using manipulatives and using her pincer grasp to pick up small objects.

Today, when Glen arrives for his scheduled session, Sue is clinging to Vanessa's leg and covering her face. Glen bends down to Sue's eye level and softly says, "I see how much you love your mom. It's great to see you again, Sue! I'll start laying out fun things on the rug. Just come over when you are ready to play!" Glen collects several of Sue's favorite small Lego people and lays them on the floor. He notices that she is watching him, with one hand still cautiously placed on Vanessa's leg. Glen eagerly begins picking up the Lego people with a child-sized pair of tongs. He laughs as he successfully drops them into a tin can and says, "Whoa! Who wants to try next?" Seeing that Sue is still reluctant, Vanessa gently asks, "Sue, are you feeling a little shy?" Sue nods. Vanessa reassures her, "It's okay to feel shy sometimes. Remember that Glen is here to help us learn new things. Would you like Mommy to go first?" Sue nods and relaxes a bit as her mom sits next to Glen to pick up and drop the Lego people. "This is fun!" Vanessa exclaims.

When Glen sees that Sue is calm, he motions for Vanessa to ask Sue if she wants a turn. "Sue, I bet you can drop more into the bucket than Mommy did!" Sue playfully sits next to her mom and tries to use the tongs. Glen offers some hand-over-hand support to guide Sue's positioning. Together they successfully pick up and drop three Lego people into the bucket. Then Sue pauses and says, "Me do it myself." Glen and Vanessa celebrate her wanting to do it independently and remain nearby, watching, as Sue makes two unsuccessful attempts. She seems visibly frustrated as she grunts, throws the tongs, and pushes the bucket over. She runs over to the couch and covers her face, crying.

Being attuned to the situation, and having talked about ways of responding to Sue in such situations, Vanessa and Glen exchange a knowing glance. Vanessa asks if Sue is ready to talk about what just happened. "No!" Sue replies. Vanessa then slowly counts aloud to 10 while modeling how to take deep breaths. Sue follows her mother's example and takes deep breaths as well.

"Nice calming down," Glen says once Sue's crying has stopped. "Are you feeling frustrated that you couldn't pick up the Lego people?" he asks. Sue slowly nods.

"I understand," Glen replies. "It's a brand-new activity—I bet if we practice a little each week, you're going to get really good at it! Can we try again two more times and then we'll do something else? You choose if you want me or Mommy to help you this time." Sue returns to the rug, willing to try again with Vanessa's help before helping Glen choose a different activity.

In this example, Vanessa and Glen work together to provide Sue with emotion coaching that includes the three components listed previously. First, they are aware of Sue's emotions; from past experience, they know she is displaying frustration, and Glen asks her if she is feeling frustrated. Second, they accept this emotion; Vanessa does not try to make Sue talk about what happened right away, because Sue is clearly too upset to do so. Finally, they provide appropriate instruction on managing emotions; Vanessa models how to calm down, and Glen praises Sue's effort to calm herself.

You may have noticed that Glen and Vanessa named the emotion they knew Sue was feeling and engaged her in conversation about it. Children are socialized to engage meaningfully in developmentally appropriate, relevant conversations about emotions both proactively and as circumstances naturally arise (e.g., labeling and explaining emotions, discussing causes and consequences of emotions). Children benefit from meaningful opportunities to share and discuss negative emotions, and they respond favorably when adults verbally label emotions, discuss others' emotional cues, respond supportively, and offer direct instruction on emotion expression (Garner et al., 2008; Gottman et al., 1996; Hooven et al., 1995; Wilson et al., 2012). Despite a plethora of research on social-emotional development, however, early childhood teachers have not been widely encouraged to understand and fully embrace their contributing role (Edwards, 2012). As will be described in greater depth in subsequent chapters, providers can reinforce adaptive emotions and enhance children's emerging repertoires for constructive ways in which to respond to, and cope with, novel or frustrating situations and experiences (Gilliom, Shaw, Beck, Schonberg, & Lukon, 2002). As you read the following vignettes, consider how one child care provider, Ms. Jackie, does this for a child named Joy, supporting Joy's family in the process.

Saying Good-Bye (Part 1): Anticipating Challenging Situations

Joy, a 3½-year-old with a mild developmental delay, was visibly excited to have extra time home with her 5-year-old brother and Mommy yesterday, with her preschool closed due to snow. The three of them baked cookies, played with playdough, and did other fun things that Joy loved to do. The next day, school is open. Joy seems fine during the first part of the morning routine at home. She hugs her daddy and says good-bye as he leaves for work. She eats her pancakes and fruit, calmly lets Mommy put on her coat, and hums along to a sing-along CD in the car.

As her mother parks the car in the parking lot and releases Joy's seatbelt buckle, Joy lifts her hands and says in a distressing tone, "Pick me up . . . no drop me off."

Her mom suspects Joy will have trouble transitioning after the unusual school closing the day before, so she calmly says, "Why don't we drop your brother off first?" This involves taking a longer route through the building to drop off her brother in full-day kindergarten. Joy's brother waves goodbye as he puts away his backpack and enters the classroom. Once her brother is no longer in sight, Joy again motions to be picked up and repeatedly says, "No drop me off . . . no drop me off!" Joy's protests become louder and more insistent as she and her mother walk through the building toward Joy's classroom.

Meanwhile, one of Joy's teachers, Ms. Jackie, is just arriving at work. As she swiftly moves through the crowded hallway, she glances in Joy's direction and makes eye contact with Joy's mother. Although Ms. Jackie is feeling a bit flustered herself this morning—she's running late, thanks to the messy roads on her daily commute—she gives Joy's mom a reassuring smile and makes a mental note that Joy seems to be having trouble making transitions.

Before reading what happens in the remainder of this vignette, pause to reflect on the following questions:

- As the caregiver, what might you do in this scenario?
- As Joy's teacher, what might you do in this scenario when you realize Joy is having trouble transitioning into the daily school routine?

Saying Good-Bye (Part 2): Validating and Addressing Children's Emotions

Joy's mother calmly walks with her daughter over to a chair she found in the hallway. After squatting to be at Joy's eye level, she holds Joy's hands and calmly asks, "You don't want to go to school today?" She is practicing validating and labeling Joy's feelings, a strategy Joy's teachers have recommended and modeled for her.

Joy nods in response to her mother's question. "But why?" her mother asks. Joy utters an approximation of "I no know; I stay with you."

"You want to stay with Mommy? But Joy," her mother says in a gentle tone, "I have to go to work. Today is Friday . . . that means they have your special snack and art class! And we'll get to see Ms. Jackie, Ms. Iris, and all your friends!" Seeing that Joy is still clinging to her, her mom says, "Come, let's go put your lunch in the fridge so it doesn't go bad." Joy tightly holds her mother's hand and walks alongside her mom toward her classroom. Her mom points out pretty wall displays: "Oh wow, look at those happy faces on the wall . . . oh, look at how soft this feels." They walk toward a closed door, and her mother suggests, "How about if you push open the door?" Joy excitedly runs to open the door. As they approach Joy's classroom, her mom hangs up Joy's backpack and helps her take off her coat and roll up her sleeves. To wash hands, her mom playfully says, "Oh, I'm going to get to the sink first!" In response, Joy laughs and runs ahead of her mom to wash her hands in the sink.

This is the final step in their routine before Joy is supposed to cross the thick red tape along the opening to the classroom door, enter the room, and say good-bye to her mom. Her mom spots Ms. Jackie in the classroom and quickly motions to the teacher from the bathroom sink, whispering, "We're having a harder time today after yesterday's snow day." Ms. Jackie smiles and nods, warmly greeting Joy and telling her what a great day they are going to have. She sees that Joy is still clinging to her mom. Knowing that Joy's older brother had already been dropped off, Ms. Jackie quietly asks, "Are you going straight to your car now?" Joy's mom nods. "Joy," Ms. Jackie enthusiastically asks, "Do you want to look out the window as Mommy walks to her car?" This is something Joy and the other children in her class enjoy doing. Joy smiles and walks slowly toward the window. Standing by the door, her mom asks, "Should I blow you two kisses or three?"

"Three kisses," replies Joy.

"Wow!" Ms. Jackie chimes in. "Let's stand by the window and watch for your mommy to blow three kisses!"

"I love you, have a great day!" Joy's mom calls, relieved that she was able to say good-bye without Joy crying. As she walks to the parking lot, she stops outside Joy's classroom window to blow her three big kisses. Joy, Ms. Jackie, and two other classmates wave excitedly. When Joy's mom calls an hour later, Ms. Jackie assures her that Joy has remained calm and is having a great day.

Think about what the mother and teacher tried in this scenario to help Joy transition to school. You might want to pause here and list their specific actions on a sheet of paper. What might have been their rationale or reason for trying each of these things? Would you have responded similarly, or tried other means of addressing Joy's emotions and behavior?

As you read and reflected on the scenario described, you may have noticed some specific effective strategies employed by Joy's mother and by her teacher. For example, Joy's mother used these strategies in her response:

- *Staying flexible.* She willingly changed their routine to drop off Joy's brother first so Joy would have more time with her.

- *Making it clear to Joy that her emotions are a priority.* When she saw Joy was upset, she paused to sit and talk quietly with her, and she allowed Joy to hold her hand.

- *Validating Joy's feelings.* She talked with Joy about Joy's reluctance to go to school.

- *Redirecting Joy's attention.* She pointed out the fun things Joy would do at school, then helped her focus on putting her lunch away, looking at the wall displays, opening the door, and racing to the sink.

- *Connecting with Joy's teacher.* Joy's mother shared her concerns and let Ms. Jackie know Joy might need her help this morning.

- *Giving Joy a sense of control.* She asked Joy how many kisses she should blow from the window.

For her part, Joy's teacher, Ms. Jackie, used these strategies in her response:

- *Keenly observing to inform her understanding.* In the hallway, she observed Joy was upset; she noticed Joy's nonverbal cues, such as clinging to her mom.

- *Communicating with mom nonverbally and verbally.* She smiled and nodded reassuringly in the hallway, and was warm and welcoming when Joy's mother called later that morning to check in.

- Via ongoing conversations, *modeling the importance of validating and labeling children's feelings.* Because Ms. Jackie had previously modeled this skill for Joy's mother, Joy's mother could apply it in a challenging situation.

- *Maintaining classroom cues for transitions.* Joy's teacher had previously taught students that crossing the thick red tape at the edge of the classroom marked the transition from time with caregivers to school day.

- *Maintaining awareness of unique family dynamics.* Joy's teacher had previously taken time to learn that Joy has an older brother at the school and that Joy's mom usually parks in the lot outside Joy's classroom window. On seeing Joy's mother dressed casually, Joy's teacher realized she might have a flexible schedule that morning and not be headed straight to a meeting.

- *Positively interacting with Joy.* She warmly greeted Joy at arrival.

- *Being flexible.* She briefly interrupted the morning routine to encourage the children to wave goodbye to Joy's mom from the window.

- *Valuing the importance of children feeling safe and supported across settings.* She helped Joy's mother get Joy settled in (rather than holding a screaming Joy as her mom ran from the room). This approach left Mom, Joy, and Ms. Jackie feeling happy and relieved.

The strategies employed by both Joy's mother and her teacher were effective in addressing Joy's difficult emotions and the resulting challenging behavior; as a result, Joy was able to enjoy a good day at school, which she might otherwise not have been able to do. This story demonstrates that yes, it really does matter when providers and primary caregivers intervene. It also matters whether every adult involved in a child's care takes responsibility for doing whatever he or she can to foster positive outcomes, as Joy's mother and teacher each did—rather than pointing fingers or blaming another adult for a child's difficult emotions or challenging behavior. This issue is further explored in the Collaborating With Families and Colleagues discussion about avoiding blame.

Collaborating With Families and Colleagues: Avoiding Blame

The fact that you are reading this book suggests you are already mindful of your shared role in emotional development. However, it is important to recognize that some key players may make comments that negate their own role and instead suggest *others* are primarily responsible for a child's challenging emotions and behavior. For example, when brainstorming why a young boy exhibited externalizing and internalizing behaviors throughout the school year, a well-intentioned teacher shared the following remark: "His dad is a dancer, so that must be why he misbehaves during music."

This child care provider was taking part in a 4-month analysis to better reflect on her role in using positive behavior interventions and supports (PBIS) in the early childhood setting (see Edwards, 2017b). Readers may connect with her desire to make sense of this child's challenging behavior. She candidly thought that perhaps acting out during music class reminded the child of his father frequently traveling out of town for dance performances. Regardless of the accuracy of this assumption, we discussed bringing the focus of her reflection back to things she was personally able to control in her immediate environment, such as:

- Her tone

- The consistency of her responses

- Her ability to set clearer expectations for appropriate behavior before going to music

- Her ability to choose preemptively which peers would be best to sit next to this child during music

- Her use of positive verbal reinforcement when seeing him sitting appropriately

This teacher was amenable to helping collect data on what was happening in the classroom before and after this child's behavior episodes, the function of behavior, and reflect on written observations of several teacher–child interactions. This process informed her increased use of teaching practices that better aligned with the child's emotional needs. By the end of the analysis, she and other teachers who went through a similar process noted a significant decrease in emotional/behavioral concerns.

Proactive Versus Reactive Approaches

Researchers, policymakers, administrators, and early childhood professionals realize the need to *proactively* minimize and address emotional and behavioral concerns as early as possible. That is, we should not wait until children begin showing challenging emotions or behavior to reflect on our role and provide guidance. Doing our part to promote a stronger foundation for all children in the first 5 years of life (regardless of behavior or disability status) is essential for healthy development (DiStefano, Greer, & Kamphaus, 2013; McIntosh, Flannery, Sugai, Braun, & Cochrane, 2008).

I previously highlighted short- and long-term adverse outcomes from early displays of challenging emotions and behavior (see Chapter 1). Fortunately, external factors can serve a protective role (Hoeksma et al., 2004; Kochanska, Philibert, & Barry, 2009) and adult socialization can help shape emotion-related physiological mechanisms in the developing brain (Hastings et al., 2008). Furthermore, it is easier to positively shape a young child's developmental trajectory than to rely on a "wait and see" approach at a later developmental stage (Alink et al., 2006; Smith, Calkins, Keane, Anastopoulos, & Shelton, 2004). Readers may have heard that the brain is more "plastic," or impressionable, in a young child. As noted in one of the seminal works on child development, "Neurodevelopmental plasticity varies inversely with maturation. That is to say, there is more multipotentiality (i.e., greater capacity for alternative developmental adaptations) in the early childhood period than in the later years" (Shonkoff & Phillips, 2000, p. 32). This plasticity can be beneficial or deleterious, depending on the quality and nature of environmental exposure. In short, it makes sense for early childhood educators and service providers to intentionally foster children's adaptive behaviors and model additional adaptive behaviors as needed to help children respond positively to situations in which they experience challenging emotions.

Unfortunately, with a few exceptions, social-emotional learning programs are mainly offered to children at or beyond age 5 (Izard, Trentacosta, King, & Mostow, 2004; Wilson, Havighurst, & Harley, 2012). To promote long-term social competence and nonaggression, we should first target the young child's emerging ability to effectively regulate emotion and focus more on early childhood educators' emotion socialization at this early age (Denham et al., 2012; Ramsden & Hubbard, 2002; Sette, Spinrad, & Baumgartner, 2016). Recall from the earlier vignette, for example, how influential the teacher was in helping to foster Joy's emotion knowledge, emotion expression, and emotion regulation (both via direct teacher–child interactions and indirectly by recommending strategies for Joy's mother to use). As noted by a clinical psychology professor (Barrish, 2013), "When we accept and value our children's emotions, we not only help them feel better, we help them *do* better, in all aspects of their lives." The next section of this book focuses on enhancing your repertoire to better support the critically important role you play.

A Strengths-Based Approach

Think about how you might respond if you heard your colleagues talking in a negative, deficit-focused way about any of the children in your care. For example, how would you feel if you heard remarks like these?

- "James doesn't know how to wash his hands, so I just wash his hands for him every morning. He is so dependent on others to get basic things done!"

- "We saw back in September that [Child] wasn't able to sit still during morning meeting, so we just stopped expecting her to sit with the group. We let her roam in the back of the room during that time. She's been doing that for the past 7 months."

These comments illustrate how teachers who focus on deficits may lower their expectations and thus not cultivate children's learning of adaptive behaviors. (Note that the second bullet point was adapted from comments made by a preschool teacher I talked with when investigating roadblocks to implementing positive behavior supports in a center-based setting; see Edwards, 2017b.)

As a teacher, do you consider a child's strengths as well as areas in need of improvement? Pinpointing and focusing on a child's strengths is an essential recommended practice in early childhood and early intervention settings. The idea underlying a strengths-based approach is to use a child's abilities, interests, or talents to help in areas where he or she is not as strong (instead of focusing on what is not working or areas in need of improvement). This is recommended when creating child portfolios (Campbell, Milbourne, & Silverman, 2001), and when working to support children's emotional and mental health (Lamb-Parker, LeBuffe, Powell, & Halpern, 2008; Laursen, 2000). Consider how this approach helps Tomas in the following vignette (based on actual events, with names and identifying details altered).

Learning to Like the Sand Table: Building on a Child's Strengths

Tomas is a sweet 2-year-old with autism. He has limited expressive language and avoids sensory activities like sand play. When the teacher opens the lid to the sand table each morning, Tomas consistently engages in hand flapping, makes high-pitched vocalizations, and quickly walks to the opposite side of the room to play with a ball drop toy. His mother feels this further isolates him because the other children in the classroom and in the nearby community park enjoy playing in the sand. Tomas's teacher reflects on how she might help him. She notices that he loves a ball drop toy. It is his favorite activity. One morning, to build on this strength, the teacher carries the ball drop toy over to the sand table. Tomas watches intently as the teacher places his favorite toy right inside the sand table. After a few minutes, he approaches the sand table to play with the ball drop toy. He refuses to touch the sand, solely focusing on the ball drop toy. When the ball drops in the sand, the teacher calmly picks it up, brushes it off, and hands it to him. This continues for over a week.

Then, one day, there is a tiny patch of collected sand still resting on top of the ball that the teacher is holding for Tomas to take. Tomas pauses, not wanting to touch it.

And then, suddenly, he reaches over on his own . . . and pushes off the sand. The teachers are ecstatic and eagerly share this news with his proud mother at dismissal. Ultimately, by the end of the school year, Tomas is willing to reach directly into the sand to retrieve the ball and is successfully playing up to his arms at the sand table alongside his peers.

In this instance, Tomas's teacher did not use his limitations as a reason to exclude him permanently from activities other children enjoy. Instead, she cleverly worked with his strengths to help him gradually learn to tolerate the feel of sand and, in time, even learn to enjoy playing at the sand table. Her approach also provides him with more opportunities to socialize with other children, at school and in the community.

WORKING TOWARD SELF-EFFICACY: THE IMPORTANCE OF REFLECTION

When reading about the importance of supporting early emotional development, it may seem easier said than done. To make this process a bit easier, it is useful for teachers to engage in ongoing reflection and dialogue. No matter what specific role you play in supporting young children's social-emotional development, this reflection can make you more effective, which in turn will enhance your sense of self-efficacy and confidence as an educator. This section will address three critical topics for reflection:

- Your work as a teacher or service provider, including your motivation, level of interest, preparedness, and self-confidence

- Your own emotions, including how you manage them and how they impact the environment in which you work

- Your views concerning children's behavior, especially challenging behavior, its causes, and appropriate responses to it

Reflecting on Teacher Motivation, Interest, Preparedness, and Confidence

Many readers of this book likely engage in some degree of day-to-day reflection about their practice. After visiting a child in the home setting, or when cleaning up after teaching multiple children in a center-based setting, early interventionists and child care providers are strongly encouraged to reflect on what went well and what they might wish to change. During this reflection, the primary focus should be on changing things *within one's control;* that is, the tone and style of one's response to a child's crying, the environmental arrangement and level of stimulation during a particular activity, and/or the approach and materials being used to work toward desired outcomes.

Teachers also benefit from engaging in reflection about their own perceived motivations, level of interest, preparedness, and self-confidence. Given that this reflection is so important, take a moment to reflect on the following questions before you continue reading:

- Do I truly believe providers and families have a shared role in emotional development? If not, can I commit to trying some of the suggested strategies to see firsthand if I may personally be able to facilitate a child's growth in this area?

- Am I highly motivated to learn and adopt new social-emotional practices? If not, why am I reluctant? Might I be receptive if these practices are likely to make me feel less stressed and more effective in minimizing and addressing negative behaviors?

- Am I comfortable reflecting on my own strengths and on areas in need of improvement? Do I already engage in this process? Might doing so on a regular basis make me a more effective provider?

- Do I respond well to constructive criticism? Might I be willing to consider altering ways in which I interact with young children if this is suggested by a supervisor, fellow provider, or recommended practice in an early learning standard?

Available research literature emphasizes the importance of first addressing early childhood teachers' motivation to adopt new social-emotional practices (Steed & Durand, 2013). As many readers may have personally experienced, challenging child behavior is linked to teacher stress (Yoon, 2002) as well as emotional exhaustion and burnout (Jennings & Greenberg, 2009). Thus, it is useful for administrators, faculty members, and individual providers to explore teachers' desire and willingness to improve reflective practice and revisit behavior-related beliefs and strategies.

Reflecting on One's Own Emotions and Behavior

Key players in a child's life, including child care and early intervention providers, must be aware of their own display of positive and negative emotions in the presence of children, families, and colleagues; in these displays, they are modeling social-emotional development and adaptive or nonadaptive behaviors for children. Thus, building on previous recommendations (Hooven et al., 1995), adults' awareness and regulation of their own negative emotions is a vital and often overlooked consideration. Proponents of sustainable change support having teachers more effectively address their own emotional displays and the overall emotional climate in the learning environment (Denham et al., 2012; Sutton & Wheatley, 2003).

Reflective Journaling   Ongoing reflection is one way adults can become more aware of their own emotions and better able to regulate them. One means of reflecting is to keep a journal. Self-reflective journaling has been recommended for early childhood educators (Kremenitzer, 2005). Teachers are not typically given opportunities to reflect on how they manage their own feelings and displays of emotion and how their emotions influence the learning environment (Garner, 2010; Marlow & Inman, 2002; Poulou, 2005; Zembylas, 2007). Adults who ignore their own emotions will likely have a difficult time supporting children with their negative emotions (Hooven et al., 1995; Ramsden & Hubbard, 2002). Given that matching of emotion correlates with early adaptive emotion regulation (Garner, 2006), reflective journaling might help align teachers with children's affect. See Figures 2.5 and 2.6 for sample templates to use for ongoing reflective practice.

How Reflecting on One's Own Emotions and Behavior Benefits Children
Children are shaped by adults' positive modeling of emotions to help with emotion regulation, social interaction, and learning alternatives to acting in a socially inappropriate manner (Bronson, 2000). Without intentional reflective practice, adults may not realize the extent to which they use a negative tone, sarcasm, negative body

A

Today's date: _____

Length of time for this reflection: _____

Specific comments/remarks I used in front of children in my class:

" _____ "
" _____ "
" _____ "
" _____ "

- *Were any of my remarks negative?*
- *Did I model using positive behavior and nonverbal cues?*
- *Did I set a positive example for children and other adults?*
- *Could I have said or done anything differently? What specifically?*

B

Today's date: _____

Pseudonym or child's initials only: _____

Location/activity: _____

Specific comments/remarks I used during my session:

" _____ "
" _____ "
" _____ "
" _____ "

- *Were any of my remarks negative?*
- *Did I model using positive behavior and nonverbal cues?*
- *Did I set a positive example for the child, siblings, and/or other adults?*
- *Could I have said or done anything differently? What specifically?*

Figure 2.5. Sample reflective journaling templates for birth–5 providers. A) Example for child care providers. B) Example for early intervention providers.

Antecedent-Behavior-Consequence (ABC) Chart and Reflection

Time: 9:00 a.m.   **Setting/activity:** Free play   **People present:** Child, me

Antecedent	Behavior	Consequence
What happened immediately before the child's behavior?	What objective, measurable terms describe the child's behavior?	What happened immediately after the child's behavior?
I asked the child to sit next to me on the rug to read a book.	*The child pushed my leg, covered his face with his hands, and screamed.*	*I sternly said, "We do not push or scream!" The child refused to cooperate.*

Teacher's Reflection

I think the child was trying to tell me he was not interested in reading a book with me first thing in the morning. He tends to push and cover his face when he is frustrated. I need to work on giving him more appropriate ways of expressing his frustration (e.g., saying or pointing to a picture that says, "No thank you").

Also, what would have happened if I gave him a choice between two books or possibly two different activities? I also think I should have been less stern and more understanding, especially because he just had a tough time saying good-bye to his dad. My response did not validate his emotions or teach him what to do instead of acting out.

Figure 2.6. Sample reflective journaling template for early intervention providers. This example presents an antecedent-behavior-consequence (ABC) chart. The ABC chart is meant to guide teacher review of one piece of data to consider what could have been changed before and/or after a child's challenging behavior.

language, and/or harsh language on an ongoing basis. Reflective practitioners may be more likely to promote positive learning environments. A reflective educator "assumes conscious and deliberate responsibility for her modeling. She is keenly aware that she, the teacher, provides the standard by which appropriate verbal and non-verbal behavior within the classroom environment is measured" (Stanulis & Manning, 2002, p. 4). As explained by Jennings and Greenberg (2009), teachers with high social-emotional competence

- Are excellent role models of desired emotions and behavior,
- Show greater empathy,
- Use less punitive or coercive strategies, and
- Display more effective, proactive management techniques (e.g., using expressiveness and verbal support to guide and manage children's behavior).

Along with promoting a strong foundation for emotional development and social competence, adult modeling of appropriate affect will likely yield personal benefits. In a parent-focused analysis, parents' emotion coaching meta-emotion structure (i.e., feelings on their own emotions, attitudes, and responses to their 5-year-old child's anger and sadness) was not only associated with the child's ability to focus attention and interact well with others, but also linked with the quality of the parents' marriage and parent–child interactions 3 years later (Hooven, Gottman, & Katz, 1995). For educators, high stress levels adversely affect their display of positive affect and quality of interactions with students (Yoon, 2002). Jennings and Greenberg (2009) advocate for more stress reduction and mindfulness programs to bolster teachers' social-emotional competencies. Encouraging adults' positive affect and being attuned to their own and others' emotions may improve relations with others within and across settings and heighten use of teachable moments.

Reflecting on One's Views About Behavior

In addition to reflecting on one's own behavioral display of emotions, it is beneficial to pause and reflect on one's current attitudes toward misbehavior. It is not uncommon to find that teachers may have somewhat different thresholds for the type of behavior perceived as frustrating. For example, if a preschool child asks you a question while you are talking to another adult, how might you respond? Teacher Angelique may stop to answer the child's question, Teacher Blanca may sweetly ask the child to please wait until the conversation is over, and Teacher Catherine may stop to yell at the child and later complain to the caregiver or other staff that this child's "rude" behavior must be stopped. Similarly, the same teacher may be fine with a lot of commotion and talking one day, but quicker to demand indoor voices or quiet another day.

As discussed in schema theory (Markus, 1977), it is useful to tap into adults' perceptions, given that early mental representations of a situation shape later attitudes and practices. In other words, teachers' current views regarding what is considered "appropriate behavior" are shaped by earlier experiences, and these beliefs may unintentionally make them respond more negatively to behavior situations that arise in the future. Thus, acknowledging one's own views, as well as engaging in ongoing reflection to continually revisit and possibly modify your reaction across children and situations, is strongly recommended. A reflective approach and openness to continually revisiting assumptions may also help minimize concern with *self-fulfilling prophecies.* This term refers to anticipating someone will act in a certain way and preemptively lowering your expectations or changing your approach so that the individual continues to act as you initially expected (Weaver, Filson Moses, & Snyder, 2016).

Teachers' views about children's challenging behaviors often include opinions about how these behaviors are influenced by other key players in the child's environment. Building on the bioecological systems theory discussed earlier in this book, it is essential to consider a systems approach to supporting emotional development, as described in the following textbox.

Collaborating With Families and Colleagues: Shared Accountability Within a Systems Approach

As many readers may have likely experienced firsthand, prolonged challenging emotional and behavioral episodes that last for several weeks or months can be complex and frustrating. A prolonged problem does not *solely* lie with the child's temperament, suspected or diagnosed disability, parents, media images—or with you. Pointing fingers only heightens defensive feelings and can result in overlooking critical pieces of information. Instead, a productive first step is to recognize the shared, contributing roles of family members, providers, and other key players.

Consider the following comment a teacher made to a parent at the end of a school day: "Your child hit someone today." Ask yourself if you would *end* this brief conversation as follows: "Your child hit someone today. Please talk with her about not hitting." Many readers may recall personally receiving such a message from their own child's teacher, or perhaps having made such a remark to a primary caregiver. Consider what may be missing here.

- Does the teacher offer insight into the particular context—what happened or what the child was trying to communicate? (No.)

- Does this option explain how the teacher responded, or offer strategies the caregiver may wish to use? (No.)

- Does the teacher seem to be insinuating it is the caregiver's responsibility to "fix" whatever is going on? (Yes—and this may make the caregiver feel inadequate, defensive, stressed, or all of the above.)

If you were the caregiver on the receiving end of this comment, how would you feel? Many might feel defensive, or perhaps embarrassed or isolated, or maybe the caregiver would direct anger toward the child, using an ineffective rapid suppression approach. Recall from Chapter 1 that early emotional and behavioral concerns may reduce caregivers' confidence in their childrearing abilities, as well as contribute to feelings of stigmatization and stress, and even marital discord (Dadds, Sanders, Behrens, & James, 1987; Levac, McCay, Merka, & Reddon-D'Arcy, 2008; Shaw, Connell, Dishion, Wilson, & Gardner, 2009; Webster-Stratton, 2015). Saying something is a problem, without engaging in a meaningful dialogue about why it might be happening or what can be done, is not the best approach to remedying a situation—and it is arguably setting the child and caregiver up for failure.

How you end a conversation like the one just described informs others of your perceived shared role in emotional development. Rather than letting "Your child hit someone today. Please talk with her about not hitting" be the end, consider that it can be merely the beginning. Reflect on the following alternative:

> Your child hit someone today. I think she was trying to tell us that she did not want to share sand toys with the other child. Have you been seeing any similar behavior at home? I bent down next to her, explained that hitting hurts, and guided her to pat nicely and 'make nice' on the hand of the child she hit. I also told her I understand that sharing is not easy, but that it's so much more fun when everyone can have a turn. I think if she hears a similar supportive message about using gentle hands and sharing from both of us, it will really help her learn to make better choices. What do you think?

The suspected reason for the behavior and strategies/suggestions offered will certainly vary based on individual considerations, but this latter option may likely be much more well received, because it

- Invites shared exchanges to reach common ground, and

- Reinforces the importance of both parties having shared accountability in supporting the child's emerging emotional development.

Developing Self-Efficacy

So far, this section has discussed three broad areas for reflection: one's teaching practice, one's own emotions, and one's views of children's behavior. Although it's helpful to consider these separately, they are, in fact, all closely interconnected. For instance, one's views about children's behavior might affect one's emotional responses when faced with challenging behavior in the classroom; whether a teacher is motivated to try new strategies might depend on whether the day's teaching has left that teacher feeling energized or overwhelmed. All of this ties in with the concept of self-efficacy—whether one feels effective and able to influence outcomes.

For example, in an anonymous unpublished survey, I asked teachers in a birth–5, center-based setting the following question: What most concerns you about a young child's challenging behavior? Think about how you would answer this question as you review some of the teachers' responses in Table 2.1.

As you can see, many providers may not yet feel competent or confident in their ability to use developmentally appropriate, evidence-based practices. In other words, they lack self-efficacy—a sense of their own effectiveness. They may also not feel confident in talking or brainstorming with families about behavior (e.g., "If I'm not sure what this is or how to help, I'm not going to be able to share insights with families"). It is essential to develop a repertoire of strategies and approaches to respond proactively and reactively across contexts, students, and situations. Teachers with lower feelings of competence in responding to behavior may have higher levels of burnout compared to those with greater self-efficacy in this area (Friedman & Farber, 1992; Skaalvik & Skaalvik, 2007).

Teacher self-efficacy is associated with job satisfaction and quality of interactions with others (Son & Sung, 2014). Building teachers' repertoires and promoting self-reflection can bolster skills, improve motivation, and minimize feelings of isolation (Barkley, 2010). Kelm and McIntosh (2012) similarly found that teachers exposed to positive behavior supports (PBS) had higher perceptions of self-efficacy compared to teachers not using PBS. Better understanding this topic and gaining familiarity with a range of universal and targeted behavior strategies can improve teacher self-efficacy and may likely strengthen provider–family collaboration.

Table 2.1. Teachers' concerns about children's challenging behaviors

Response From Other Peers

"That other children will copy their behavior"

"Losing the attention of the whole class when one or a few students are disruptive"

"When children are hurt by the 'challenges'!"

"I worry mostly about the safety of all the children."

"How it affects the other children in the class"

"That other children will be affected by the negative behavior–physically or emotionally–of one child"

"Tantrums or physical aggression resulting in injury to the child or other children"

"The child's safety and everyone around him"

"How to address challenging behavior so it doesn't . . . waste time for students not presenting with challenging behavior"

Student's Well-Being

"Child's future cognitive development"

"What can we do to stop the behavior?"

"Concerned child will get hurt"

Teacher's Perceptions/Actions

"How to cope and have patience with a challenging classroom"

"Loss of control of the classroom"

"Keeping order while still staying positive"

"Not showing negative behavior, modeling proper strategies when dealing with a behavior"

"How to address challenging behavior so it doesn't exhaust me . . ."

"If a concerning behavior happened repeatedly, what is the best course of action to take to ensure the safety, happiness, and possibility for growth with said child?"

"Finding strategies that result in improvement over time! Sometimes feels very trial and error!"

"I feel that we recognize positive behavior but rewards shouldn't be given each time someone does something good. I think children expect to be rewarded and if they aren't, they continue misbehaving!"

Talking With Caregivers

"How to discuss behavior with parents without them becoming upset."

Responses obtained from a survey conducted for an unpublished study (Edwards, 2014c).

Chapters 1 and 2 have laid a foundation for readers' understanding of early emotional development and the role of key players in a young child's life. (See the supplemental exercises at the end of both chapters to deepen your understanding.) Chapters 3 and 4 will provide specific strategies that can be used, with consideration for both center- and home-based settings. The evidence-based, practical recommendations are intended to build readers' repertoires to more successfully tailor responses, improve self-efficacy in addressing behavior, empower more families, and improve child outcomes.

QUESTIONS FOR REFLECTION

1. Reflect on a recent instance when what you said or did positively or negatively affected a child. Then, reflect on a recent instance when a young child said or did something that positively or negatively affected you. In each case, what action had a noticeable positive or negative effect? What was the effect? Why do you think this effect occurred?

2. As an educator or service provider, how would you categorize your connections with other key players across systems/environments? Are your interactions mostly positive or negative? Consider specific examples. What might you try to possibly improve the quality of certain interactions?

3. In the recent past, what negative or unsupportive remarks have you heard providers or caregivers say to a child? How did hearing them make you feel? How did the child respond? Have you personally made such comments to a child? What could you have said instead?

4. Who were the key players during your childhood? Take a moment to reflect on five individuals who may have directly influenced you during your earliest years of life. For each, list the person's name and his or her contributions to your emotional development, positive and/or negative.

5. Consider a child you personally know. Identify and describe the influential adults who interact directly with this child on a regular basis. Reflect on each of their current contributions to this child's emotional development. If you see any opportunities for improvement, reflect on what specifically you would want to see this adult do more consistently (and the supports/resources that might be needed to achieve this goal).

6. Review the teachers' responses to the described survey, which asked them to answer the question, "What most concerns you about a young child's maladaptive behavior?" How would you personally answer this question? How do your own thoughts compare to what this sample of teachers reported?

7. How might journaling help facilitate self-reflection? List at least three ways.

SUPPLEMENTAL EXERCISE:
FOSTERING CHILDREN'S EMOTION EXPRESSION

It is common to hear early childhood practitioners telling children, "Use your words." For a child who is developmentally and cognitively able to do so, this can provide wonderful insight into what happened and how a child may be feeling. Consider, however, how children's ability and willingness to verbally express themselves can widely vary across situations and settings—as in the following scenario.

> *George has been student teaching in the inclusive toddler room for the past 2 weeks. He sees that Andrew, Shana, and Eduardo are fighting over a toy vacuum. George intervenes by saying, "It has to go away if we can't share nicely." George quickly places the toy on a high shelf and notices that all three children respond differently: Andrew cries and knocks over a block tower; Shana lowers her head and quietly wanders to another center; and Eduardo crosses his arms and exclaims, "I don't like that!"*

Based on this scenario and your own experiences, answer the following questions:

1. If you were George, how would you have responded to the children not sharing the vacuum? Did he help the children's emotional development by doing what he did?

2. Do you think he should respond to each of the children? If he says nothing, might this be a missed teachable moment to help them better understand and express their emotions?

3. What could he say/do in response to each of the children's reactions? For Andrew or Shana, who did not use their words to express themselves, what additional support(s) would you suggest that George give them?

SUPPLEMENTAL EXERCISE: REFLECTING ON BEHAVIORAL CONCERNS

Reflect on a child you know who is age 5 or younger and exhibits concerning behavior. Complete the following activities:

1. List the behaviors you find concerning, frustrating, or confusing.

   - Avoid using subjective, "red flag" words such as *aggressive, rude, defiant, silly,* etc. Only use objective wording to describe exactly what the child is doing, in neutral, matter-of-fact terms (e.g., "Puts head down on table"; "Yells 'no!'"; "Plays with carpet strings during read aloud").

   - Did you list internalizing behaviors, externalizing behaviors, or both? Are these new behaviors or have they been persisting for weeks/months?

   - *Why* are you so concerned about each of the listed behaviors? Take a moment to reflect on and write down the underlying worries you have (e.g., "If he keeps covering his eyes during small-group instruction, he will miss important information, and this could affect his learning"; "If she continues biting other children, she will hurt them and have a harder time socially with peers").

2. Share this list with another person who does not know the child. Does this person agree the listed behaviors warrant attention? Is this person similarly concerned?

3. Finally, reflect on these questions and write down your answers: What are this child's strengths? What is he or she good at? What does the child enjoy doing? How might you use the child's strengths to help address behavior concerns? (For example, "Because Child A loves story time, maybe I can use extra story time with a favorite adult to help reinforce more adaptive behavior.")

ONLINE RESOURCES

See the online companion materials for Chapter 2, available at www.brookes publishing.com/edwards/materials to learn more about the following topics:

- Abuse
- Adults' Role in Early Emotional Development
- Ecological Systems
- Early Learning Standards
- Theoretical Frameworks for Understanding Behavior
- Toxic Stress

II

Supporting
Social–Emotional Growth

3

Guiding Principles

Section I of this book provided an overview of how young children's emotional development progresses, which environmental factors may place children at risk, and what role teachers and service providers play in early intervention. Section II (Chapters 3 and 4) will present guiding principles and practical strategies educators can use to foster healthy emotional development and adaptive behaviors.

Chapter 3 will discuss core principles for nurturing emotional growth, teaching adaptive behaviors, and better understanding challenging behaviors. Chapter 3 situates these topics in two related, evidence-based frameworks that are well established as being highly effective in early childhood educational settings: *positive behavior interventions and supports (PBIS)* and the *Pyramid Model* of tier-based intervention. This chapter will describe both in depth, including a discussion of the evidence supporting each model and the connection between the two.

Recall that Chapter 2 emphasized the importance of self-reflection in being an effective educator and developing a sense of self-efficacy. Chapter 3 revisits this theme by discussing how self-reflective questioning can inform educators' approach toward emotions and behavior within PBIS and the Pyramid Model. Finally, this chapter will emphasize the value of a proactive, prevention-oriented method and discuss specific components of this approach.

WHY EDUCATORS NEED
A COHESIVE SET OF PRINCIPLES AND STRATEGIES

The previous section highlighted the importance of early emotional development and the role of providers and primary caregivers. To be most effective, it is crucial for providers to have a store of evidence-based strategies, based in explicit principles, to foster children's emotional growth and adaptive behavior. One birth–5 program administrator who shared insights with me during an audiotaped focus group (Edwards, 2017a) described this necessity as follows:

> [There should be] a tool kit—a teacher having a tool kit, not literally, but something that they could pull at with little tricks of the trade when the going gets tough instead of saying "no" would be a great idea. Truly a great idea. Teachers tend to revert back—even though they sat at the training—they revert back to the comfortable style that they've always had.

Even with the best of intentions, it can be difficult for teachers to apply effective evidence-based practices consistently or to know what to do if one's usual strategies aren't working. During a different focus group I conducted (for a study currently under review for publication), one home-based early intervention provider commented, "[It] would be nice if there was a designated time during the week...to sit down and bounce [ideas] off of someone," while a center-based preschool teacher who participated in a separate analysis (Edwards, 2017b) noted, "I wish someone were over my shoulder, telling me exactly what to do."

Insufficient Training and Follow-Up

Perhaps you have heard providers make similar remarks, or you may be able to relate on a personal level. Many providers may have experienced insufficient pre-service or in-service training. Even when providers do receive this training, fol-low-up may be inadequate, leading to difficulties applying what was learned in the training.

Begeny and Martens (2006) found that providers may not have had exten-sive training in behavioral instruction practices at the preservice level. A survey of faculty from 2- and 4-year higher education programs in nine states suggested graduates were prepared to work with families and support social-emotional devel-opment, but were less prepared to work with preschool children with challenging behaviors (Hemmeter, Santos, & Ostrosky, 2008). At the in-service level (when working full-time in the education field), researchers who assessed 1,126 provid-ers (only 20.1% of whom worked in early childhood education) found that receiving at least 8 hours of professional development in a 3-year period strongly correlated with teachers' perceived ability to adapt instruction for students with diagnosed disabilities, compared to those who received less than 8 hours (Kosko & Wilkins, 2009). Unfortunately, in-service providers tend not to have sufficient professional development opportunities in their current positions. DeSimone and Parmar (2006) noted that available professional development workshops on inclusion often con-stitute only a few hours' worth of training. When compared to those with lengthy in-service training, those with little or no training on working with students with special needs have significantly less positive views on inclusion (Avramidis & Kalyva, 2007). (Readers are encouraged to consult their program administrator for relevant state or federal accrediting body guidelines concerning the number of required professional development hours per year and topics covered in core train-ing expectations.)

Even when teachers have received preservice or in-service training they may not be able to apply what they have learned consistently. Providers may not read-ily recall content learned from undergraduate or graduate coursework (Fink, 2013). They may not know how to meaningfully generalize or apply content to respond to a child's emotions/behavior once a training has ended (see Zaslow, Tout, Halle, Whittaker, & Lavelle, 2010). Researchers increasingly emphasize the importance of direct coaching and follow-up beyond offering isolated workshops (Fox, Hemme-ter, Snyder, Binder, & Clarke, 2011). For example, in a study of 113 prekindergarten teachers, those receiving online consultation on specific interaction skills had bet-ter quality teacher–child interactions than teachers who just reviewed online infor-mation and video clips (Pianta, Mashburn, Downer, Hamre, & Justice, 2008).

Effects on Self-Efficacy and Responses to Challenging Behaviors

When teachers are not adequately prepared to foster children's positive emotional development and behavior, the teachers may lack self-efficacy with regard to their confidence in their ability to minimize and address early social-emotional concerns. In addition, they may not be able to recommend effective approaches to family members. This can make both teachers and family members more likely to fall back on "go-to" techniques, which may unfortunately include the ineffective and punitive rapid-suppression approaches discussed in Chapter 2.

Figure 3.1 provides examples of thoughts a center- or home-based provider might have if he or she feels unprepared to address challenging behaviors. If a teacher's or therapist's repertoire is limited, he or she may continue to do what is familiar, even if it is not considered best practice or effective at minimizing concerns. An administrator in a focus group I conducted (Edwards, 2017a) commented, "I have seen time-outs being used. . . . I see more of it at the end of the day. The child is tired. They've been there since 7:30 in the morning, ya know, it's 5:30 at night. It's a long day for everyone and it's just easier sometimes. And I'm not saying that as a favorable thing. . . ." Providers who rely heavily on familiar, but not necessarily effective, approaches may consequently not know what ideas or strategies to offer to family members or may not feel comfortable offering them. Thus, parents or other primary caregivers may not always have as much information as they need to implement effective strategies for coping with challenging behaviors. In a survey that included urban mothers of preschool children in Head Start, which was conducted so as to better understand their perceived role in early emotional development, some mothers made the following comments when

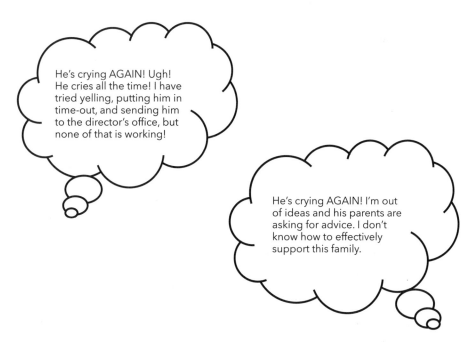

Figure 3.1. Potential thoughts from center- and home-based providers if not feeling prepared to address challenging behavior.

asked face-to-face questions about this role or their perceived role in emotional development (Edwards, 2010, 2012):

- "I beat my son when he don't listen—doesn't always work. I spank [him] and sit him in the corner and he wants to get up."

- "Being a boy, everyone wants me to spank him—but he's at the age where he doesn't understand—but you don't want them to run over you."

- "I'll smack her hand then put her in the corner for 5 to 10 minutes then talk to her . . . [but] then she'll do it again."

- "I try to put her in the corner, but that doesn't always work—[with spanking], I hate to do that to her—I cry when I hit her but she has to listen to me."

- "From experience, spanking is very unhelpful. Behavior gets worse from spanking—you rebel and get scared of that parent—I know as a child of abuse. My kid is bad but I try not to get to that point."

These remarks may be surprising. Consider how you might respond as a teacher if a parent of one of your students made similar remarks to you. As discussed in Chapter 2, rapid-suppression approaches fail to teach new skills or produce long-term success; moreover, negative verbal responses and routine physical punishment may have last-ing negative effects on emotional development and behavior.

Rapid-suppression, punitive responses do not always involve physical punish-ment. Consider a scenario where 15 preschool children are playfully screaming and running around indoors. For some adults, a spontaneous reaction might be to yell, "Stop running and making so much noise!" An adult who responded this way might be understandably worried about safety and/or ensuring safe, adaptive behavior. In the immediate, short-term context, this approach might appear to work temporarily—especially if children abruptly stop running and become silent. However, this is not really the best response. After all, what is this statement actually contributing to the learning environment? The adult's tone and approach are not positively modeling how individuals should talk to each other.

A better approach would be for the adult to do something *proactive* before the same behavior occurs again. Always consider how adults in any child care setting should use a nonpunitive, prevention-oriented approach to lay a solid foundation for early development and promote a more supportive learning environment. Further-more, keep in mind that to help build each family's capacity and support all young children, providers must first understand emotional development, enhance their own repertoire of recommended strategies, and confidently serve as models for others to promote self-regulation and emotional development (Edwards, 2012).

Building a Strategy Toolkit: Benefits and Limitations

This section has highlighted the need for educators to develop a "toolkit" of cohesive principles and strategies for fostering emotional growth and adaptive behavior. The remainder of Chapters 3 and 4 will discuss specific principles and strategies in detail. Note that while it is certainly beneficial for more teachers to have this toolkit, the strategies included have their limitations. Readers might sometimes wish there was one strategy that always worked well with every child, but there is no single infallible response or technique that will. (Be wary of anyone making such claims about any strategy.) Moreover, a strategy that works one day may not be effective the next day. This section is *not* intended to serve as a cookie-cutter, one-size-fits-all, exhaustive list of strategies, but rather, a source of different ideas and techniques you can try. Always keep in mind the need to be flexible and respond to individual children's strengths and needs.

Ideally, all key players in the life of a developing child should consistently use a nonpunitive, data-driven, and responsive approach. The remainder of Chapters 3 and 4 will equip readers with a more complete (but nonexhaustive) sampling of guiding principles, reflective questions, and strategies to use proactively and in response to challenging emotions and behavior. With greater understanding of development, a guiding framework, and a toolbox of resources and strategies, providers may find themselves looking forward to:

- Collecting objective data
- Brainstorming with other key players
- Thinking on their feet to support emotional development in an individualized, developmentally appropriate, and culturally responsive manner

High-quality early childhood and early childhood special education (EC/ECSE) administrators, teachers, and therapists should be celebrated! These dedicated individuals accept and even *embrace* day-to-day variability and uncertainty in young children's emotions and behavior. As previously discussed, this demands ongoing reflective practice, sensitivity to verbal and nonverbal cues, and awareness of developmental strengths and needs, as well as a commitment to modeling emotion coaching, collaborating with others, and tailoring recommended practices to maximize each child's full potential.

PBIS AND THE PYRAMID MODEL

Recall from Chapter 1 that children are expelled from preschool at a rate 3.2 times higher than the *combined* rate for all students in kindergarten through twelfth grade, with higher rates for older preschoolers and African Americans, and with boys being 4.5 times more likely to be expelled than girls (Gilliam, 2005). What might we do to minimize the number of young children who are expelled? Vinh, Strain, Davidon, and Smith (2016) sought to address the concerning expulsion rate in one state by incorporating components aligned with the Pyramid Model (see the following vignette). As you read the vignette, consider the impact a teacher might have on individual students' lives by choosing to take a positive, proactive approach to challenging behaviors.

You Have Given Me a New Child: The Importance of Positive, Proactive Approaches

Ms. Terri has a master's degree in early childhood special education and is the lead teacher in a self-contained, center-based class for toddlers with diagnosed delays and disabilities. Halfway through the school year, the center director notifies her that a new child, Matthew, has qualified for early intervention (EI) services due to a sensory and speech-language delay and has been enrolled in her class. The next morning, Matthew and his mother enter Ms. Terri's classroom for the first time. Matthew is watchful as other toddlers arrive and begin playing. He remains quiet, clinging to his mother's leg. Ms. Terri warmly greets Matthew and his mother. She puts various toys and puzzles on the table for Matthew to explore.

After a few minutes, Matthew's mother shares that she is late for work and is fearful that she will lose her job because of everything that has been happening with Matthew. "Yours is the third preschool program he has been in this year," she explains. "If you tell me he can't stay, I don't have any other options." Ms. Terri learns that due to Matthew's externalizing behavior (e.g., noncompliance with teacher requests, pushing staff and peers), he was asked to leave two other child care programs in the same urban neighborhood. Ms. Terri is aware of the high expulsion rate in early childhood settings, but this is the first time she has met a family directly affected by this.

Over the remaining months, Ms. Terri and the assistant teacher, Ms. Diana, develop a supportive, trusting rapport with Matthew. This rapport develops within the positive, orderly, and safe classroom environment they have established for all of their students. They set clear, appropriate expectations for all students before they enter the room in the morning (e.g., getting to eye level and having students touch picture cues or repeat the statements, "First we hang up our coats, and then we sit on the carpet"). They also do so throughout daily classroom activities, especially during transitions.

For example, before Matthew transitions to working one-on-one with his speech-language pathologist, Ms. Bonnie, Ms. Terri hands him two rectangular pieces of cardboard, with Velcro attaching a fork to one and a yellow ribbon to the other. She says, "Matthew, in 2 minutes we're going to put away our puzzles. Do you know what comes next?" "Look, Matthew," she says, prompting him to touch the fork, "First, we're going to have lunch." She guides him to touch the yellow ribbon as she explains, "Then, Ms. Bonnie will work with you in her room for a little bit." After lunch, when Ms. Bonnie arrives, Matthew is guided to peel the yellow ribbon from the cardboard to hand to her. When they walk together down the hall, Matthew notices that Ms. Bonnie has the same yellow ribbon on the outside of her door. This process required some advance planning and commitment to adhering to a predictable schedule, but it helps Matthew and his peers understand what is happening next and transition more smoothly between activities.

Ms. Terri and Ms. Diana also validate, reinforce, and redirect emotional displays when needed, provide Matthew and his classmates with meaningful opportunities to make choices, and model emotion coaching and responsiveness when they are distressed. They use a feeling chart, posted on the back of the classroom door, and picture cues as needed. For instance, one day another student leaves school early with her father. Immediately afterward, the teachers notice Matthew cover his eyes and start to cry. Ms. Diana gently guides him to the posted feeling chart and says, "Can you point to the picture that shows how you're feeling right now?" Matthew points to the crying face. "It looks like you're feeling sad," says Ms. Diana, encouraging Matthew to echo, "I feel sad." He nods when she asks if he misses his mommy. She validates that it's okay to feel that way and assures him he will see his mom later that afternoon. The teachers praise Matthew for letting them know how he feels, redirect his attention by asking him to choose between two of his highly preferred activities, and stay nearby to give extra attention as needed.

Ms. Terri and the other service providers take detailed notes on what progress Matthew is making in working toward desired outcomes. Within a few months, they have become keen observers of his strengths and emerging skills. Compared to when he first started, he increasingly uses adaptive wording to functionally communicate thoughts and feelings (e.g., "I feel sad"; "Help please"). He follows more one- to three-step directions with minimal verbal or gestural prompting and transitions more calmly between activities. The teachers enthusiastically praise him for his increased willingness to share with peers, take turns, and participate in small-group activities. They also arrange time to call and/or meet with Matthew's mother, the speech-language pathologist, and the occupational therapist to brainstorm ideas, share progress updates, and encourage continuity in strategy use across people and settings. At the end of the year, when it is time to assess eligibility for preschool special education, Matthew's mother is amazed that he does not qualify for services. "I can't believe it," she tells them. "You have given me a new child!"

Notice how in this vignette Ms. Terri and Ms. Diana embed many developmentally appropriate components in their teaching practices, such as setting clear expectations and incorporating multiple modalities so children not only hear instruction, but also see visual cues and touch tactile cues to help enhance understanding. Ms. Terri also highly values team collaboration and facilitates ongoing meetings for service providers and Matthew's caregiver to share ideas and progress updates. Do you think Ms. Terri would have been as effective in helping Matthew if the other adults were inconsistent and/or punitive in their interactions with him?

Consider how much of an effect Ms. Terri's approach likely had, in conjunction with the efforts of other team members. Were Matthew's improvements due solely to his maturing, or did the EI team's work make a difference? In what ways did their approach probably differ from approaches used by his previous teachers? Consider, also, the effect on Matthew's mother. How might she have felt walking into Ms. Terri's class, knowing this was Matthew's third child care placement in 1 year? Even though Ms. Terri was primarily supporting Matthew in the classroom, how did his mother also benefit from Ms. Terri's efforts?

Overall, Ms. Terri is laying a strong foundation for her students that nicely aligns with the positive behavior interventions and supports framework that will be discussed in the next section.

PBIS

Readers may have varying familiarity with *positive behavior interventions and supports (PBIS)*, sometimes known as positive behavior support or PBS. PBIS builds on *applied behavior analysis (ABA)*, which is "the application of behavioral principles, to everyday situations, that will, over time, increase or decrease targeted behaviors" ("Getting to Know ABA," n.d.). In other words, it is using one's knowledge about behavior to get someone to do a specific thing more often, or less often. PBIS is considered "the application of behavior analysis to . . . social problems" (Horner, 2000, p. 97). This approach is not just a handful of techniques or strategies. PBIS represents an evidence-based *framework* to guide our understanding of and approach to behavior.

The PBIS model is proactive and focused on creating learning environments that help to prevent challenging behaviors from arising. Within this model, instead of trying to stop or fix a concern, teachers focus on redesigning the learning environment to effectively support emotions and behavior. Horner (2000, p. 97) reminds us that "effective environments make problem behaviors *irrelevant, inefficient,* and *ineffective.*" For example, imagine that a toddler, Ruby, is not able to align pieces in a wooden shape-sorting toy independently and throws the pieces onto the floor with a visibly angry expression. A teacher might put Ruby in time-out, but if Ruby is behaving this way because she is frustrated and wants to stop the activity, what would be the point? Relying solely on this approach may just reinforce Ruby's behavior because she will learn that this is an effective way to get out of a frustrating situation. This approach will not teach her a new, more adaptive way of communicating her emotions when similar situations arise. Suppose that, instead, the teacher ignores the throwing behavior, quietly picks up the pieces, guides Ruby to communicate, "Help please," and encourages her to try again. This approach makes Ruby's challenging behavior *ineffective* in getting the teacher to let Ruby stop the activity, and also *inefficient*. Ruby will realize that if she wants to get this activity over with, she needs to just do it.

Moreover, suppose also that the teacher uses tape to cover over all but two of the holes in the shape-sorter and plans to give Ruby the two corresponding pieces. Using errorless teaching, she gently taps the edge of the first hole. Ruby smiles broadly as she correctly inserts the corresponding block. Then the teacher hands her the remaining block, which Ruby inserts on her own. The teacher celebrates her effort while removing tape from two more holes in the shape sorter. This process continues until Ruby has successfully completed the entire puzzle. This adjustment to the puzzle task makes Ruby's earlier behavior *irrelevant*. She no longer needs to throw the blocks to avoid a frustrating activity because it is no longer frustrating. The teacher has eliminated the frustration by reducing the number of stimuli and using errorless teaching to help her feel immediately successful. If Ruby does get frustrated, she now knows to ask for help. The combination of strategies Ruby's teacher used work together to make Ruby's challenging behavior ineffective, inefficient, and irrelevant.

In addition to taking a proactive, preventive approach to challenging behaviors, researchers like Horner and Sugai (2015) stress that PBIS embraces *person-centered planning,* meaning that the intervention aligns with the person's strengths and talents, uses readily available supports, and intentionally considers other factors that influence the person, including family views (Kincaid, Knab, & Clark, 2005). Researchers, such as Wheeler and Richey (2014), highlight how interventions based on person-centered planning use positive ways of:

- Modifying the environment
- Teaching alternative behaviors
- Using tailored consequences
- Working toward meaningful outcomes

The PBIS framework is not intended only for those children with concerning or challenging behaviors; rather, it is set up so that *everyone* benefits from embracing it. This framework has multiple tiers, or levels, to best support the needs of each learner. Typically, there are three tiers, each providing a different level of support. At the first level (Tier I), universal, proactive strategies are developed and regularly revisited to support everyone in the child care setting, including children with and without disabilities, children with and without challenging emotions and behavior, and even staff and family members (i.e., caregivers, siblings, extended family). Roughly 80% of children in a center-based class will thrive and not need additional support beyond this initial, universal tier (Sugai & Horner, 2002). At the second level (Tier II), children may need additional interventions, such as small-group supports. Approximately 15% of children will benefit from these secondary small-group or individualized Tier II supports (Sugai & Horner, 2002). The third, most intensive level of support, constitutes Tier III. A much smaller percentage of children (approximately 2% to 4%) may warrant comprehensive and intensive targeted Tier III supports across settings (Sugai & Horner, 2002). Chapter 4 provides a sampling of strategies across tiers and settings.

Implementing PBIS involves multiple components, including the following steps.

Build a behavior support team. It may come as no surprise that behavior plans developed collaboratively (i.e., with fellow service providers and family members working together) are highly recommended whenever possible. In a study of 58 elementary school personnel, for example, participants viewed vignettes of collaboratively devised behavior support plans (i.e., team members alone or by a team with a behavior specialist) as more highly preferred (e.g., improved contextual fit), over plans solely developed by a behavior specialist (Benazzi, Horner, & Good, 2006).

Engage in person-centered planning. (See prior description.)

Use proactive, Tier I, universal supports for all learners. This includes learners with and without special needs and challenging behaviors. (Specific strategies are discussed in depth in Chapter 4.) Support at Tier II and Tier III is likely to involve the additional steps that follow.

Conduct functional behavioral assessments (FBAs) as needed. For children who exhibit prolonged social-emotional concerns, you will need to define the behavior objectively and systemically collect data using widely available forms. (Many of these forms can be located online; see the links in the online companion materials for this chapter.) The goal is to identify *patterns* in when the behavior occurs/doesn't occur, which key adults or peers may be present when the behavior occurs, the function or purpose of the behavior, and what may be happening before or after each behavior episode to trigger the behavior and make it more likely to continue. (For more information about the FBA process, see Watson & Steege, 2003.)

Develop a hypothesis about the behavior based on the information gathered through the FBA. Following completion of data collection, you should be able to articulate a data-driven summarizing paragraph or statement on the frequency/duration of the target behavior displayed, what typically happens before and afterward (e.g., what activity is the student engaged in; what is said or done by specific staff members, family members, siblings, or peers), and the purpose(s) served by the target behavior (see Blood & Neel, 2007; Scott, Anderson, & Spaulding, 2008).

Work with your team to develop an intervention. Once you have collected objective data on the behavior's apparent function and others' roles in making the behavior circumstances more or less likely to happen, you're ready to create a data-driven intervention (i.e., behavior support plan). Based on the collected data, think about which strategies and/or techniques can be meaningfully embedded within the child's everyday routine and activity settings to minimize triggers, teach the child new skills, and help the child find a more adaptive way to achieve whatever outcome the behavior currently functions to bring about. This can involve outlining and committing to specific changes at the Tier I, Tier II, and/or Tier III level. Tier I supports might include changes like rearranging the room, posting the daily schedule, consistently using warning time, and providing a transition cue to help children end their current activity. Tier II support might include building students' skills through individual or small-group teaching, then providing tailored reinforcement within the setting. The more intensive and comprehensive adjustments made at the Tier III level might include outlining a consistent response and reinforcement schedule when the child attempts to use the challenging behavior at home, with the babysitter, and in child care. (See Chapter 5 for discussion of reinforcement schedules; for more information about developing behavior support plans, see Killu, 2008.)

Monitor and evaluate outcomes. With the help of your behavior support team, it is important to reflect on and assess their satisfaction with the devised behavior support plan, as well as its effectiveness (see Bradshaw, Reinke, Brown, Bevans, & Leaf, 2008; Wheeler & Richey, 2010). Questions to ask may include the following: Are you seeing an improvement in the child's use of desired, adaptive behavior? Is there data to indicate that the challenging behavior is decreasing? Are the selected strategies being consistently used by key adults and are they easy to implement? Are there aspects of the intervention plan that need to be tweaked? Is it time to start systematically fading or reducing the selected reinforcement and/or certain prompts?

The Pyramid Model

The multilevel Pyramid Model involves the application of PBIS (or PBS) in early childhood settings (Fox, Dunlap, Hemmeter, Joseph, & Strain, 2003) and emphasizes early childhood educators' role in young children's social-emotional development. More specifically, according to Hemmeter, Ostrosky, and Fox (2006, p. 583), the Pyramid Model comprises the following four key components:

1. Building positive relationships with children, families, and colleagues
2. Designing supportive and engaging environments
3. Teaching social and emotional skills
4. Developing individualized interventions for children with the most challenging behavior

Like PBIS, the Pyramid Model can be thought of in terms of levels or tiers. A positive, thoughtfully designed learning environment is beneficial for children's social-emotional development in general. A smaller proportion of children benefit from more specific instruction to address social-emotional development. A still smaller proportion of children will require more intensive support. Consider the illustration in Figure 3.2.

Most of our efforts should focus on the bottom two levels of the pyramid; that is, the universal levels to support all learners. Here, the emphasis should be on relationship building and designing our learning environment; for example, the quality of our teaching practices; rapport with children, families, and colleagues; proactive strategies to promote a positive learning environment; and responsiveness to others' needs. The next level up addresses the needs of children at risk for challenging behaviors by explicitly teaching social-emotional strategies; for example, how to take turns, how to ask someone to play, or how to label various emotions. The next level above that (at the top of the pyramid) involves an individualized and more comprehensive approach for children with prolonged, severe challenging emotions and behavior. It is at this highest level of intervention that teachers would need to implement more intensive steps, such as conducting a functional behavior assessment, forming a hypothesis statement, and implementing and monitoring a behavior intervention plan.

It is important to remember that these levels build on each other. It may seem counterintuitive for some readers, but rather than immediately intervening at one of the top levels for every concern, providers should spend most of their efforts strengthening the quality of teaching practices and relationships at the bottom of the pyramid to best support social-emotional development. (For a more detailed overview of each pyramid level, see Hemmeter, Ostrosky, & Fox, 2006.)

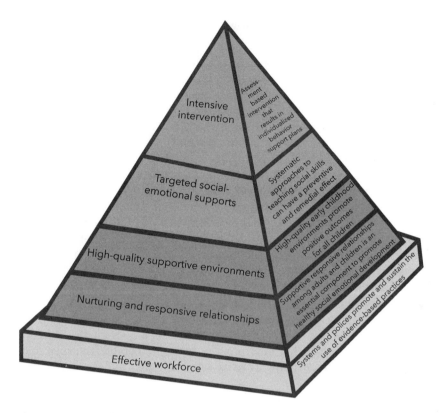

Figure 3.2. The teaching Pyramid Model. (From Center on Social and Emotional Foundations for Early Learning at Vanderbilt University. [2003]. *Pyramid Model for promoting social and emotional competence in infants and young children.* Nashville, TN: Author.)

Usefulness of PBIS

A great deal of research supports use of this multitiered, prevention-oriented framework across K–12 settings (see Wheeler & Richey, 2014) and early childhood settings (see Benedict, Horner, & Squires, 2007; Fox et al., 2003; Fox & Hemmeter, 2009; Frey, Boyce, & Tarullo, 2009; Hallett, Strain, Smith, Barton, Steed, & Kranski, 2016; Hemmeter, Fox, Jack, & Broyles, 2007; Stormont, Lewis, & Beckner, 2005). Empowering early childhood teachers to use specific verbal praise, for example, is linked with more appropriate behaviors and fewer challenging behaviors (Fullerton, Conroy, & Correa, 2009). Using Pyramid Model practices has also been associated with higher quality toddler classrooms (see Branson & Demchak, 2011).

Use of PBIS has been strongly encouraged in disability law as well. As of its 1997 and 2004 reauthorizations, the Individuals with Disabilities Education Act requires the following (Positive Behavior Interventions and Supports, 2018):

- The IEP team to consider the use of Positive Behavior Interventions and Supports for any student whose behavior impedes his or her learning or the learning of others (20 U.S.C. §1414(d)(3)(B)(i)).

- A functional behavioral assessment when a child who does not have a behavior intervention plan is removed from their current placement for more than 10 school days (e.g., suspension) for behavior that turns out to be a manifestation of the child's disability (20 U.S.C. §1415(k)(1)(F)(i)).

- A functional behavioral assessment, when appropriate, to address any behavior that results in a long-term removal (20 U.S.C. §1415(k)(1)(D)).

What is the purpose of PBIS—to minimize or replace concerning behavior? To help children identify and effectively express emotions? To improve overall quality of life? Certainly, the first two outcomes are desirable. But for educators successfully and appropriately implementing this framework, the *best* answer to the question is the third outcome: to improve overall quality of life. The true intent of PBIS is much broader and more holistic than just minimizing social-emotional concerns. Its focus should be on achieving lifestyle enhancement and improving overall quality of life (Bambara, Cole, & Koger, 1998; Wehmeyer & Schwartz, 1997; Wheeler & Richey, 2014). Recall from Chapter 1 the adverse effects that may ensue for a child with early-onset difficult emotions and challenging behavior, such as how these may potentially affect caregiver expectations, academic performance, social interactions, and later employment. By intervening early using PBIS within the multilevel Pyramid Model, educators can help lay a stronger foundation for emotional development and help positively alter developmental trajectories. Figure 3.3 demonstrates how it is essential not to ignore early concerns. It contrasts the two developmental paths a child might follow, depending on whether this framework was used to address early behavioral concerns, by offering alternating outcomes.

The best intervention is *prevention*. Establishing a high-quality, positive, nurturing, and engaging learning environment with predictable routines and clear expectations, where all key players are valued and supported at a developmentally

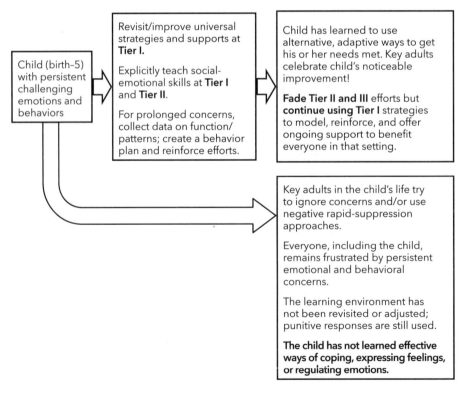

Figure 3.3. Alternating outcomes depending on whether the Pyramid Model is used to address concerns.

appropriate level, will likely minimize the emotional and behavioral concerns children might otherwise exhibit.

Teachers' Feedback on the Pyramid Model and PBIS

Although evidence from research supports use of the Pyramid Model and PBIS across settings, readers may also be curious what actual educators in the field say about this approach. Hutchinson and colleagues (2014) have demonstrated how tailored workshops on these approaches can improve teacher attitudes, empathy, and self-efficacy when they work with students with disabilities who have behavior challenges. In another study, a consultant helped a teacher reframe her beliefs to see how providing clear consequences for problem behavior is, in fact, a way to show that she cares about her students. This realization led to the teacher's increased use of this practice (Coles, Owens, Serrano, Slavec, & Evans, 2015). Similarly, when teachers of children under the age of 5 attended an in-service workshop I conducted on PBIS, one commented, "It is a very positive way of dealing with all behaviors. It is very 'clear and precise' [and] allows teachers to improve in an 'easy' way—it is an excellent guide." Another remarked, "It helped show us how to correctly help children without just ending with 'stop.'" A third noted that the workshop helped teachers understand "how to turn a negative behavior into a positive situation by speaking to the child." Finally, one teacher found the workshop helped her "remember how important we are and how we can make changes."

Later chapters of this book will discuss how specific strategies aligned with this framework might actually look in practice. Even teachers who are initially skeptical about PBIS may come to see its benefits. After completing my Positive Behavior Support Systems course, one student said, "A lot of the information I took away from the PBS course you taught, I incorporate into my classroom. I will be honest, I was skeptical of the model while learning it, but am a true believer in it during my first year of teaching. I have built great relationships with my students and they have greatly improved from years past, behaviorally and academically. Rapid-suppression approaches are a thing of the past and I hope the new wave of teachers keep PBS going strong."

REFLECTIVE QUESTIONS TO INFORM PROVIDERS' APPROACHES

Embedded within this prevention-oriented framework is a key consideration that may unfortunately be overlooked in practice: We must value the importance of self-reflection and embrace *our contributing role* in establishing a positive and responsive climate at Tier I, and helping colleagues and families support individual children at Tiers II and III. Recall the importance of being a reflective practitioner overall. This section presents a sampling of reflective questions intended to enhance readers' understanding of the Pyramid Model and PBIS process, and inform their implementation efforts.

Consider the following common scenario. Your colleague, Ms. Smith, is complaining or venting to you, and perhaps to other colleagues as well, about a child who exhibits a specific challenging behavior. What might you be likely to say in response?

1. "Ugh! I know a child who does that. So frustrating!"
2. "Oh, you should try X, Y, and Z. That always works when I do it."
3. "Hmmm . . . sorry to hear that. Tell me more."

Perhaps you, or another of your colleagues, would respond in a way similar to the first example, in an attempt to validate and commiserate with Ms. Smith's concerns. Unfortunately, this response may perpetuate feelings of frustration, and it fails to move the conversation forward in a more positive, reflective direction. This choice does not empower Ms. Smith to address the situation effectively (except, perhaps, to complain and/or seek an alternate placement for the child).

You also likely know people who would respond along the lines of the second example, in an attempt to "fix" the situation by offering specific techniques or strategies they have personally found effective. However, there is a problem with immediately responding in this manner. The *unique features* of the particular situation must be taken into account before assuming that certain techniques/approaches will work. Although well-intentioned, this response could set Ms. Smith up for failure by applying piecemeal, random strategies to a situation without first considering the context or developing a tailored approach to the problem based on reflective inquiry and objective data collection.

Ideally, administrators and providers will choose option 3, which invites Ms. Smith to elaborate more on the issue. This elaboration then becomes *the beginning* of a meaningful conversation that will likely empower Ms. Smith and yield more thoughtful, individualized insights to inform the next steps she takes.

What follows should be probing questions to help Ms. Smith embrace shared accountability and make sense of what is occurring. (Note: If there is no one to ask, Ms. Smith could certainly engage in this initial process of reflective inquiry on her own.) Here is a nonexhaustive sampling of possible follow-up questions to encourage Ms. Smith to elaborate and reflect, depending on the situation and context:

Is there anything you could change or improve at the Tier I level for all children? This question is *not* intended to ignore Ms. Smith's valid child-specific concerns. (Questions specific to the child's particular challenging emotions and behavior follow.) On the contrary, backtracking to ask about the teacher's role in implementing universal Tier I supports may shed light on areas in need of improvement within the early childhood setting. Addressing these areas may potentially resolve this particular child's emotional/behavioral concern—*without* requiring extensive data collection or a detailed behavior intervention plan—and also simultaneously benefit other children in the setting (e.g., peers, siblings).

Chapter 4 will provide a detailed description of possible teaching strategies to apply across home- and center-based settings at the Tier I level and will address other relevant considerations at the Tier I level (e.g., tone, expectations, scheduling, interaction style). For instance, depending on the situation, being more consistent in using positive expectations and visual cues might help a particular child, and all other children in that setting, understand and/or be reminded of what is expected.

Can you define or describe the behavior in objective, measurable terms? If someone is venting about a child's behavior in subjective, vague terms, this can be problematic when it comes to data collection or determining next steps (Edwards, 2017b). Saying "She is hostile" or "He is difficult," for example, may mean different things to different people. If adults in the child's life want to see how often the behavior is occurring (i.e., through recording frequency data), something one adult might count as "being difficult" may not align with what someone else marks as "being difficult." The use of "red-flag" words (e.g., *difficult, aggressive, angry, rude, defiant, mean, frustrating, bored*) is unhelpful for data collection purposes and may potentially make family members feel defensive (e.g., "My son is not difficult!"). For this reason, providers are strongly encouraged to avoid these "red-flag," subjective words when defining behavior.

Thus, in a scenario like the one about Ms. Smith presented here, it is best to guide the teacher to state the child's behavior in neutral, objective, and measurable terms. Everyone should understand what to look for, both to collect data and to share progress updates. Here are some examples of specific behaviors colleagues might decide to target: "Covers his eyes with his hands." "Takes toys from other children." "Cries and kicks teaching staff during transitions."

"Opens and closes cabinet doors in the family's home." "Throws food onto the floor from highchair."

What is the context for the behavior? Regardless of the tier of support involved, the context or setting in which challenging emotions and behaviors occur must not be overlooked (see Baker, Grant, & Morlock, 2008; Lucyshyn, Dunlap, & Albin, 2002). To gather information about the context for the behavior, educators might ask any or all of the following subquestions:

- Where does this behavior take place? Does it occur only in the child care, only in the home, or across settings?

- During which parts of the routine, or during which activities, is this behavior typically taking place? (For example, does it mostly happen after saying good-bye to a family member at arrival, during outdoor play, or before bedtime?)

- Who is usually present when the behavior is happening? Which other children, care providers, or family members are there?

- Is this typically how the child responds to this situation? Is anything unusual happening? Examples of unusual setting events might include such things as rain during the time the child typically plays outside, the mother's or father's departure on a business trip, the presence of an unfamiliar teacher, the child's not feeling well or being interrupted during naptime, or the birth of a sibling.

Such setting events do not mean we should excuse or ignore challenging emotional displays or behaviors, but sensitivity to these considerations can help plan for additional supports that might be warranted when unique situations arise.

Especially when moving toward the upper level of the Pyramid Model; that is, the level for addressing the needs of children with more persistent, prolonged social-emotional concerns, teachers must embrace the importance of "data-driven" interventions. In the sample scenario provided earlier, Ms. Smith should complete various observations, interviews, and forms as part of a functional behavior assessment to collect data on context, patterns, etc. (see Blair, Fox, & Lentini, 2010; Williford & Shelton, 2014). Recall the sample antecedent-behavior-consequence (ABC) analysis shown in Chapter 2. The online companion materials for this chapter direct readers to additional, free, widely available data forms to help with the corresponding process of reflection. Also, keep in mind that even when applying child-specific strategies at the upper levels of the pyramid, administrators and providers must *continue* to reflect on whether high-quality instruction, strong rapport, and effective strategies are being used to support all key players at the universal (Tier I) level.

What would worry you the most if this behavior doesn't improve? What "skills" might need to be improved to help this child in the long run? It is possible that this individual child (or perhaps a small group of children) needs to be explicitly taught specific skills to be successful in a particular setting or environment. Recall that strategies within this preventive framework should not only reduce emotional/behavioral problems, but actually *increase* overall social competence.

Reflecting on *why* a behavior is concerning can help teachers determine how best to address it. Consider the sample teacher reflections presented in Figure 3.4.

DeAndre cries and covers his eyes whenever he separates from his parents.

I am really worried about his ability to

- Make transitions calmly
- Cope when distressed
- Attach to and be comfortable with providers and peers

Lisa pushes and hits peers and adults throughout the day.

I am really worried about her ability to

- Express herself appropriately using picture cues or words
- Use gentle hands with adults and peers
- Use self-regulation to calm her body and make good choices

_____ **[YOUR child's behavior].**

I am really worried about his or her ability to

_____

_____

_____

Figure 3.4. Sample teacher reflections about children's concerning behaviors.

As you might notice from the examples in Figure 3.4, it is important to reflect on why you are truly worried or frustrated by a particular behavior. The issues are not just simply about DeAndre's crying or Lisa's pushing. When you help a colleague like Ms. Smith reflect on the underlying worry regarding a particular social-emotional concern, you will likely gain insight into specific skills that need to be explicitly taught and/or reinforced to improve long-term developmental outcomes.

PRINCIPLES INFORMING A PREVENTIVE APPROACH

One goal of this book is to support readers' efforts to implement a more proactive framework for early social-emotional growth and development. To effectively navigate challenging emotions and behavior, a thoughtful, individualized approach is needed. Providers must embrace *shared accountability* in what is occurring; that is, they must avoid narrowly "blaming" the child, parent, and/or another reason beyond providers' control. Although it is true that certain diagnoses or environmental risk factors may adversely affect language, cognition, executive function, attention, impulsivity, and/or emotion regulation, providers can do so much to minimize concerns and improve outcomes. Before moving on to the discussion of multitier strategies and techniques in Chapter 4, consider the following principles that are part of a *preventive* approach to addressing challenging behaviors:

1. Assume ALL children can learn!

2. Ensure that expectations are appropriate, well-articulated, and visible.

3. Use prompt hierarchies.

4. Focus concern on the emotion/behavior, not the child.

5. Always think about a behavior's function.

Take a moment to consider your intuitive understanding of each of these principles before reading the detailed explanations that follow. They may be a quick reminder of what you are already doing well, and they may also help you identify certain opportunities to improve current practice. Each principle is explained further next.

Assume ALL Children Can Learn!

Erroneously thinking that a child doesn't "belong" or cannot thrive in a particular setting can be deleterious for children and their families (see Doubet & Ostrosky, 2015). This first consideration may seem simple, but it is arguably often overlooked when providers and families talk about emotional/behavioral concerns. All young children can learn to manage their emotions and use adaptive behavior to get their needs met in a socially and developmentally appropriate manner. The speed and extent of progress within a certain period of time can certainly vary, depending on a range of factors, and this progress will likely require consistent support that is more extensive at first and gradually faded over time. By establishing appropriate expectations, high-quality engagement, positive reinforcement, and effective scaffolding from others, providers and families will likely see notable gains in each child's skills and abilities, as illustrated in the following vignette.

She's Not Making Progress: The Importance of Patience

This was Ben's second year working in an urban EI program. He loved the variety in his home-based caseload, and he appreciated working with diverse children and families in their everyday natural learning environments. One particular family on his caseload, seen once a week, included a single mother and her 2-year-old daughter, Jiao-Lin. When Ben was first assigned to this family, he learned as much as he could about Rett syndrome, the suspected diagnosis listed on Jiao-Lin's individualized family service plan. Due to the mother's disdain for Jiao-Lin's previous providers, Ben was the third early interventionist to work with this family. Jiao-Lin had a sweet smile and enjoyed being around others, but she was also nonverbal and visibly frustrated by not being able to communicate. In addition to using other strategies, Ben introduced a few basic signs. When Ben held up a desired toy, for example, he would gently pull it back, guide Jiao-Lin's hand to make the sign for "Give me," and then exclaim, "Great job saying 'Give me,' here you go!" while handing her the toy. Similarly, when a musical toy stopped playing, Jiao-Lin would start making visibly agitated grunting sounds. Ben would ask, "Do you want more?" while using hand-over-hand prompting to guide her to make the sign for "more."

Ben continued working on other desired outcomes while meaningfully incorporating such signs when appropriate. After several months, however, Jiao-Lin continued to stare silently when asked if she wanted something, and she remained fully dependent on Ben's hand-over-hand prompting to sign. Ben grew increasingly doubtful that Jiao-Lin was developmentally ready to make these signs independently. Then, during one visit in Ben's fifth month of working with this family, he held up a desired toy that made Jiao-Lin eagerly extend her arm. He paused, held back the toy, asked, "What do you say?" and waited. Jiao-Lin smiled. She slowly moved her arm back to her body, opened her palm and tapped it on her chest, signing, "Give me." Ben and Jiao-Lin's mother cheered! Over the next several months, Jiao-Lin began to meaningfully initiate other signs for Ben and other key adults in her life in appropriate contexts (e.g., "more," "help," "stop," "yes"). Her distressed grunts and crying notably decreased as she was now able to communicate wants and needs more effectively.

The takeaway message from this vignette is that educators should never be too quick to assume a child cannot learn or is not making any progress. Suppose Ben had become discouraged and dismissed his practice of using sign language after just 1 month? In that circumstance, Jiao-Lin would likely have continued to struggle to communicate and continued to feel frustrated. Can you think of a time when you or someone you know tried a new strategy for just a week or two, and then decided it wasn't working? If so, a valuable opportunity might have been lost. Conversely, you can probably also think of a time when you helped or saw a young child reach a certain milestone or goal. How did it feel to see that? How do you suspect it felt for the child?

Ensure That Expectations Are Appropriate, Well-Articulated, and Visible

Adults may have expectations for behavior that are not necessarily clear to the children in their care. When a provider or caregiver says a child is showing "inappropriate" emotions/behaviors, this certainly suggests there is an *expected* way of expressing one's emotions or behavior in a particular context.

Figure 3.5 shows three different settings: a playground, a family's dinner table, and a circle time meeting area in an early childhood classroom. Take a moment to think about which emotions/behaviors would typically be considered "appropriate" in each setting. Consider how some "expected" or "appropriate" emotions and behaviors might differ across settings, while others might be the same across multiple settings, as indicated by the areas of overlap in the figure. Compare and contrast your expectations across activities and/or settings.

The key question is: To what extent are we making our expectations known to young children? That is, rather than reactively reprimanding a young child for not

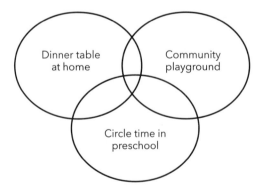

Figure 3.5. There are likely differences and areas of convergence in expected ways of behaving across settings in a child's natural environment. Consider the extent to which we clearly communicate and regularly reinforce compliance with these expectations in a developmentally appropriate manner.

behaving appropriately, let's instead set the child up for success by being more intentional and explicit in teaching and reinforcing what is expected across settings and activities (Carter & Pool, 2012). Ideally, readers should be able to say "yes" to each of the following questions:

- Are all adults in the child's life consistent in what they expect within a given setting or during a certain activity?

- Are these expectations made known to the child *before* entering that setting or starting the activity?

- Are expectations realistic, developmentally appropriate, and stated in positive terms? (For example, it is better to say "Use walking feet" and "Use gentle hands" than to say "No running" or "No hitting.")

- Are simple, visual pictures and/or songs used to help young children remember the rules?

- Do you *frequently* remind the child of expectations in a supportive, nonpunitive manner?

Use a Prompt Hierarchy

Prior to beginning a PBIS workshop for birth–5 educators, one anonymous respondent wrote about wanting to better understand "how to properly 'physically' move a child out of a situation." Recommended practice, regardless of whether there are any emotional/behavioral concerns, is that teachers should use a *prompt hierarchy* when interacting with children. That is, the level of prompting used should progress in a hierarchy of intensity/intrusiveness. In the context of PBIS, educators should begin with the least intensive or intrusive type of prompt, and use more intensive/intrusive prompting only if prompting at the less intensive level is unsuccessful. As part of everyday practice, teachers, therapists, and care providers should be mindful of using "less intrusive or intensive" prompts (e.g., gestures, visual cues, verbal cues), with less reliance/dependence on physical prompts whenever possible (see Lane, Gast, Shepley, & Ledford, 2015; Wong, 2013). For example, suppose a provider wants a child named Roberto to sit down, but Roberto is not sitting. Figure 3.6 shows the hierarchy of prompts, from least to most intensive, that the provider might use to help Roberto to sit.

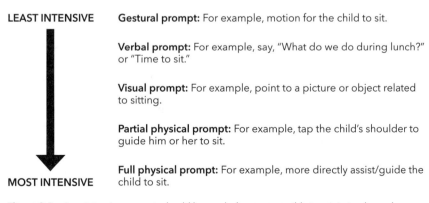

LEAST INTENSIVE   **Gestural prompt:** For example, motion for the child to sit.

Verbal prompt: For example, say, "What do we do during lunch?" or "Time to sit."

Visual prompt: For example, point to a picture or object related to sitting.

Partial physical prompt: For example, tap the child's shoulder to guide him or her to sit.

Full physical prompt: For example, more directly assist/guide the child to sit.

MOST INTENSIVE

Figure 3.6. Less intensive prompts should be used whenever possible to minimize dependence on the adult and work toward greater mastery/independence in emerging skills.

Guided by this prompt hierarchy, adults should not typically react or respond to a situation by assuming a physical prompt is needed. If this more intensive level is currently being used with a child in your center or on your caseload, what should be done? One goal should be to prioritize *fading or lessening* reliance on this level of prompting. Work toward gradually having the child respond effectively to less intensive prompts (Wheeler & Richey, 2014).

Focus Concern on the Emotion/Behavior, Not the Child

Although many readers likely already know this one, it seems worthwhile to emphasize. It can certainly be frustrating or concerning when a child displays brief or prolonged challenging emotions and/or behaviors. To look at the situation more objectively, remember that the *emotion or behavior* may be "inappropriate," "frustrating," or "bad," not the child! Building on the ecological framework discussed in Section I, consider a holistic view of the child's behavior and emotions, with each child having varying strengths, talents, interests, and needs, nested within the context of his or her family unit and community. Think of a child's selected emotional display(s) in terms of *choices* (e.g., Marshall, 2005). We need to help a child make a better choice.

Always Think of a Behavior's Function

It is essential that more early interventionists and early childhood educators embrace this important concept in their everyday practice. Before considering possible ways of responding to challenging emotions and behavior, we must first ask: What is the behavior's function?

That is, what *purpose* is the behavior serving? Consider this fundamental idea: All behavior is a form of communication. When trying to determine a given behavior's function, put words to what you think the child is telling you, such as, "What was the child trying to tell me when [behaving in that way]?" This can help you notice patterns and brainstorm next steps.

Children's challenging behaviors can serve many different functions (e.g., Gable, Park, & Scott, 2014). Several common functions are to solve a problem, to get attention, to obtain sensory stimulation, to get access to something tangible, to escape or avoid something undesirable, and simply to entertain oneself or play. As noted by Carr (1994, p. 393), "[t]he functional control of problem behavior is generally conceptualized as involving attention, escape, sensory reinforcement, and tangible factors . . . [and] we need to explore the role of context, including social factors such as group interactions, sequencing of tasks and activities, presence or absence of specific individuals, and crowding; as well as biological factors, such as physical illness . . ."

Wheeler and Richey (2014) offer PASTE-P as a creative acronym for remembering behavior functions: problem solving (P), attention seeking (A), sensory stimulation (S), access to tangibles (T), escape/avoidance (E), and play/entertainment (P). These functions are illustrated by the image of the bird in Figure 3.7.

Bear in mind that the same behavior may serve a different function depending on the context. It may serve a different function for the same child at different points during the day, or serve different functions for different children. For example, young children's repertoires may be limited in terms of communicating emotions. Thus, crying might serve different functions for the same child at different times of day. During free play, crying may mean, "I need your help," whereas crying during arrival at the child

Common Functions of Behavior

> **Problem solving:** "I was just curious about how to use my beak to open the cage door."
>
> **Attention seeking:** "I want to fly closer to my owner!"
>
> **Sensory stimulation:** "It feels so good to flap my wings!"
>
> **Access to tangibles:** "I want to reach the berries on that branch!"
>
> **Escape/avoidance:** "I don't want to stay in this small cage!"
>
> **Play or entertainment:** "It's so fun to fly to and from my cage!"

Figure 3.7.   Illustration of common functions of challenging behaviors.

care setting could mean, "I don't want to stay!" The same behavior may also serve different functions for different children. For example, suppose three different children are frequently trying to bite others during the school day. Amira bites to say, "I want to stop doing this activity!" Benicio bites to say, "I am teething—my gums hurt!" Carmen bites to say, "Give me attention!" What might happen if an adult responds to biting in the same way for all three of these children? Doing so would be inappropriate, because the three children have different needs, even if they are using the same behavior to communicate those needs. Similarly, if two different children are screaming, one might be trying to communicate, "I want the grown-up to give me a hug!" while another might be trying to communicate, "I want the other child to stop touching my toy!" Again, responding in the same way to both children would not be appropriate, because they are expressing different needs.

Take a moment to consider different possible functions of behavior. The underlying reason for some emotions or behaviors may seem relatively obvious. For example, think about how you might answer the following questions about your own behavior: Why did you eat breakfast this morning? Why did you hit your snooze button six times this morning? Why did you cry during the sad movie? Why did you walk away when your colleague or friend made a rude comment? These questions are probably easy to answer.

Other times, the function or purpose of someone's behavior may be much less clear. Consider how a teacher might answer the following questions when reflecting on the behavior of children in that teacher's care: Why did she bite him? Why did he hit me? Why did she run out of the room like that? Why did he start crying during that activity? Why did she pull her hair? Why did he dump the bucket of toy cars on the ground? Why does she keep getting out of her seat? (Very likely, you can come up with similar questions about other behaviors among the children in your care that concern you.)

Consider the wide array of possibly emotionally heated situations that might lead to children displaying challenging behaviors. As you read each of the following, keep in mind that tailored data collection will help shed light on the *underlying purpose or function* of any prolonged problem behavior (e.g., to attain or avoid sensory stimulation, attention, or another function, as discussed earlier) within and across naturally occurring components of the day:

- *Making transitions:* Bobby is watching cartoons on TV when his care provider, Ms. Harris, arrives at his home. His father says, "Bobby, look who's here. Let's shut off the TV and go sit with Ms. Harris."

- *Following directions:* Alexandra is playing with a toy as the class gets ready to go outside. She doesn't respond when her teacher directs her to bring her jacket. The teacher says, "Alex, Ms. Karen asked you to get your jacket."

- *Staying on task:* Emma's teacher is about to start storytime. Emma is fidgeting as she gets settled in. Emma's teacher, Ms. Jackson, says, "All eyes on me. Emma, please sit nicely in your chair."

- *Waiting:* Rashid and Jorge just finished drawing pictures. Rashid is now telling their teacher, Mr. Jones, about his picture. Jorge interrupts to talk about his own picture, and Mr. Jones responds, "Jorge, you need to wait your turn while Rashid is talking."

- *Sharing:* Two siblings, Melissa and Jack, are playing at home as their provider, Ms. Daniels, watches. Ms. Daniels says to Melissa, "You've had those toys for 10 minutes. I think your brother would like a turn." (Sharing toys calmly, as the child in Figure 3.8 is doing, does not come naturally to all children.)

Figure 3.8. Not every child will calmly share with siblings or peers. This is a skill that may need explicit scaffolding and positive reinforcement.

When I conducted a workshop on positive behavior supports for birth–5 center-based providers, I asked them to list examples of social-emotional concerns. They mentioned concerns such as the following: "[Child] cries because they are not first in line." "[Child] cries for the gross majority of the school day . . . disrupting and upsetting the others." "[Child] sits or lies down on the floor and refuses to move." "[Child] refuses to transition (whether to a special, going home, or even just washing hands) by laying on the floor, acting out if anyone gets close, refusing to take part in daily routine . . ." "[Child has] excessive tantrums." "[Child] simply does not listen." "[Child] throw[s] a tantrum with physical aggression . . . play[s] aggressively . . . [controlling]." "[Child] is a young toddler who pushes/bites." "[Child] randomly approaches peers and hits them with hand or toy, or kicks them." Consider the extent to which you, or your colleagues, have observed or felt personally concerned by these behaviors in a birth–5 setting.

Rather than immediately suggest strategies for colleagues to use, how would you respond? Certainly, encourage the reflective questioning discussed in Chapters 2 and 3. Furthermore, determine exactly how each behavior can be defined in objective, measurable terms (e.g., saying "pushes peer with one or both hands" is more objective and measurable than saying "aggressive"). Then, collect data to identify each behavior's purpose. Understanding the underlying function of concerning emotions/behaviors will likely require close observation and data collection. (See the links provided in this chapter's online companion materials for a sampling of tools you can use for data collection.)

Keep in mind, also, that when collecting data about a behavior, it's important to gather information about the behavior, its antecedent, and its consequence (see Table 3.1.). When the same challenging behavior continues to happen, most likely this is because it is working! That is, the child is getting a certain need met by repeatedly exhibiting the particular emotion/behavior over an extended period of time. It can be humbling to realize that something we are doing, as caregivers and providers, may possibly be perpetuating the display of difficult emotions and challenging behaviors.

Consider the following two scenarios, where adults are unintentionally helping difficult emotional displays and challenging behavior to continue:

- Two-year-old Rosa has just started attending a center-based program. This is the first time she has been away from her mother. When Rosa purposefully drops to the floor, crying, the assistant teacher runs over to give hugs. This provider continues to respond in this way when Rosa uses the same behavior at other parts of the day. This teaches Rosa an important lesson: "If I want more hugs and attention, all I have to do is start crying!"

Table 3.1. Antecedent-Behavior-Consequence (ABC): Rather than just focus on the child's challenging emotions and behavior, consider other individuals' contributing role in what is happening before and/or after the behavior.

Antecedent	Behavior	Consequence
What did the adult or peer say/do *before* the behavior? What was happening in the context (e.g., what was everyone doing)?	Describe the child's behavior using *objective* wording (i.e., state exactly what you saw the child do).	What did the adult or peer say/do *after* the behavior? How did the child respond?

- Four-year-old Terrell is having a difficult time listening during group storytime. When he pushes another child to show his frustration, he is quickly sent to the director's office down the hall. The teachers continue to "warn" him of this consequence if he pushes again. Terrell is learning an important lesson: "Whenever things are boring and I want to leave the room, all I have to do is push someone!"

For these reasons, when children present challenging behaviors, it is important to ask reflective questions such as:

- What was the child trying to say by acting in this way?
- Did my comments/reaction before or after the behavior affect what happened?
- Are my words/actions making it more or less likely that this child will use this same behavior whenever a similar situation occurs?

It is essential to collect data to determine what purpose the display of emotions or the behavior is serving, then teach/reinforce a more appropriate way of communicating that want or need.

Readers should now have a better understanding of positive behavior interventions and supports, the Pyramid Model, and key guiding principles for fostering healthy social-emotional development and adaptive behavior—including the importance of asking reflective questions. It is also important to individualize supports to align with the setting, the culture, and the unique strengths, interests, and needs of each child. Keep these principles in mind as you read Chapter 4, which will build on the foundation provided in this chapter by highlighting a sampling of recommended, multitiered strategies to enhance providers' repertoires across a variety of early childhood educational settings.

QUESTIONS FOR REFLECTION

1. Identify three ways you usually react or respond (or anticipate responding) to challenging emotions/behavior. Next, identify three things you do (or anticipate doing) *proactively* to minimize or prevent social-emotional concerns before they start.

2. Review the components of the positive behavior interventions and supports model (e.g., identify your team, embed proactive supports for all learners, conduct a functional behavior assessment on prolonged behavior, create a data-driven behavior support plan, monitor and evaluate your plan). How might they look in your early childhood educational setting? Think about how you would implement these steps with a particular child or group of children.

3. The Pyramid Model comprises four key components: building positive relationships, designing supportive and engaging environments, teaching social and emotional skills, and where needed, developing individualized interventions for children with the most challenging behavior. Think about an EC/ECSE program in which you have observed or currently work. How well does this program address each of these four components? What improvements could be made?

4. Just as people apply sunscreen before going to the beach, or childproof their home before a baby is born, so do teachers sometimes anticipate problems in advance and take steps to address them before they can arise. Think about a time you intentionally altered your teaching practice *before* there was a problem. What did you change and why? Did the change help forestall a potential behavioral problem,

and if so, how? How could you proactively adjust your approach for a new family on your caseload or to get ready for a new school year?

5. Recall that when targeting a particular challenging behavior to address, it is important to define the behavior in specific, objective terms. Think of a child you know who exhibits challenging emotional displays and/or behaviors. What specific behavior(s) could you target for intervention? Describe them in measurable, objective terms. Share this list with others on your team to see if they agree with your choice of a particular behavior (or behaviors) to target for intervention.

6. Remember that it is important to consider, and build on, a child's strengths when intervening, so as to minimize challenging behavior and teach functionally equivalent alternatives. One way to frame issues is as follows: "*In terms of strengths, Sarah is very creative and makes thoughtful comments during storytime. She does not always make good choices in* how she copes with disappointment or shows her feelings." Think about a child in your care whose emotional displays and/or behavior concern you. Complete the following sentences:

   • Some *strengths* this child has include . . .

   • This child *does not always make good choices* when it comes to . . .

   Brainstorm how the strengths you listed can be used to help the child in areas where he or she needs improvement.

7. Review the most common functions of challenging behaviors. Now think of two children you work with who exhibit challenging emotional displays and/or behaviors. How could you apply the functions discussed previously to concerning emotions/behaviors you observe in these children?

SUPPLEMENTAL EXERCISE: UNDERSTANDING THE FUNCTION OF A BEHAVIOR

Read the scenarios that follow. As you read, think about whether each adult's response in each scenario makes sense, and why it does or doesn't. Answer the following questions for each scenario:

• What is the likely function of the child's behavior?

• Considering the behavior's function, is the adult's response likely to be effective? Why or why not?

• If the adult's chosen response is not likely to be effective, what alternative approach could be taken instead?

Scenario A

Barry does not like having to clean up toys after playtime. Every day, when playtime comes to a close and his teacher asks him to help the other children clean up, Barry angrily starts throwing toys. His teacher responds by putting him in time-out.

Scenario B

Jasmine, age 4, is an only child. For most of her life, her grandmother supervised and cared for her during the day while her parents worked. Recently, her family moved. Because her grandmother is no longer close by, Jasmine's family has enrolled her at a local child care center. Unlike Grandma, Jasmine's teacher cannot always give her undivided attention. Whenever Jasmine feels lonely, she starts to cry. The teacher's aide responds by taking her out into the hallway for one-on-one conversations.

Scenario C

Three-year-old Kayla has some developmental delays that may interfere with learning to communicate. Nevertheless, she is fascinated by books—including the books her brother, Jake, a kindergartener, is learning to read. One day Kayla grabs her big brother's book right out of his hands. Their care provider tells Jake, "Just give her the book."

Scenario D

Ben does not like to sit still for long periods, including storytime with his early interventionist. Ben says his body feels "funny" if he sits still for too long. One day, as Ben's early interventionist reads a lengthy story to him, Ben starts shaking his leg. The early interventionist insists that Ben keep his body very still "so he can concentrate" on the story, but the shaking continues.

ONLINE RESOURCES

See the online companion materials for Chapter 3, available at www.brookes publishing.com/edwards/materials to learn more about the following topics:

- Data Collection Forms
- Function or Purpose of Behavior
- Functional Behavioral Assessment
- Positive Behavior Interventions and Supports
- Pyramid Model

4

Strategies Supporting
Social–Emotional Growth

Section I of this book discussed early social-emotional development and the role that teachers and other care providers play in fostering this development. In Section II, Chapter 3 presented core principles for nurturing children's social-emotional growth, teaching adaptive behaviors, and minimizing or addressing challenging behaviors. It also provided an overview of positive behavior interventions and supports (PBIS) and the Pyramid Model, guiding reflective questions to embrace shared accountability and tailor support to children's needs, and key principles to guide implementation of a prevention-oriented approach to social-emotional development. Building on this content, Chapter 4 will highlight how a sampling of recommended strategies might be used with young children across home- and center-based settings. This array of strategies is not intended to be exhaustive; readers should always be wary of any falsely proposed "one-size-fits-all" approach. Responses must be individualized in light of particular children's and families' strengths and needs, and any considerations unique to the particular setting or context.

This chapter will bolster teachers' sense of self-efficacy by expanding their repertoires of possible ways in which to minimize and address social-emotional and behavioral concerns for children at any intervention tier. It presents proactive strategies that can be used across settings to support all young children's social-emotional skills, along with secondary or tertiary strategies that can be used across settings to address prolonged emotional/behavioral concerns. For each strategy in this chapter, discussion includes a user-friendly, evidence-based rationale for the strategy's role in supporting emotional development, along with examples of how it may be used in practice.

PRIMARY PREVENTION STRATEGIES TO
SUPPORT SOCIAL-EMOTIONAL GROWTH

Take a moment to reflect on strategies you or other providers have used to help ensure the school day or session goes smoothly for everyone in the setting. As noted in Chapter 3, it is vital to work toward establishing a positive, trusting rapport with children and families and use reflective practice. Other proactive strategies include "[providers making] changes *within themselves* (e.g., tone, consistent responses), *the physical environment* (e.g., moving a meeting time seat, posting rules at eye level), and/or *the curriculum* (e.g., incorporating more motivating content)" (Edwards, 2017b, pp. 11–12). Recommended strategies should be embedded and used in conjunction with inclusive, culturally sensitive, high-quality instruction.

This section presents a small sampling of evidence-based primary (universal, proactive) intervention strategies that build on the PBIS framework and Pyramid Model presented in Chapter 3. These strategies, which I have personally found to be both highly effective and not consistently used in practice, include:

- *Communicating expectations:* Communicate expectations before transitioning to a new activity.
- *Redirection:* Redirect children to what they should do.
- *Providing choices:* Embed meaningful opportunities for choice making.
- *Emotion coaching:* Model and encourage emotion talk.

As stated in previous chapters, proactive social-emotional strategies are intended to promote adaptive emotional development for *all* young children, regardless of whether they have developmental delays or diagnosed disabilities, or present difficult emotions or challenging behaviors. Application of these strategies should certainly be tailored to children's developmental level. Also consider adapting these strategies in ways that will be well received by and feasible for providers and caregivers in each setting.

Proactive Strategy: Communicate Expectations *Before* Transitioning to a New Activity

To help children make smooth transitions between activities and ensure they understand what to do during each activity, it makes sense to communicate expectations *before* the transition.

Description and Rationale   Sometimes providers and caregivers move to the next step in the daily routine without clearly communicating expectations. Just hoping for the best, or assuming that by a certain age or time of the year children should simply know what to do—and then reprimanding them if not behaving as expected—fails to set young children up for success. Instead, aim to provide realistic, developmentally appropriate expectations for behavior and emotional expression *before* entering each activity or step in the routine (see Hemmeter, Fox, Jack, & Broyles, 2007; Nelson, Colvin, & Smith, 1996; Safran & Oswald, 2003).

Certainly, a teacher's expectations might vary across different contexts, such as the playground, storytime, naptime, center time, and mealtime or snack time. For each of these contexts, try to identify two rules or expectations a teacher would expect a child of a particular age to remember. Consider how the teacher could communicate these expectations to children. For example, one expectation for naptime might be that children do not talk during this time, and that they lie down to sleep or rest. A teacher could verbally convey these expectations as follows: "Before we have naptime, what do we need to remember? Keep quiet as a mouse so we don't wake anybody up. Lie down and either go to sleep or just rest."

After children have heard these expectations, then depending on a given child's age and ability level, the teacher might consider pausing to see if the child is able to complete his or her sentence. For example, the teacher could say, "Remember, during naptime, we keep . . ." ("Quiet as a mouse!") "Instead of walking, standing, or sitting, we . . ." ("Lie down and go to sleep or just rest.") This technique can be easily adapted for teaching children expectations for appropriate behavior in other public settings; for example, a home-based provider might use it to teach rules or expectations for how to behave at the grocery store or in a restaurant.

Expectations must be consistently applied and explicitly made known to young children (Lane, Stanton-Chapman, Jamison, & Phillips, 2007). Using multiple modalities with young children has been recommended in areas such as literacy instruction (Roskos, Christie, & Richgels, 2003) and science (Siry, Ziegler, & Max, 2012). Similarly, instead of solely relying on our words to teach behavioral expectations, it can be helpful to use multiple modalities, either in succession or paired, such as brief statements, modeling, tactile cues, visual cues, and/or actual photos of what is expected (see Bevill, Gast, Maguire, & Vail, 2001; Knight, Sartini, & Spriggs, 2015, p. 157). Also recall the prompt hierarchy discussed in Chapter 3, which reminds us that less intensive prompts like gestures or verbal cues should be used before more intensive prompts like physical cues. For example, suppose children have been taught the following expectations for sharing: If Child A has something that Child B would like to look at or use, Child B should approach Child A and ask, "Can I see?" Child A should count to five and then give the item to Child B.

These expectations can be reinforced through visual cues, as shown in Figure 4.1. The teacher can reinforce expectations through dialogue like this:

- "How do we share with each other? Let's look at this picture." [Point to the first picture shown in Figure 4.1.]

- "If you want to see what another child has, open your hand and say, 'Can I see?'"

- "Let's try it together: 'Can I see?'" [Point to the second picture shown in Figure 4.1.]

- "If another child asks to look at something you have, slowly count to five, and then share it with them."

- "Let's try it together: 'One . . . two . . . three . . . four . . . five. Okay, it's [other child's] turn!'"

Figure 4.1 demonstrates how using visual cues can be a useful, developmentally appropriate way of explaining expectations to a young child.

Recall the importance of ongoing reflection. If an adult notices certain problematic emotions/behaviors during an activity, this should inform the type of friendly reminders given to the child before that same activity takes place again. For example, if the child previously started giggling or singing to himself during naptime, it would make sense to remind the child *before* naptime begins that it is important to keep quiet during this time so everyone can rest.

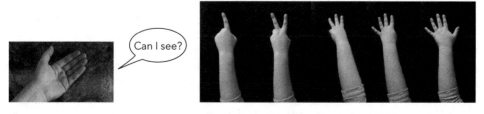

Figure 4.1. Using visual cues can be a useful, developmentally appropriate way of explicitly showing a young child what is expected.

To promote success, it is helpful not only to use developmentally appropriate wording to specify what is expected, but also to share, briefly, the anticipated consequences after the behavior occurs (and then to be consistent in following through with what is said). Researchers refer to this as *contingent reinforcement,* or the relationship between a response and consequence in which the consequence is offered if and only if the response occurs (Hart, Reynolds, Baer, Brawley, & Harris, 1968; Skinner, 2014). Adults, for example, may use *"If X . . . then Y"* wording to clarify connections between choices and consequences, regardless of whether the behavioral choice and the related consequence are positive or negative.

This serves as a means of preemptively reinforcing adaptive choices. An adult might tell a child, "If I see you do X, then we will do Y," and follow up later with, "Okay, nice job doing X, so now we can do Y!" For example, the adult might say, "If you share nicely with the other children during this game, then you get to play with it some more during free play." Then, if the child shares nicely, the adult can follow up with, "Okay, nice job sharing with the other children! Now you can have more time to enjoy the game at free play!" Conversely, the same formulation can be used preemptively to caution against challenging behavioral choices (again, with consistent follow-through). An adult might tell a child, "If I see you do X, then we will do Y" and follow up later with, "Because you did X, what does that mean? Right, by doing X, you need to do Y." For example, the adult might say, "If I see you hit another child when we are on the playground, then you will have to sit on the bench for the rest of recess." Then, if the child does choose to hit one of his or her peers, the adult can follow up by saying, "Remember, hitting hurts. We need to pat nicely and use our words. Because you hit someone, what does that mean? Right, because you hit someone on the playground, you need to sit on the bench for the rest of recess. Let's remember to make better choices next time."

Application Across Settings   This strategy of clearly communicating expectations can be applied in both center- and home-based settings. For example, consider these four scenarios.

Scenario 1: The teacher in a prekindergarten, center-based setting greets the children by the door of the school and waits until all buses have arrived. She presses her finger to her lips and gives reinforcing thumbs up as they quietly walk against the side wall toward the classroom. *Before* opening the door, she asks a volunteer to share what they are expected to do every morning as soon as they walk inside ("Put your bag in your cubby, pick a book from the shelf, and do a picture walk on a carpet square.") The children are reminded of what is expected and calmly begin their day.

Scenario 2: It is the beginning of mealtime in the infant room in a center-based setting. In recent weeks, several of the children (aged 9 to 12 months) have been loudly banging on their trays to get their food faster. Today the teachers try something different to make mealtime less stressful. Before the children's arrival, the teachers taped a small picture of a fork and a picture of a sippy cup to the corner of each child's tray. Before lifting each child into his or her highchair, they bend down to the child's eye level and say, "No banging. Gentle hands please! Touch the picture to show what you want." Throughout mealtime, the teachers ignore any tray banging, instead quickly redirecting the child to gently tap the picture (using hand-over-hand guidance as needed). They use task-specific verbal praise when children do what is expected: "Good using gentle hands, Kevin! Good touching the picture of a cup—let's get you your sippy! You are showing me you are ready . . . Here's your food!"

Scenario 3: Jayden, who receives services in his home, has been testing limits during mealtime lately. His service provider decides to model for the caregiver how to talk about mealtime expectations *before* going to the kitchen table. After Jayden wakes up and the service provider helps his caregiver with the process of getting Jayden dressed, his service provider pauses and sits down with him on a nearby chair. "Jayden," his service provider softly says, "We are going downstairs to have breakfast. I want us to make better choices when we're eating. Do we throw food and scream?" [Jayden quietly shakes his head.] "Should we jump all around or stay in our seats until we're finished?" [Jayden says, "Stay in our seats."] "What should we say if we don't want something?" [Jayden is guided by his provider to repeat, "No, thank you."] "Okay, we know you can make good choices . . . We'll be watching! Let's go have a nice breakfast!"

Scenario 4: Katherine receives home-based services. After playing in her back-yard with her older sister for the past 45 minutes, Katherine is thirsty. She runs inside and abruptly screams, "I want my milk!" Instead of hurrying to give her milk when she makes this inappropriate demand (which may make it more likely that Katherine will try this approach again), and instead of yelling at her, her service provider takes a different approach. She ignores Katherine's screamed request, looks away, and says calmly and clearly, "May I have milk, please?" This reminds Katherine of what is expected when requesting something. She softly echoes, "May I have milk please?" Her provider immediately looks up, smiles, thanks her for using such nice words, and pours her a cup of milk.

As part of communicating expectations, the "If X, then Y" strategy can also be applied across settings. For example, a teacher might say, "Remember to use walking feet in the hallway on our way to Music. If anyone runs in the hallway, then we will have to return to the classroom and try again. . . . Because three of our friends were running in the hallway, we all need to go back to our classroom and try again. This means we will have less time in our special. Remember, walking feet!" In a home-based setting, a service provider might say, "If you eat most of your lunch, using nice words and keeping the food on your plate, you will get to choose the dessert! . . . You did a great job eating lunch today and remembering to use nice words and not throw your food. Because you ate so nicely, you get to choose the dessert!"

Proactive Strategy: Redirect Children to What They Should Do

Instead of focusing on what a child is doing that is problematic or inappropriate, often educators can simply redirect children to do what is appropriate.

Description and Rationale   A teacher in a birth–5 program once anonymously asked me, "What can we do to stop negative behavior?" How might you respond to this question? I encourage readers to never end a conversation by telling a child what he or she should stop doing. Statements like "Stop running!" "No more screaming!" and "Stop crying" are not very effective, as such negative statements contribute to a harsher, more punitive learning environment.

Furthermore, we cannot assume young children necessarily know what they should be doing or know how they should more appropriately express their emotions. Recall from Chapter 3 how all behavior serves a particular *function*, such as problem solving, attention seeking, sensory stimulation, access to tangibles, escape/avoidance, or play. Because all behavior, whether adaptive or not, has a purpose or function, it is essential to validate what the child is trying to communicate and teach replacement behaviors (as illustrated in Figure 4.2), regardless of whether the provider chooses to use words, visuals, gestures, and/or modeling.

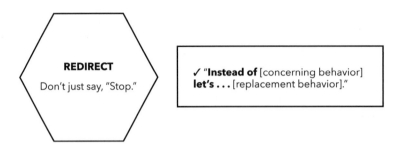

Figure 4.2.   Challenging emotions and behavior cannot just be "stopped," only redirected or replaced with a functionally equivalent alternative.

For example, suppose children find playing with blocks to be fairly dull, and as a result, when given blocks to play with, they throw them around. Simply saying "Stop throwing blocks!" is not likely to be effective. Rather, it's important for the teacher or service provider to identify the function of the children's behavior (escape from an undesirable activity). Once this function is identified, what could the teacher *teach* children to do to communicate their desire to end block play more appropriately and/or help them brainstorm alternative, engaging ways to play with blocks?

To consider another scenario, suppose that after children have been sitting for 45 minutes they start jumping up and down because of an inner desire for movement; that is, they need sensory stimulation. How effective will it be for an adult to simply insist that they all sit quietly? How might the children likely respond? Instead, a much more effective way to address their jumping and appropriately meet their needs might be to guide the children to do a quick movement activity (see Pica, 2006) and revisit the length of activities within the daily schedule/routine.

In short, rather than trying to just stop challenging behavior, it is much more effective to focus instead on how behaviors can be redirected (Fettig, Schultz, & Ostrosky, 2013; Voorhees, Walker, Snell, & Smith, 2013), as in the example shown in Figure 4.3. One way to work toward establishing a positive climate for all children is to identify replacement behaviors that meet the following criteria:

- They are *developmentally appropriate* in terms of the child's abilities and needs.

- They are *socially acceptable* in that particular setting (i.e., replacement behaviors that key players would be happy to see the child display, such as raising a hand to ask a question instead of calling out).

- They *serve the same function as the concerning emotion/behavior* being displayed.

Application Across Settings   This strategy can be applied in both center- and home-based settings. For example, consider these four scenarios.

Scenario 1: Lily, a child in a center-based setting, hits another child, Alice, who is holding a toy Lily wants. Their teacher says, "We do not hit. Hitting hurts. Let's pat Lily nicely on her arm and ask if she's okay. Did you want the toy she was holding? Hold out your hand and say, 'Can I see?'" (Note: This technique can build the skill set for a child with emerging expressive language. Alternatively, guide this child to point to a picture card or use a gesture/sign.)

Scenario 2: Two co-teachers in a center-based setting hear a loud noise from another part of the room. A child named Andy is sitting on the floor screaming. The change is so sudden that neither teacher knows what precipitated it. One teacher walks

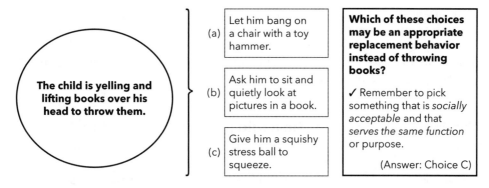

Figure 4.3. When replacing behavior, alternative options must align with what is deemed appropriate and well received in a particular setting and what would serve the same function (e.g., attention seeking, avoidance, sensory stimulation, and access to tangibles).

over to Andy. Andy shakes his head when asked if he is hurt, but persists in screaming loudly. The teacher says, "Screaming on the floor is not okay—let's calm our bodies. Let's take a walk to the office to get some paper." Later, when Andy is visibly calmer, the teacher says, "Great job calming down. Are you ready to talk about what happened?" (Note: This technique can help with self-regulation.)

Scenario 3: Isaiah, a child who receives services in a home-based setting, always has a lot of energy, and often he expends this energy by jumping on the couch, which frustrates his parents. His service provider tells Isaiah, "Jumping on the couch is not a good choice—let's jump on the floor. Let's see if you can jump 10 times . . . 1, 2, 3, 4, 5, 6, 7, 8, 9, 10! Good jumping on the floor! Are you ready to sit calmly on the floor or do you first want to do five more jumps?" (Note: This technique can possibly help to satisfy the function of sensory stimulation.)

Scenario 4: Recall the example presented earlier: children in a center-based setting throwing blocks to escape the activity of block play. Perhaps one reason they find block play boring is that they don't really know how to do it. The teacher might say, "Someone can get hurt if we throw blocks—let's see who can build the tallest tower!" (Note: This technique can help the child learn an alternative, more appropriate way of playing.)

As suggested in the following vignette, instead of using a punitive response, there are many naturally occurring opportunities to redirect a child and teach foundational skills.

Wanting a New Song on the Radio (Part 1): A Teaching Opportunity

Toward the end of the day, 4-year-old Sam and his aftercare provider, Christian, are singing a popular song as they wait for Sam's parents to come pick up Sam and his brother, Jack. Jack, who is 30 months old, starts screaming from his highchair, "I no want this song! I no want this song!" Christian quickly presses a button to play a Mickey Mouse sing-along CD. This makes Jack immediately happy. He smiles and begins singing along to the music. Sam, however, complains, "Hey, I was singing the other song! Jack always gets his way!" At the end of a long work day, Christian is tired. He abruptly shuts off the music and says sternly, "Fine, then we will just not have any music while we wait." Both boys sniffle and whine as they wait for their parents to arrive.

What do you see as some of Christian's strengths in this scenario? What are some concerns or missed opportunities? Do you suspect Jack has learned another way to request a song, or is he likely to continue screaming when he wants the music changed? How might you have handled things differently? Consider the alternate approach illustrated in the following vignette.

Wanting a New Song on the Radio (Part 2): Using Redirection

Toward the end of the day, 4-year-old Sam and his care provider, Christian, are singing a popular song as they wait for Sam's parents to come pick up Sam and his brother, Jack. Jack, who is 30 months old, starts screaming from his highchair, "I no want this song! I no want this song!" Christian lowers the music, takes an audible deep breath, and says slowly and calmly, "Jack, screaming is not a choice. We need to calm down. When you show me you're calm, I can turn it back on. Let's count to five: 1 . . . 2 . . . 3 . . . 4 . . . 5 . . . [long pause] Are you ready?" Jack quietly nods that he is ready.

Christian replies, "Okay, good calming down. If you want another song, you need to say, "New song, please." Christian waits patiently. "New song, please," Jack echoes softly. "Nice using your words, Jack!" Christian exclaims. "Your brother is listening to his song. After Sam's song is finished, you can pick the next song. Okay, Jack?" Jack smiles and says, "Okay!" Sam happily resumes listening to the music and sings along with Christian. As promised, Christian switches to one of Jack's sing-along CD songs when Sam's song is over. Both boys are calm and happily singing as they wait for their mom and dad to come pick them up.

What was different about this second vignette? Did you notice that Christian seemed more confident and empowered in this scenario? Following the strategy of redirection helped Christian take a source of daily stress and turn it into a calmer, more positive experience. Moreover, think about the wonderful new skills Jack is learning from this modeling and instruction. To support his emerging skill set, he is now receiving a nightly reminder from a trusted caregiver on how to do the following:

- Self-regulate and make better choices when frustrated, such as calming himself down and using his words instead of screaming
- Share and take turns
- Take another's perspective, such as understanding how others want to hear different songs (this emerging skill is related to sharing and turn-taking)
- Improve his expressive and receptive language in a meaningful context

Proactive Strategy: Embed
Meaningful Opportunities for Choice Making

Whenever possible, educators can give children appropriate, well-defined choices and let them decide among these choices.

Description and Rationale   Skilled providers recognize that young children tend to respond favorably when given options or choices within clear parameters set by trusted, familiar adults. Certainly, there are some children who will not get upset if told exactly where to sit or what color crayon to use. However, it is not uncommon for young children to become visibly frustrated and/or test limits if they are *rarely* given any choices. This can lead to unnecessary power struggles and a harsher climate (e.g., remarks from adults such as "I said you need to sit here! You are not being a good listener!"). Proactively planning for ways to strategically embed meaningful opportunities for children to express personal preferences is strongly advised. This will likely have the following positive effects:

- It will minimize defiance and limit testing by tapping into young children's increasing desire for autonomy and control (Ruef, Higgins, Glaeser, & Patnode, 1998; Smith & Bondy, 2007).

- It will encourage communication (i.e., expecting children to make verbal or nonverbal requests) (Rogers et al., 2006).

- It will improve performance on school readiness and assigned tasks (Denham, 2006; Moes, 1998). One study suggested toddlers with autism had improved engagement (time on task) when allowed to self-select a toy, compared with instances in which they played with a teacher-selected toy (Reinhartsen, Garfinkle, & Wolery, 2002).

- It will enhance quality of social play with other children (Carter, 2001).

- It will reinforce the importance of person-centered planning (Denham et al. 2012; Reid, Everson, & Green, 1999).

- It will promote self-determination earlier in development (Erwin & Brown, 2003; Palmer et al., 2012; Shevin & Klein, 1984).

Allotting for increasing independence and choice making is developmentally appropriate and highly recommended. The key is to meaningfully and creatively embed choice making *within parameters or parts of the established, consistent routine set by providers and caregivers*. Note that overarching parameters are set by the adult, not the child. For example, one would *not* ask a child, "Do you want to eat lunch or go play on the playground?" because broad decisions like this, which involve thinking about how best to structure the day and schedule activities, go beyond what is developmentally appropriate. Answering such a broad question, or having to choose among too many different alternatives, may be overwhelming for the child. Instead, the adult can say it is lunchtime, then brainstorm opportunities for the child to choose from X, Y, or Z (e.g., choosing which chair or which cup), making sure these opportunities make sense for that particular mealtime context.

Application Across Settings   Allowing children to make choices within developmentally appropriate parameters is a strategy that can be applied in center- and home-based settings. For example, consider these scenarios:

Scenario 1: When giving children in a center-based setting the direction, "It's time to sit," use embedded choices to keep the process orderly. For example, say, "If you are wearing [a bow in your hair], please walk over here to choose a carpet square . . . Now, if you are wearing [green socks], please find a carpet square . . ." In a home-based setting, try embedding a choice such as, "Do you want to sit on the floor or on the couch?"

Scenario 2: At snack time, provide choices like "When the snack helpers come to your seat, please choose either the crackers or the pretzels" or "Let's get a drink. Do you want this green cup or this blue cup?"

Scenario 3: For play activities, give a choice such as "Which crayon do you want?" or "We're going to explore with playdough. Which color do you want, red or yellow?"

Scenario 4: When planning two different consecutive activities, give children a choice of which one to do first. For example, say, "In a few minutes, we will put on our coats. We want to take a nature walk and play on the playground. Which one do you want to do first?"

This kind of choice can also be embedded with daily-living activities in home-based settings. For example, "We need to comb your hair and brush your teeth. Which one do you want to do first?"

To ensure that the choices incorporated into the everyday routine clearly reflect individual preferences (i.e., things children strongly prefer or enjoy doing), readers are encouraged to complete a *preference assessment* on each child with whom they work, or ask caregivers to help fill it out. (See the online companion materials for this chapter for more information about this type of tool.) Choice making is important for *all* children, with and without disabilities (Jolivette, Stichter, Sibilsky, Scott, & Ridgley, 2002). We must "provide young children with choices within a variety of home, school, and community settings and activities" (McCormick, Jolivette, & Ridgley, 2003, p. 3). Readers may be surprised to learn, however, this has not always been the case. For example, students with severe disabilities have historically not been explicitly taught in school how to make choices (Shevin & Klein, 1984). The extant literature largely highlights the benefits of choice making for children with a range of disabilities, such as visual impairment (Clark & McDonnell, 2008), autism (Reinhartsen, Garfinkle, & Wolery, 2002), and orthopedic impairment (Liso, 2010). Research suggests an improved quality of life and behavior outcomes for individuals with disabilities when there is "the provision of choice and identification of preferred stimuli" (Tullis et al., 2011, p. 576).

Proactive Strategy: Model and Encourage Emotion Talk

Explicit modeling and encouragement of discussing emotions can help decrease children's challenging behaviors, and even very young children can be taught ways to do this. For example, consider the following authentic anecdotes involving my own two children. Jacob, at age 5, after having been guided to use self-soothing strategies since he was 15 months old, once commented on the usefulness of an emotion-regulating strategy he'd learned called Stop and Think (see Elliot, 1995; Rimm-Kaufman et al., 2014). He remarked, "'Stop and Think' can really help you . . . It's about thinking about what you did. You have to sit there until you're ready to come back. I think that helps me because you can think about what you're doing, and when you think about it, you'll never do it again. *Who should use 'Stop and Think'?* Whoever needs it. Anyone can be in 'Stop and Think.' Time-out isn't really where you think about what you did, and 'Stop and Think' really has something to think about what you just did. *How old can you be?* Little kids can even do it!"

Similarly, my son Sean, when he was 3, learned from a teacher how to use a "balloon" strategy for self-soothing that involves taking a deep breath, lifting one's arms above one's head, and then breathing out slowly while lowering one's arms to one's sides. One day, when his playmate's tower of blocks fell, I observed Sean's teacher tell the child, "I see you're very upset that your tower just fell!" Sean added, "Let's do the balloon." They proceeded to follow the motions of "doing the balloon" together.

Afterward, Sean asked his playmate, "Do you feel better?" The child nodded and helped Sean and the teacher pick up the fallen blocks.

Description and Rationale   To proactively lay a strong foundation for emotion socialization at the universal level for every child, it is important to explicitly teach, model, and positively reinforce adaptive emotions and behavior (Edwards, 2012; Merritt, Wanless, Rimm-Kaufman, Cameron, & Peugh, 2012; Ritz, Noltemeyer, Davis, & Green, 2014). All young children benefit from repeated opportunities to constructively share and discuss negative emotions (e.g., being asked questions like "Are you feeling sad that . . . ?") and they respond favorably when adults verbally label/validate emotions, discuss others' emotional cues, respond supportively, and offer developmentally appropriate guidance on emotion expression (Garner, Dunsmore, & Southam-Gerrow, 2008; Gottman, Katz, & Hooven, 1996; Hooven, Gottman, & Katz, 1995; Ramsden & Hubbard, 2002; Wilson, Havighurst, & Harley, 2012).

Moreover, providing children with repeated opportunities to practice emerging regulatory skills meaningfully should increase the generalizability of these skills across situations, settings, and people (Lochman & Lenhart, 1993; Ramsden & Hubbard, 2002). One such strategy, for example, involves taking advantage of emotion-related picture cues, such as asking which face shows a certain emotion or captures how the child is personally feeling in a particular situation. As Fox and Lentini (2006) explain, children with a larger vocabulary of feeling words have improved emotion expression. Even if children have a limited vocabulary or do not speak, they can be taught how to use nonverbal means of communicating about emotions, such as referring to an emotion chart posted where they can easily see it, as shown in the following vignette.

Posting an Emotion Chart at Eye Level: Helping Children Express Emotion Nonverbally

Ms. Janice worked with older infants and young toddlers with significant speech delay in a center-based setting. One child, Morris, was a tall, sweet child who had extremely limited oral language. He was exposed to English at school and Spanish at home, and he learned a few signs to communicate across settings (e.g., "more," "open," "help," "finished"). Ms. Janice decided one day to put a colorful emotion chart on the back of the classroom door, at eye level. Morris closely examined the images. As he eagerly pointed to them, a staff member would provide the word used to label the corresponding emotion. Later in the day, when someone took his toy, or when it was time to move to an activity he did not like, Morris initiated walking to the door and repeatedly pointing to the sad face. This sparked comments from his teacher about his feelings, and he gradually began meaningfully using such labels to express himself appropriately without the visuals.

Another strategy to elicit emotion talk in the natural environment is to use emotion-focused books. Using a wordless picture book, for example, researchers have shown how a sample of low-income preschoolers' emotion situation knowledge was positively predicted by caregivers' empathy-related statements on what occurred in the book. Furthermore, preschoolers' emotional role-taking ability correlated with caregivers' explanations about causes and consequences of emotion in the book (Garner, Jones, Gaddy, & Rennie, 1997). Similarly, Schickedanz (2014) emphasized the importance of rethinking story reading across settings to address not only story comprehension but also social-emotional learning.

Application Across Settings   In any setting children can be taught to discuss emotions and to label and communicate their own emotions verbally or through other means, such as pictures. For example, consider the following scenarios.

Scenario 1: When using a poster or other visual support that shows faces to represent various emotions, a teacher can make comments such as the following. To introduce the poster, the teacher can say something like, "Children, I just bought this poster that shows different emotion faces! Who can point to the face that shows sadness? Which face looks happy? Which one looks surprised? Who can share a time that they felt [emotion]?" Later, when a child seems upset but the teacher does not know what is wrong, he or she can ask: "What's wrong? Can you point to the face in our emotion poster that looks like how you feel?" [Child scans and points.] "Ah, it seems you are feeling sad. Is that right? Can you say, 'I feel sad'?" (Note: This is helping to validate and label how the child is feeling.)

Scenario 2: When a child seems upset and the teacher has some inkling of what is wrong (e.g., seeing a child pouting in the corner on arrival), the teacher can say: "Are you feeling sad that your dad just left?" [Child nods.] "I understand. Would you like to draw a picture for him so we can surprise him at pick up? Or maybe you want to help me get ready for Morning Meeting?" (Note: This approach validates and labels what the child may be feeling, and it gently offers options that might help the child transition to the school day.)

Scenario 3: If the teacher is aware of something that may be negatively affecting his or her own emotions (e.g., suddenly having a terrible headache and waiting for medication to take effect), the teacher can acknowledge it directly: "Children, I have a booboo in my head. It will feel better soon, but right now it is making me very sad and a little cranky. Do you ever feel that way? Let's listen to this soft music and see what quiet activities we can do before lunch. I think whispering and playing quietly right now might really help!" (Note: Ideally, a provider would have help from another staff member, but this is not always feasible. Rather than not saying anything to the children and risk becoming visibly irritable as they loudly enjoy free play, offering just enough information helps reinforce that it is okay to feel unpleasant emotions sometimes. It also models an adaptive way of coping and communicating when not feeling well.)

Scenario 4: A teacher might also share an emotion picture book with a child, discussing the feelings shown and connecting them to real-life experiences in a way appropriate for the child's developmental age and the context. For example, the teacher could say: "Let's look at the pictures together. How do you think [the character] feels in this picture? Can you say, 'Happy'? Remember how happy you were when we did . . . ?" "How does [this character] feel? She looks frustrated. Have you ever felt that way? I felt frustrated the other day when the applesauce jar lid was stuck. Do you remember that?" (Note: It can be helpful to draw connections between the characters in the picture book and what the child/caregiver experience in real life.)

Each of these four samples can also be applied within home-based settings by service providers and by family members to help children communicate emotions and to model how to communicate emotions effectively.

SECONDARY STRATEGIES FOR
PROLONGED CHALLENGING EMOTIONS AND BEHAVIORS

Readers are encouraged to use the previous universal strategies proactively with all children, regardless of any behavior concerns. In contrast, secondary strategies are used more reactively, either one-on-one or in a small group, in response to prolonged behavioral concerns and as part of a data-driven behavior intervention plan.

When there is a pressing social-emotional concern, providers and family members alike may feel a strong desire to "fix it quick." It is not unreasonable for a well-intentioned adult to feel this way. However, remember that PBIS is not simply a collection of recommended strategies. It is a framework, or holistic way of looking at, approaching, and supporting social-emotional development. Tiers or levels in this framework build on each other. That is, even when experiencing frustration or concern about prolonged challenging emotional displays/behaviors, adults must *continue* to ensure Tier I prevention-oriented strategies are used consistently and with high fidelity (Farkas et al., 2012). In other words, providers who want a quick fix, hoping to ignore or skip Tier I universal suggestions and just pick a higher-level strategy, should be cautioned against doing so.

As noted earlier, when planning interventions for a child exhibiting prolonged challenging behaviors, first consider whether high-quality, culturally responsive instruction is already in place, along with prevention-oriented, relationship-building, and high-quality teaching practices. A reflective approach to incorporating multiple levels of support aligns with the PBIS framework and will likely reduce the need for extensive data collection and comprehensive individualized social-emotional strategies. It is important to explore all tiers rather than engaging in "partial or piecemeal implementation of PBS" to "make targeted change or to sustain that change over time" (Benedict, Horner, & Squires, 2007, p. 176). Once providers feel they have exhausted universal strategies with little change in a child's challenging behaviors, they should then proceed with *child-specific data collection* on an objective/measurable prolonged target behavior (see Chapter 3 for clarifying details). Providers should look for behavior patterns by conducting a functional behavioral assessment (FBA), which then informs details included in a behavior intervention plan, such as replacement skills to teach the child, recommended responses to the child's behaviors, and reinforcement strategies.

The following nonexhaustive sampling of strategies is intended to heighten awareness of what strategies might be included in a behavior intervention plan, *if warranted*. As with universal strategies, secondary strategies—such as changing what happens before and after the behavior (antecedent and consequence), or targeted social skills training in specific topic areas—must be adapted based on the child's age, ability, needs, and interests, and on what works best in the setting. Also recall how home- and center-based providers need to tailor each devised intervention plan to align effectively with the function or purpose of the child's emotional display of behavior (e.g., escape, attention seeking, problem solving, play, obtaining tangibles, or sensory stimulation) (Rispoli, Burke, Hatton, Ninci, & Sanchez, 2015; Wheeler & Richey, 2014). Thus, teachers are creating a data-driven plan that taps into all of the contextual nuances related to the child's behavior; accounts for the child's strengths, interests, and needs; and aligns with evidence-based recommendations.

The following highlighted strategies include scripted stories, individualized visual cues (e.g., activity schedules, self-monitoring charts), and peer coaching.

Secondary Strategy: Create Scripted or Social Stories

The use of scripted stories or Social Stories (Gray, 2018) can help children learn adaptive behaviors appropriate for a particular situation or type of social interaction that presents challenges for a particular child or group of children. (The terms *scripted stories* and *Social Stories* tend to be used interchangeably in the literature.)

Description and Rationale   In addition to rules and expectations established for all children in the particular setting at the universal level, some children may benefit from something more explicit and tailored to their unique emotions/behaviors. The evidence supporting this strategy's effectiveness for changing behavior is mixed (Leaf et al., 2015); however, it is one approach to consider, if it is warranted based on the data collected for a specific child or group (see Sansosti, Powell-Smith, & Kincaid, 2004; Swaggart et al., 1995). Such stories highlight issues, concerns, or dilemmas faced by a child or group of children; for example, being more empathetic toward peers, understanding others' need for personal space, waiting to speak when someone else is talking, cleaning up after playing with toys, or making better choices when feeling upset. These stories are written to emphasize what behavior is typically expected, along with alternative options that are developmentally and socially appropriate as well as functionally equivalent.

This strategy could be used at the universal level to support all learners; for example, devising and presenting to the class a story about how important it is to include everyone during open-ended play, if this is a class-wide issue. However, scripted stories are more typically used as a secondary strategy with individuals or smaller groups of children. Just as personalized books may enhance word acquisition (Kucirkova, Messer, & Sheehv, 2014), use of targeted, personalized stories may improve social functioning and reduce challenging behaviors (Karkhaneh et al., 2010). Although there can be different outcomes when individualizing stories for each child, Karkhaneh and colleagues (2010) suggest that the same scripted story targeting a specific skill or behavior can be effectively used among different children.

Application Across Settings   Use of scripted stories is a strategy that can be applied in center- and home-based settings. The story can be presented to the child as a print or electronic text and read aloud, or recorded as an audio file. Such a story typically has only one to two lines on each slide or page, with simple visuals. If it is not feasible to read the story to the child directly, the child could listen to a prerecorded version on an electronic device, using headphones if needed. Consider the following scenarios in which scripted stories might be used.

Scenario 1: Barbara, a center-based early childhood educator, is concerned that one of the children, Blake, continues to run in the halls and the parking lot despite universal efforts to have each child use "walking feet." Based on collected data, Barbara and her team decide that part of the behavior intervention will be to write a brief scripted story that can be read to Blake on arrival. They devise the following story: *"It is safer to walk than to run. // When people run, they can trip and fall. I will use walking feet when I am in the hallway. // I will also remember to hold my babysitter's hand when it is time to leave at the end of the day. Running in the parking lot is not safe. // I will stay close to my babysitter, hold her hand, and always look both ways before walking together to her car. // My teacher and babysitter will be so proud of me for using walking feet! I know that using walking feet will help keep me safe."*

(Note that the story is written in a positive manner, reminding the child what he *should* do instead of running.)

 Scenario 2: Danielle receives services from a home-based provider. Despite her family and provider reminding her not to throw food at mealtime and snack time, she has continued to do so for several weeks. As part of the data-driven behavior intervention plan, the home-based provider has created a brief scripted story that every adult in this setting has agreed to read to Danielle before each meal or snack over the next 2 weeks: *"I love to eat in my highchair. // Momma, Dadda, Grandma, and Grandpa all take turns helping me eat my food. // Sometimes I eat cereal and bananas. Sometimes I eat applesauce. // When I throw food on the floor, this makes a big mess and makes everyone sad. // I want my family to be happy. I will keep my food on my tray. // If I don't want it, I will say, "No more!" // If I am finished, I will say, "No more!" // If I say, "No more," my family will take the food away. // I will use my words and keep my food on my tray. Everyone will be so happy!"*). (Note: Again, this story is reminding Danielle what she *should* do instead of throwing food on the floor. If using such a story with a child who is unable to verbalize short phrases like "No more," suggest alternative ways for the child to communicate, such as pointing to a "No more" visual, gesturing, using sign language, or pressing a button on a communication device, depending on what is agreed on by the team.)

Secondary Strategy: Use Individualized Visual Cues

Use of individualized visual cues can be helpful with individual children in a variety of situations that might present emotional or behavioral challenges.

Description and Rationale Although visual cues were noted earlier as part of a prompt hierarchy and in supporting efforts to proactively establish expectations for a large group of children, tailored visuals can also be useful at the secondary level to address prolonged concerns. Alternative and augmentative communication systems such as the Picture Exchange Communication System (PECS) provide a way for those with limited functional speech to communicate (Bondy & Frost, 2002; Preston & Carter, 2009). Furthermore, visual cues can help children who may have noteworthy difficulty delaying gratification or smoothly transitioning across activities or parts of the daily routine (Bondy & Frost, 2002; Hayes et al., 2010). Such visual cues may take varying forms, including activity schedules, visual timelines, and self-monitoring that incorporates a visual tracking system. Discussion of each of these options follows.

Activity Schedules Activity schedules are a form of visual support that can be used with a child or group of children during a particular part of the daily routine that is causing confusion, frustration, or stress. An activity schedule includes visuals displayed in a *linear sequence* as a reminder of what to do first, second, third, and so on during a particular activity or routine. The visual cues might be photos, stick figure drawings, or other images to help promote understanding of the sequence of events, as shown in Figures 4.4 and 4.5. These can be affixed with Velcro so they are removable. This allows the child to peel and stick a laminated card onto a new step in the routine to help reinforce what is next. For more complex routines, any individual component within the routine can be assigned its own activity schedule with visual cues, if needed, with a breakdown of tasks to reinforce what is expected and enhance success. The schedule can be placed on the child's desk or cubby in a center-based

Eat
breakfast

Get
dressed

Drive to
preschool

Sing "Bye-Bye"
song with
Mom and Dad

Play at
school

Figure 4.4. Drawings or photographs can be used as a primary prevention strategy (with all children) or a secondary prevention strategy (for one child or small group of children) to reinforce expectations and/or enhance understanding of steps in a predictable routine.

setting; within a home, it can be moved around or posted at eye level in a high-traffic area. Having a clear, predictable schedule is considered one of the indicators of an effective early childhood program in helping *all* young children (Webster-Stratton & Reid, 2004) and research has highlighted the influence of activity schedules on children with varying disabilities. For instance, among children with autism, using activity schedules has been found to decrease maladaptive behavior, with some variation in effectiveness based on setting, level of functioning, and ability to communicate (Lequia, Machalicek, & Rispoli, 2012). They are considered an evidence-based practice to "increase, maintain, and generalize a range of skills of individuals [with autism spectrum disorder] from preschool through adulthood" (Knight, Sartini, & Spriggs, 2015, p. 157). In addition, picture activity schedules have been shown to increase on-schedule and on-task behavior of older students with moderate intellectual disabilities (Spriggs, Gast, & Ayres, 2007) and increase cooperative behavior in a preschool child who was displaying disruptive behaviors during transitions (Dooley, Wilczenski, & Torem, 2001).

Visual Timelines   Although not as widely discussed in the literature, visuals can also be used to highlight the passage of time for young children. The ability to engage in episodic future thinking, or preexperience a future event, typically begins to emerge at age 3 or 4 (Atance & O'Neill, 2005). Thus, "visual timelines might . . . help young children to begin to compare different events occurring at the same point in time" (Jantz & Seefeldt, 1999, p. 165). Available research literature also stresses the need for more teacher training to discuss imagery in early childhood settings. Visual literacy

Eat
breakfast

Get
dressed

Drive to
preschool

Sing "Bye-Bye"
song with
Mom and Dad

Play at
school

Figure 4.5. Drawings or photographs can be used as a primary prevention strategy (with all children) or a secondary prevention strategy (for one child or small group of children) to reinforce expectations and/or enhance understanding of steps in a predictable routine.

or visual communication can be especially helpful in fostering communication skills among English language learners (Britsch, 2010).

For example, suppose a parent or teacher is preparing for an upcoming conference. Certainly, there can be added stressors or emotional strain when a trusted adult in the child's life has to travel (Espino, Sundstrom, Frick, Jacobs, & Peters, 2002). When the adult says, "I'll see you in 2 days," what might this mean to a child who does not yet think in such an abstract way? I have found it be a much smoother transition when I sit with the young child in advance to create a stick figure drawing of what both the child(ren) and adult will likely be doing while they are in two different locations. Figure 4.6 is a sample visual similar to what I have shared with my sons. It may not only help enhance understanding of when the child will see the trusted adult again, but also reassure the child that all logistics will be taken care of (e.g., that another adult will bring him or her to preschool; that the child will do the same activities with the substitute teacher).

Self-Monitoring   Teaching self-monitoring is widely acknowledged in the research literature as an effective intervention (see Amato-Zech, Hoff, & Doepke, 2006; Briesch & Chafouleas, 2009). Self-monitoring "is a procedure that students can be taught, whereby they observe and record specific aspects of their own behavior . . . [which] often results in positive changes in the behavior being self-monitored" (Cole, Marder, & McCann, 2000, pp. 122–123). In other words, you would use this strategy when you want the child to be more mindful or increase personal awareness of how he or she is behaving in certain situations. Rather than solely relying on an adult to tell the child he or she was not using an adaptive response, this technique places shared responsibility on the child in evaluating how he or she behaved (e.g., "Did I share nicely with my friends and/or brother? Did I raise my hand before asking a question? Did I calmly wash my hands after outdoor play?"). For this intervention to be the right fit, the child needs to understand what is expected, be able/willing to reflect on his or her actions (with guidance from an adult), and make some kind of mark to track a predefined behavior, such as making a happy face or tally mark, coloring a circle, or using a sticker.

Application Across Settings   The different types of visual supports described previously can be implemented in different center- and home-based settings, as shown in the following scenarios.

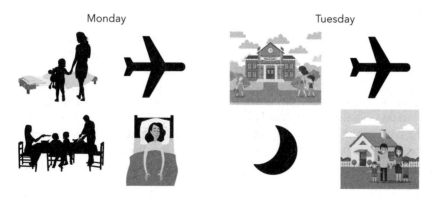

Figure 4.6.   Sample visual timeline to help a young child see what is happening (especially when there is a change in the routine, such as a trusted adult going on a business trip).

Scenario 1: Bryson is a 28-month-old who just relocated to a new child care program from another state. When Bryson stands in the doorway with his father, hesitant to enter, the teacher warmly smiles and brings a visual activity schedule over to him, kneeling to his level. "Hi, Bryson!" she says. "It's nice to see you again. We're so happy to have you in our class! I want to show you what we'll be doing this morning." [She directs his attention to the first image on the linear activity schedule.] "Do you know what this is a picture of?" Bryson softly says, "Washing hands." The teacher praises his response, and they use the visual schedule to discuss a few other morning activities. "Bryson, for Centers, see how you will get to pick water play, puzzles, or blocks. Which one is your favorite?" Bryson touches the picture of blocks. "I like that, too!" says the teacher. "Can you help me build a really tall tower?" Bryson nods. "Okay, let's start by washing hands. Give Daddy a big hug good-bye so we can wash hands and build that tower!" Bryson smiles, hugs his daddy, and walks toward the classroom sink with his new teacher.

Scenario 2: Elizabeth receives home-based services in the late afternoon with an occupational therapist, Gary. Elizabeth's grandmother tells Gary that after Elizabeth's daily afternoon nap, she gets upset that her parents aren't home and repeatedly asks for them. Gary understands that both parents have a long commute and don't get home until after Elizabeth's dinner and bath. Glen suggests they try a visual activity schedule. He takes out a pack of sticky notes from his bag. He asks Elizabeth's grandmother what types of activities they usually do after her nap. As she lists activities that may vary depending on the day (e.g., playtime, watching TV, taking a walk, dinner, bath, story and cuddle time with Mommy and Daddy), Gary draws a simple stick figure drawing on each sticky note and writes the corresponding word. He shows the grandmother how she can rearrange, add, or remove them, depending on the sequence of events they are planning to do each day. "As soon as she wakes from her afternoon nap," Gary suggests, "sit with Elizabeth to arrange the sticky notes in a straight line on a piece of paper. Let her see all the fun things you will be doing together before her parents get home. For some of the activities, let her choose the order. If she gets upset, ask her to count how many activities are left before they get home." The grandmother is excited by this suggestion and commits to using this approach over the next week. When Gary returns, the grandmother shares a positive progress update.

Scenario 3: Three-year-old Gavin is very attached to his older sister, Reneé, who is getting ready to go to sleepaway camp for 2 weeks. The home-based provider, Tricia, sees that Gavin is becoming increasingly agitated and repeatedly asking where Reneé is going and when she'll be back. Tricia helps the children's parents create a visual timeline to show activities that both Gavin and Reneé will be doing, separately, during that 2-week period. They draw simple stick figures and paste on some computer-generated images to represent the children's activities, with each column representing a different day. Gavin watches intently as Tricia and his parents narrate each daily activity (e.g., "See, when your sister is swimming at sleepaway camp, you'll be swimming in our backyard pool! When Reneé is eating lunch with the kids who bunk with her at camp, you'll be eating lunch with your friends at preschool."). When Reneé leaves for sleepaway camp, Gavin is comforted by the visual timeline, using it to see what activities Reneé is doing and how many days are left before she returns.

Scenario 4: Tamika, a 4-year-old who attends full-day preschool, has been hitting her peers, and her teachers would like to encourage her to use "gentle hands" instead.

Morning
*Did I use **gentle hands**?*

Afternoon
*Did I use **gentle hands**?*

Figure 4.7. Sample self-monitoring chart. Notice how the question in the chart focuses on the desired positive behavior instead of the negative behavior ("Did I hit today?").

The teachers decide that for the next 2 weeks they will use a simple self-monitoring chart, as shown in Figure 4.7. Right before lunch, the teachers can guide Tamika to put a happy face in the left-hand box if she used gentle hands all morning. Right before dismissal, she can put a happy face in the right-hand box if she used gentle hands all afternoon. If she hits anyone during either part of the day, she won't be permitted to put a happy face in that box and her teachers will talk with her about making better choices. They will also share Tamika's self-monitoring chart with her grandmother when she picks Tamika up each day. The teachers decide to laminate the chart so they can easily wipe it clean to start fresh each day. Self-monitoring data collected over multiple days will be recorded separately to track Tamika's progress.

Scenario 5: Two-year-old Noah, who receives services at home from an early intervention (EI) provider, has been throwing toys and crying when asked to clean up after playing. As part of Noah's behavior intervention plan, the family and EI provider agree to try a simple, age-appropriate, self-monitoring intervention to give him more positive attention for cooperating during clean up (see Figure 4.8). Because Noah loves stickers depicting cars, they create a self-monitoring chart with spaces large enough for Noah to place a sticker. Every time clean-up time naturally arises in the home routine—which might be once a day or several times a day, depending on the activity—the adult supervising Noah will bring the self-monitoring chart to Noah's eye level. If Noah helps clean up, he will get to choose one of his favorite car stickers to

Did I help clean up my toys?				
Yes, I helped!	*Yes, I helped!*	*Yes, I helped!*	*Yes, I helped!*	*Yes, I helped!*

Figure 4.8. Sample self-monitoring chart. Again, notice how the question in the chart focuses on positive behavior within the child's ability level that is not yet occurring consistently.

place on one of the spots on the chart. His family and provider also plan to give verbal praise and encouragement each time he is successful.

For additional information related to the visually supported self-monitoring strategy, see the discussion of tailored reinforcement in Chapter 5.

Secondary Strategy: Encourage Peer Coaching

Young children vary widely in their social and emotional development, even when they are approximately the same age. One child may have developed skills in this domain that a similar-age peer has not yet learned. Thus, if a child who lacks these skills exhibits prolonged challenging behaviors, peer coaching can be used to help the child learn more adaptive behaviors for interacting socially and for managing one's emotions.

Description and Rationale   From birth to age 5, children grow across several developmental domains, including social interaction skills. Typically, children also have a natural propensity to imitate and learn from others (Vygotsky, Luria, & Knox, 2013). Adults can use this propensity to their advantage; for example, by intentionally praising another child for doing something they would like the child to copy (see McLeod et al., 2017). In addition, when providers and caregivers have social-emotional or behavioral concerns about a child, they can pair that child with a peer who is more skilled in expressing or regulating emotions in a particular context (Miller, 1994; Oden & Asher, 1977; Vilardo, DuPaul, Kern, & Hojnoski, 2013). Children may respond differently to suggestions or directions when prompted by another child instead of their teacher. According to a synthesis of research findings on this topic, "optimal classrooms may be those in which children have the opportunity to learn from peers with advanced skills" (Diamond, Justice, Siegler, & Snyder, 2013, ix). Furthermore, such an approach builds in opportunities for people other than the teacher or service provider to provide some modeling and reminders throughout the day, which can arguably reduce children's reliance/dependence on the teacher and, therefore, concerns related to teacher burnout (see Zinsser, Christensen, & Torres, 2016).

Application Across Settings   Peer coaching is a strategy that can be applied in various settings to foster adaptive behavior. Following are sample scenarios in which this strategy might be useful.

Scenario 1: Rachel's teacher, Ms. O'Reilly, is concerned, because over the past week, Rachel has been repeatedly jumping instead of sitting during storytime. Sternly saying, "Rachel, stop jumping and sit down!" has not been working. From her experience working with Rachel, including 2 weeks of consistent, objective data collection to look for patterns in the times when her challenging behaviors happen and in what happens before and after these behaviors, the teacher realizes that Rachel often displays challenging behaviors when she wants attention. The teacher decides to try focusing instead on another child who is doing what she wants Rachel to be doing and have that child support Rachel. Rachel's classmate Pedro always sits calmly, so during storytime, Ms. O'Reilly pairs Rachel with Pedro. As the children are sitting down, Ms. O'Reilly quietly addresses Pedro and Rachel: "Oh, I love how nicely you are sitting, Pedro. Thank you! I know Rachel can sit nicely like you. Pedro, I want you to sit with Rachel today so she can see how to sit nicely. Rachel, sit nicely with him." (Note that the effectiveness of the strategy will depend on the function of Rachel's behavior. In this instance, because Ms. O'Reilly knows Rachel likely is seeking attention, she has helped Rachel understand that sitting calmly can result in her getting positive attention like the praise Pedro received.)

Scenario 2: Jenna, age 5, repeatedly sings and calls out during teacher-led activities and quiet activities at preschool. Having the teacher constantly interrupt what she is doing to ask Jenna to stop has not been working. In addition to planning other strategies, the classroom team assigns Jenna to sit next to Kendra, a peer coach. Kendra is more skilled at staying quiet and on task during quiet activities, and the two girls have a nice connection. The teacher speaks with Kendra privately, and Kendra agrees to help Jenna by sitting next to her during quiet activities and gently tapping her own lips and/or Jenna's arm if Jenna starts to sing or call out. Kendra's modeling of expected behavior, her close proximity, and her gentle reminders seem to be working.

Scenario 3: Thirty-month-old Charles is an only child who receives caregiving services in his home. Charles is having a difficult time making friends. His parents worry that when he transitions to a center-based setting in 6 months, his discomfort around other children will make it harder. The service provider asks if any nearby children can come to the next EI session. The following week, a neighbor down the hall in the same apartment building and her 4-year-old son, Louis, visit and stay for the session. Louis is coached by the provider to say certain phrases to help Charles play with him (e.g., "Can I see?" "Can I play with you?" "Look what I am doing!"). When the more skilled peer coach uses these phrases in their play interaction, Charles is guided to respond appropriately. Ultimately, in the course of numerous visits from Louis and other playmates, Charles begins to initiate social interactions using the same scripted phrases.

Sections I and II of this book were intended to enhance your understanding of children's social/emotional development, educators' contributing role, and multilevel strategies that may be used as part of a data-driven, tailored behavioral intervention plan to foster adaptive development. Before you proceed to Chapter 5, take a moment to reflect on specific strategies you might use, and strategies about which you wish to learn more. In Section III of this book, you will explore roadblocks or obstacles to implementing PBIS across settings (Chapter 5), along with recommendations for working with diverse stakeholders—including families, colleagues, and agencies—to ensure you are communicating effectively and implementing strategies consistently (Chapters 6 and 7).

QUESTIONS FOR REFLECTION

1. Consider how your expectations for appropriate behavior might vary across each of the following contexts: on the playground, during storytime, during naptime, at mealtime or snack time, or on a field trip to the zoo. Depending on the age of the children you work with, select an age between 1 and 5. For each listed activity, identify two rules or expectations you would want a child of that age to remember. (For example: "Before we go to the zoo, what do we need to remember? . . . Either walk next to the teacher or walk with our friends, so everyone in our class stays together.")

2. Think of times during the day or within your session when you, or another teacher or provider you have observed, typically allow children to make meaningful choices. List at least three. Then, consider whether your classroom or session routine might include any missed teachable moments when a child is not given an opportunity to express individual preferences. List two additional ways you might build in more opportunities for children to make meaningful choices throughout the day.

3. Briefly explain why it is important to 1) implement primary, universal strategies, and 2) assess the effectiveness thereof, as a means of addressing challenging behaviors. Why is it important to do this even when you really would like to get a child to stop behaving in a certain way, rather than just automatically moving to a secondary strategy?

4. Review the strategies discussed in this chapter and respond to the following questions:

    •   List one strategy you could implement right away—even tomorrow. With whom would you try this strategy, and why?

    •   List one strategy you want to discuss with your colleagues. Why is it an important strategy to talk about with them? What ideas do you have for how you and your colleagues might implement this strategy in your setting?

    •   List one strategy you still have questions about. What would you like to know about the rationale for this strategy or ways to apply it?

SUPPLEMENTAL EXERCISE: EVALUATING BEHAVIORAL RULES/EXPECTATIONS

Choose an age group you currently work with or have worked with in the past (e.g., infants, toddlers, preschool, prekindergarten). Reflect on the usual daily routine you follow with children this age. Identify three rules or expectations you might want children to follow, either throughout the day or at a particular time of day. List each rule and the reason why it is important for children to follow it. Then, consider the following questions for the first rule/expectation you listed:

•   Is it realistic and age appropriate?

•   Is it positively worded to tell children what they *should* do?

•   Will it be posted at eye level? Where?

•   In addition to posting the rule itself, could you use photos or other visual supports to help children follow it successfully? If so, what visual supports would you use, and how?

•   Do you expect all adults and children in this setting to understand and agree with this rule?

•   Will this rule be revisited over time?

Next, work through these questions for the other two rules/expectations you listed. Then consider whether any need to be revised or clarified in any way.

ONLINE RESOURCES

See the online companion materials for Chapter 4, available at www.brookes publishing.com/edwards/materials to learn more about the following topics:

•   Implementing a Functional Behavioral Assessment and Behavior Intervention Plan

•   Preference Assessments

•   Room Arrangement

•   Rules and Expectations

•   Social-Emotional Intervention

•   Scripted or Social Stories

III

We Can't Do It Alone

Anticipating and Overcoming Obstacles

5

Potential Roadblocks
to Implementing PBIS

In Section I of this book, you learned about different facets of children's early social-emotional development and how it can be influenced by teachers, other service providers, and family members. Section II introduced positive behavior interventions and supports (PBIS) and the Pyramid Model, presented general principles for fostering early emotional growth and adaptive behavior, and then presented specific strategies for doing so, which included the following:

- Universal *primary strategies,* which can be used proactively with an entire group to help foster social-emotional development and minimize or prevent challenging behaviors

- *Secondary* or *tertiary strategies,* which can be used when a particular child or small group of children exhibits challenging behaviors over a prolonged period and primary strategies are not effective in curbing these behaviors

These strategies are evidence-based, effective, and easy to understand. With a little planning and reflection, you can begin using them to help foster healthy social-emotional development and adaptive behaviors among the children who are in your care. However, as with any other kind of instructional planning, it is important to anticipate potential obstacles to implementation and plan for ways to overcome these obstacles. Doing so requires teamwork, collaboration, and a shared commitment to evidence-based, reflective practice.

Building on the first four chapters, Section III of this book focuses on addressing obstacles and embracing opportunities to collaborate with key stakeholders to support young children's emerging emotional development. Roadblocks and setbacks are inevitable, and no practitioner can successfully handle them all on his or her own. To implement PBIS successfully, it is crucial to have two elements in place:

- Strong lines of communication among the adults who play a key role in a child's world, including teachers, other service providers, and family members

- Consistency in how these adults implement recommended strategies within the guiding framework for fostering social-emotional development and use of adaptive behaviors

Section III will focus on anticipating possible obstacles to implementing PBIS and working with families, colleagues, and agencies to ensure you are communicating effectively and applying strategies consistently. Chapter 5 will discuss specific roadblocks you might encounter in using PBIS and collaborating with colleagues and families to support early emotional development. Chapters 6 and 7 will address how you can overcome these roadblocks through communication and consistency. Specifically, Chapter 6 discusses effective family–provider communication and Chapter 7 offers next steps for meaningful, sustained improvements over time.

MODELS FOR SERVICE DELIVERY

The principles and strategies discussed in Section II may be applied in a variety of child care settings and contexts. Varying types of service providers and child care options serve roughly 11 million children under the age of 5 (National Association of Child Care Resource and Referral Agencies [NACCRRA], 2012). Birth–5 direct service professionals include early childhood teachers, aides, early childhood special education teachers, paraprofessionals, service coordinators, behavior consultants, school psychologists, and therapists (e.g., occupational therapists, physical therapists, play therapists, vision and hearing specialists, and speech-language pathologists) (Allegheny County Family Resource Guide, 2016; Council on Children and Families, 2017). Settings may include the following:

- Inclusive early childhood settings
- Early Head Start programs (birth–36 months) (Head Start, 2017)
- Home- or center-based early intervention (EI) programs under Part C of the Individuals with Disabilities Education Act (birth–36 months)
- Head Start classrooms (3–5 years) (Head Start, 2017)
- Family child care homes

Each option for children younger than 5 years of age has its strengths and challenges. In this chapter, we will explore considerations across settings that, if not effectively addressed, may result in missed opportunities to improve child and family outcomes. We will focus primarily on concerns with implementing PBIS in various settings. Another focus of this chapter is concerns pertaining to fostering meaningful family partnerships. For each concern addressed, we will consider possible roadblocks or obstacles that are unique to center- or home-based settings, as well as those that are likely to occur across settings. However, keep in mind that concerns listed for a particular setting are *not* absolute. That is, there is within-group variability in any one type of setting. What a provider experiences in one center, or through one agency that provides home-based services, may vastly differ from what that same provider may experience in another center or agency. Child care policies vary by state (Kim, 2015), and providers' experiences are influenced by multiple factors, such as internal support structures, interpersonal dynamics, child-rearing beliefs, quality of the physical environment, or emphasis on family capacity-building (Dunst, Bruder, & Espe-Sherwindt, 2014; Vandell, 1996).

POTENTIAL ROADBLOCKS

The narrative this book has provided on the guiding PBIS framework may seem simple or straightforward at first glance. It is not uncommon, however, for providers to experience roadblocks or obstacles when trying to implement PBIS in practice

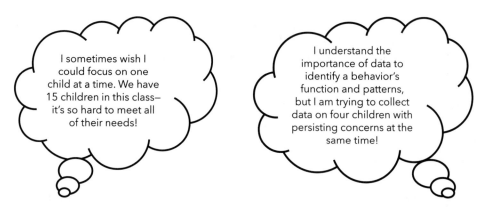

Figure 5.1. Sampling of potential teacher concerns when trying to help multiple children with social-emotional challenges at the same time. Have you ever felt this way?

(Bradshaw, Reinke, Brown, Bevans, & Leaf, 2008; Edwards, 2017b; Fox, Hemmeter, Snyder, Binder, & Clarke, 2011; Muscott, Pomerleau, & Szczesiul, 2009). A nonexhaustive list of concerns related to implementation, which will be addressed later, includes considerations unique to center- or home-based settings as well as concerns that span both. For example, in a center-based setting, there may be numerous children in the same room with notable social-emotional needs or minimal opportunity to collaborate with diverse professionals. In a home-based setting, the service provider may see the child only on a weekly, biweekly, or monthly basis. In either setting, adults' dispositions and baseline knowledge may vary. They may have difficulty defining concerns or revisiting assumptions. They may not embrace the idea of data collection or may not feel there is enough time for this. They may not use a tailored reinforcer and/or reinforcement schedule. Finally, in either setting, communication and consistency across team members may vary. This may be a particular concern for home-based settings because different providers typically work with the family at different times and direct interaction between providers may be difficult to arrange. Each of these concerns is discussed in this chapter.

Numerous Children With Varying Social-Emotional Needs

Recall from Chapters 3 and 4 that the largest, foundational level of the guiding social-emotional framework includes rapport-building with key stakeholders and implementation of proactive strategies to benefit all children, with a smaller percentage needing targeted, individualized support (Fox, Carta, Strain, Dunlap, & Hemmeter, 2009). Nonetheless, providers may feel it is challenging to collect progress-monitoring data and juggle diverse needs and levels of supports for multiple children at the same time (Bagnato, 2007; Edwards, 2017b; Ingram, Louis, & Schroeder, 2004). This idea is conveyed by the sample quotations from teachers shown in Figure 5.1.

Although this concern is valid, recall that social-emotional and behavioral strategies implemented for one child or a small group of children—such as posting a visual reminder of what activities are coming next or using task-specific verbal praise to reinforce specific behavior you want to see—may benefit others at the same time, depending on the function of the children's behavior. Furthermore, there are ways to make the process feel more manageable, such as the following:

- Asking others (such as staff members, paraprofessionals, student workers, assistants/aides, co-teachers, or a supervisor) to help with data collection

- Being strategic about when functional behavioral assessment (FBA) data are collected once recognizable patterns in these data emerge (e.g., collecting data on one child, Alison, during midday transitions; on two other children, Bernardo and Catherine, at arrival/dismissal; and on a fourth child, Deshawn, during whole group gatherings/meetings)
- Having data forms printed and readily accessible in a predetermined location (using initials or a fake name to protect the child's privacy)

Review the online companion materials for Chapter 3 for data collection resources. See the following sections for additional data-related concerns.

Minimal Opportunity to Collaborate With Diverse Professionals

Settings vary to the extent in which there is opportunity to collaborate and brainstorm with other professionals meaningfully. Just as child–child peer coaching can be beneficial, adults can also benefit from situations in which diverse providers guide one another and share expertise (Tschantz & Vail, 2000; Vail, Tschantz, & Bevill, 1997). Rush, Shelden, and Hanft (2003, p. 33) explain that "coaching provides a supportive structure for promoting conversations between family members, childcare providers, and early interventionists to select and implement meaningful strategies to achieve functional outcomes that focus on the child's participation in natural settings." An example of when adult–adult coaching might be helpful is provided in the following vignette.

Why Is He Drawing All Over the Table? The Value of Peer Coaching

Valerie is a new special instructor in a Part C EI center-based setting. She sits at a small table with four children, trying to engage them in a drawing activity. Bharavi eagerly grabs a jumbo-sized crayon from the box and proceeds to make large lines and scribbles. Valerie is concerned when he extends his lines beyond the perimeter of the white paper, onto the table itself. "No, Bharavi," Valerie says, trying to redirect, "Not on the table, let's color only on the paper. Look how nicely Alex is staying on his paper." Despite this verbal prompting, however, Bharavi continues to scribble on the table. Building on her training, Valerie considers the behavior's possible function. She thinks to herself, "Is he trying to leave the activity and escape? Is he seeking negative attention from me?" Fortunately, during this episode the program's vision therapist, Juan, enters the room to see another child from Valerie's class. Valerie motions for Juan to notice what Bharavi is doing with his crayon. Juan nods and comments, "See how the table is light wood and the paper is white? Bharavi has a visual impairment. He is having a hard time seeing the border of the paper. Here, why don't we put this red tray under his paper—that will help give him clearer contrast." Bharavi immediately proceeds to color only on the paper. Valerie watches in amazement. She thanks Juan for pointing out something that she would otherwise have never considered.

This situation illustrates how beneficial it is when a teacher can be advised by a qualified peer on site who has a different base of knowledge or professional experiences to call on. However, this is not necessarily the norm. For instance, family child

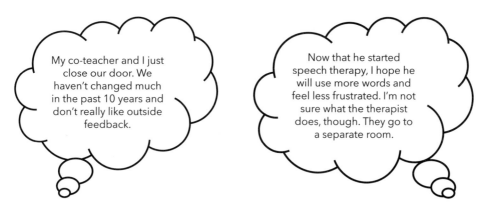

Figure 5.2. Reflect on the extent to which you seek insights and learn new strategies by brainstorming with diverse professionals.

care providers have few or no colleagues at their worksite (Gerstenblatt, Faulkner, Lee, Doan, & Travis, 2014). Lower levels of communication and social support among center-based providers may contribute to burnout (Goelman & Guo, 1998). (Consider the situations depicted in Figure 5.2 as examples of why this might happen.) In any setting, child care providers are likely to have few or no peers to consult regarding mental health concerns. Despite consultation being linked to positive child outcomes and less expulsions, many center-based providers have insufficient access to mental health consultants (Carlson et al., 2012; Perry, 2011; Perry, Allen, Brennan, & Bradley, 2010). As explained by Hemmeter, Ostrosky, and Fox (2006, p. 596),

> Although public preschools and Head Start programs may have access to a behavior spe-
> cialist or mental health consultant, many child care programs do not have the expertise,
> or resources for expertise, related to behavior and mental health. Thus, developing a
> program-wide model in a child care program will require looking beyond the program to
> community resources that may be available such as community mental health providers,
> child care resource and referral agencies, and school psychologists.

When a therapist such as Juan is available on site to work with children in your care, it is best to minimize use of pull-out services in which the therapist and child work on isolated skills in a separate room. Instead, encourage more push-in or integrated therapy in the natural, everyday learning environment (McWilliam, 1996). In addition to benefiting the child, having providers see firsthand what strategies are recommended within the actual routine will likely promote generalizability or application of strategies beyond the therapist's weekly session (Rush et al., 2003).

Seeing the Child Infrequently

Whereas a center-based provider can directly convey the same consistent message and reinforce emerging skills on a daily basis, home-based providers may feel somewhat limited in only seeing the child and caregiver once or twice a week, or once a month (Vismara, Colombi, & Rogers, 2009). Session frequency for infants and toddlers (birth–36 months) in Part C EI, for example, is determined by the team and written on the child's individualized family service plan (IFSP) (see Dunst & Bruder, 2002).

The intent of home-based EI is to build each family's capacity to embed family-centered recommendations within the natural environment (Campbell & Sawyer, 2007; for a comprehensive overview of Part C EI, see Dunst, 2007). Technically, the length or frequency of an EI session should not matter; that is, it should not matter whether the service provider visits 4 days a week versus just 2 days a week, and so on, because the focus is less on provider–child interactions and more on what the child does within the family unit. Empowering caregivers has been shown to enhance the benefits of EI (Dunst & Trivette, 2009; Trivette, Dunst, & Hamby, 2010). If families are effectively coached, true learning and impact on desired outcomes will be influenced by what happens during engaging activity settings, both when the provider is there and between EI sessions, when caregivers are alone with the child (Dunst et al., 2001). This coaching is an interactive process of observation and reflection (Mahoney et al., 1999; Rush & Shelden, 2011). As one attendee in my focus group for home-based EI providers noted (Edwards, 2018), "I think that a lot of families do learn and follow through because our kids are making progress, and we see it!"

Caregivers may be dissatisfied with the level of support they have in developing and implementing strategies (Iversen, Shimmel, Ciacera, & Prabhakar, 2003). For example, I conducted a needs assessment study (Edwards, 2018) with families receiving home-based EI services in a primarily urban region. When asked how EI can improve, 19% of 195 surveyed families requested extended session length and/or frequency. As one mother wrote, "I would like them to have longer sessions. My son would do better, faster, if they were allowed to be here longer." Notice how even if the length or frequency of sessions does not "technically" matter, it may nevertheless matter to the caregiver in the family. Such concerns may arise if families are not effectively informed of or do not fully understand the rationale underlying the intent of EI services and the expected, contributing role of primary caregivers.

In addition, some EI providers may share in these kinds of concerns. Depending on the state and service model used, the EI providers may feel current options do not suffice for tailoring session duration and frequency to each family's needs. As noted by one attendee during a 60-minute focus group I conducted in the previously mentioned study, "[I would like more] flexibility . . . [for] units to be able to go up and down [to] fit a child, fit a family. . . . It would be a benefit to the county, a benefit to the family, a benefit to us . . ." To align with recommended practice, decision making regarding the "dosage" of services should be individualized for each family. Dosage includes "more than just number of hours or days of service provided. The essential learning activities that occur within and between those service contacts must happen with appropriate frequency, focus, and intensity for families and children, resulting in meaningful growth for the participants" (Kuhn & Marvin, 2015, p. 2).

How, then, can home-based services be set up for maximum effectiveness, with both the care provider and the family fully aware of their roles? Ideally, expectations should be established by the service coordinator and individual providers *early* in the process, before accepting and beginning services, with consistency in family-centered expectations and frequent dialogue to validate and address concerns throughout service delivery. If caregivers are not made fully aware of the importance of actively participating and practicing recommended strategies during and between the EI sessions, dissatisfaction is likely to arise, as described previously.

Providers may then be concerned that this familial dissatisfaction may reduce the family's willingness to consistently follow the service provider's recommendations when the provider is not there.

Variable Team Communication and Consistency

Levels of communication and consistency may vary within and across center- and home-based settings. When several different team members are involved in providing services to a child, it is important for them to communicate with each other and ensure that intervention plans and recommendations are implemented consistently. In a study of 544 child care staff (including directors, teachers, and assistant teachers), staff meetings focused on discussing child guidance and staff development issues enhanced job satisfaction among all three groups and indirectly helped to minimize emotional exhaustion (Stremmel, Benson, & Powell, 1993). Similarly, home-based providers in Part C EI may vary to the extent in which they experience this concern. This may partly be due to state variability in the philosophy or model used, and also due to the extent to which teaming is encouraged and compensated (Spiker, Hebbelel, Wagner, Cameto, & McKenna, 2000). As you read the following vignette, contrast the experiences of the two providers, José and Darrell.

Varying Part C EI Service Models: Effects on Team Communication

José is a special instructor under a traditional model of Part C EI service delivery. He has eight families on his part-time caseload, and sees each of these families in their home at varying frequencies, depending on what is written on each child's IFSP. Some of these families only see José and a service coordinator. Others, however, have several providers who each come to the family's home on different days and at varying times during the week. For these families, José makes comments in a notebook that he hopes other providers will read. Sometimes they write back, but often they do not. The extent to which they review José's comments is unclear. Some caregivers have expressed frustration that they are getting mixed messages on what to do from different providers who come to their home. José is not allotted any time or compensation through the home-based agency to meet with fellow providers, and he often feels there is little collaborative brainstorming or support.

Darrell is a special instructor under a primary service provider (PSP) service model. He too has eight families on his part-time caseload and sees each family at varying frequencies, depending on what is written on each child's IFSP. As the PSP for these families, he is the only provider who directly works with them, besides the service coordinator who visits periodically. In the particular state in which Darrell is employed, there are weekly, compensated team meetings. At these meetings, Darrell and other PSPs share progress updates and questions with a diverse team of providers (occupational therapists, physical therapists, speech-language pathologists, and special instructors). By pooling their expertise, they are able to offer constructive suggestions that Darrell is then able to take back to each respective family. At times, some family members question whether it is appropriate that Darrell make suggestions that seem outside his area of expertise (e.g., a family might see recommendations related to crawling as falling within the purview of a trained physical therapist). Darrell tries to assure them that his recommendations are based on collaborative team input to best support the child's functional skills within the family's everyday routines.

As you can see, there are pros and cons to both models of service delivery. In a traditional model, for example, families have direct access to multiple specialists on an ongoing basis, but they may receive mixed messages from providers, and the collaboration among providers may be poor. In a PSP model, the family has to build a trusting rapport with, and arrange schedules to accommodate visits from, only *one* service provider. Arguably, this model allows for more team collaboration, but there may be some caregiver or provider hesitation depending on the match between the provider's area of expertise and the child's developmental needs. Furthermore, there is variation in what providers may experience *within* each model. For example, some providers working within a traditional model might be compensated for collaborating with other providers, or individual providers might be actively committed to connecting with and ensuring continuity across providers, even if they are not compensated for doing so.

Regardless of service model, home-based providers may at times feel isolated from other providers. They may desire more meaningful exchanges and collaborative brainstorming. As one focus group attendee shared with me: "[It] would be nice if there was a designated time during the week . . . to sit down and bounce [ideas] off of someone . . . [I would like more] joint decision making, joint teamwork" (Edwards, 2018). Reflect on the extent to which you have personally seen such collaborative decision making among birth–5 professionals in your field-based placements and/or work experience.

Providers' Variable Dispositions and Knowledge Base

For all providers who work with children 5 years of age or younger, regardless of setting, adults' natural dispositions and their preservice and in-service training may influence the extent to which PBIS is implemented with fidelity. Consider the following vignette.

Two Ways to Respond:
How Disposition and Training Affect Responses

Four toddlers are standing around a small table, stacking blocks. Mr. Connor watches as Stephanie's tower falls down. Stephanie gasps and begins to cry. Mr. Connor's response will depend on his disposition and training. If he is easily irritated, and/or if he is not adequately trained in how to work effectively with very young children, he might roll his eyes and sigh dramatically, saying, "Seriously, we're not doing this again! Blocks fall down. We've talked about this! If you are going to get this upset during block play, you shouldn't play with blocks for a while. Go pick a different activity." For her part, Stephanie is likely to remain tearful, because now, in addition to having her tower fall, she has been scolded by an adult.

In contrast, suppose Mr. Connor has a patient disposition, high-quality professional training, or both. If so, he is more likely to get down to Stephanie's eye level and say something like, "I'm sorry. You look sad. I would feel sad too if my tower fell." He might say, "That's okay, try again!" He can encourage Stephanie to softly echo, "That's okay, try again" and offer verbal praise as she begins to rebuild.

Which reaction seems most supportive and helpful in this situation? Why? Consider what might happen if Mr. Connor and other key players in Stephanie's life repeatedly choose either the first reaction or the second.

Providers like Mr. Connor could take a course and/or complete a workshop on effective ways of communicating with young children. At the same time, although someone's personal disposition can be difficult to define and measure, it is important to acknowledge the role of each provider's disposition, or "internal hidden trait[s] . . . that can influence behavior," that may result in the extent to which they use one of the previous reactions (Murray, 2007, p. 383).

There is increasing interest in understanding how early childhood educational providers' psychosocial characteristics, such as emotional expressiveness, mental health status, and personality traits, correlate with the quality of the learning environment and providers' views toward children with challenging emotions and behaviors. For example, Bullock, Coplan, and Bosacki (2015) investigated personality traits in a sample of 395 early childhood educators. They found personality predicted participants' classroom management self-efficacy above and beyond number of years teaching. More specifically, "[h]igher levels of extraversion and openness to experience were found to uniquely predict greater classroom management self-efficacy" (Bullock et al., 2015, p. 175). Perhaps not surprisingly, providers' positive affect, mindfulness, and self-compassion have been positively linked with providing emotional support in the preschool classroom. Conversely, experiencing depression and emotional exhaustion correlates with providing less emotional support (Jennings, 2015).

Although teacher education programs strive to bolster teacher candidates' knowledge, skills, and dispositions, the extent to which dispositions can be changed is unclear. In a study of 99 early childhood teacher candidates, researchers found that "dispositions can be 'taught' if there is intentionality with effective teaching methods related to dispositions" (Cummins & Asempapa, 2013, p. 99). Although more research is needed, it is promising that training and professional development may be able to influence the degree to which service providers display the characteristics described previously. Professional development initiatives, for example, need "to promote mindfulness, reduce distress, and support teachers' social and emotional competence and well-being" (Jennings, 2015, p. 732). This may be achieved through a combination of efforts, such as building repertoires via relevant lectures and readings (e.g., webinars or in person) (Dodge, Colker, Heroman, & Bickart, 2002), administrative support (Fox & Hemmeter, 2009), reflective exercises (Kremenitzer, 2005), mental health consultation (Raver, 2003), and peer modeling and coaching (Fox et al., 2011). Steed and Durand (2013) examined an "optimistic teaching" intervention that involved combining traditional PBIS coaching with a cognitive-behavioral component addressing teachers' self-efficacy among a sample of preschool teachers. Their study suggested that, compared with traditional coaching, the optimistic teaching intervention resulted in an improved self-efficacy and capacity for using PBIS. They further noted the importance of the provider's level of motivation in adopting PBIS-related practices.

In addition to inconsistencies among a host of other variables—including provider dispositions and mental well-being, administrative support, access to resources, and part- or full-time status—birth–5 service providers do not experience uniform preservice and in-service training and support. Providers vary with regard to education level, the licensing requirements they must fulfill, and their qualifications (Edwards & Gallagher, 2016; Fox & Hemmeter, 2009; Herzenberg, Price, & Bradley, 2005). Furthermore, the extent to which recommended practices are emphasized within training programs across EI-related disciplines varies (Bruder & Dunst, 2005). As emphasized by Bruder (2010, p. 351), we need "a highly qualified and collaborative workforce, across natural and inclusive settings."

The quality of preservice and in-service professional development may influence teacher self-efficacy and retention (Bobeck, 2002; Darling-Hammond, 2003). Teacher education programs can help establish a stronger foundation for resiliency and persistence among preservice teacher candidates by providing diverse field experiences and encouraging critical reflection (Yost, 2006). At the in-service level, Part C (IDEA) legislation mandates a comprehensive system of personnel development (see Bruder, 2010; for more about this topic, see this chapter's online companion materials). In one study, Head Start providers had less depression and more job satisfaction and felt more supported in managing social-emotional concerns when given greater access to training, resources, curriculum, and consultants (Zinsser, Christensen, & Torres, 2016). Koplow (1996, p. 249) explained, "Without supportive practices, it is likely that staff members will feel overburdened and emotionally overwhelmed, leading to burn out and high rates of staff turnover."

Recall the importance of self-efficacy, or confidence in one's ability to do something effectively; in this case, to address diverse social-emotional needs. It is important to build one's repertoire in terms of theory, principles, reflective questioning, and evidence-based practices. Both provider and administrator self-efficacy may influence multitiered PBIS implementation. Consider the following feedback received through a series of surveys and focus groups I have conducted on this topic:

- "Teachers seem to have a limited bandwidth for children who have trouble adapting to the program schedule." (Anonymous survey feedback from a child's caregiver when asked to rate level of satisfaction across multiple components of the early childhood education [ECE] program; this respondent's child attended a northeastern birth–5 setting) (Edwards, 2017a).

- "...teachers feel that they're disappointing the parents when they continually give accident, incident reports for the same type of thing. So, again he did that? Again, he hit somebody, she bit somebody—and I think to lessen the blow, they seemed in the past not to always want to [fill out a report]." (ECE administrator focus group attendee when asked to respond to the aggregated family satisfaction data) (Edwards, 2017a).

- "They could use more guidance than I could give." (ECE administrator, when asked to provide written reflection on giving feedback to teaching staff on a data-driven practice exercise, following a 2-hour tailored PBIS workshop for birth–5 providers) (Edwards, 2014c).

Difficulty Defining Concerns or Revisiting Assumptions

Teachers may find it difficult to define precisely their social-emotional/behavioral concerns about a given child. And, if they can objectively articulate these concerns, they may find they make assumptions about the child that are difficult to revisit, even when revisiting these assumptions would be appropriate.

Results from a 4-month study I conducted on this topic were presented in an article entitled, "Teacher Perceptions Impeding Child Behavior Assessment in an Early

Childhood Setting" (Edwards, 2017b). One of the points I illustrated was that concerns can be very difficult to define. As part of this study, six co-teaching dyads were guided to implement multitiered PBIS on teacher-selected 4-year-old children with year-long emotional/behavioral concerns. Despite agreeing on which child should be selected, each dyad had difficulty explaining why. That is, co-teachers differed in how they defined the behavior, disagreed on word choice (e.g., whether the child was "defiant"), and/or did not have a clear sense of where to start.

Recall that the data collection process necessitates first articulating the objective, measurable behavior, such as "pulls on pants strings," "puts hands over eyes," or "yells, 'No' when asked to clean up." It is important to describe the behavior *without* using subjective language and red-flag words such as *frequent shutdowns* or *aggressive*. Collecting data, detecting patterns, identifying functions, and proposing an intervention are contingent on first pinpointing the target behavior(s) (Barnhill, 2005; Casey & Smith, 2014; Crone, Hawken, & Horner, 2015). Poorly defined concerns preclude effective implementation of PBIS.

Not revisiting assumptions about a child also hinders effective implementation of PBIS. Pause for a moment to consider a time when a well-intentioned family member made a false assumption about you as an adult based on how you may have acted as a child. Readers should be wary of colleagues who do *not* revisit their assumptions about how a child will express emotions or behave in certain situations. A self-fulfilling prophecy, or anticipating how a child will behave based on early perceptions, can adversely affect adult–child interactions and child outcomes (Dobbs, 2007; Jussim, 1986; Peth-Pierce, 2000). Providers in the study mentioned earlier (Edwards, 2017b) did not revisit expectations until guided to reconsider views and consider alternatives, as explained in the following excerpt:

> When assumptions were challenged . . . teachers were pleasantly surprised; Megan, for example, was "amazed" and said it was as if they had a different child in the classroom. I encouraged them to make specific changes in classroom practices that would reexamine assumptions that emerged during the audiotaped interviews (e.g., "Why was Ken permitted to wander at the back of the room during Circle Time when all other children were expected to sit? What would happen if the teachers repositioned him at the front of the room? Why was James singled out throughout the year as the one child in the class who needed to run up and down the hallway or run hills on the playground? What would happen if more gross-motor activities were embedded in the natural routine for all of the children? Why was verbal praise no longer used with James? What would happen if they tried it again to reinforce his positive exchanges? If you know Ethan loves telling facts about dinosaurs, how might peer relations be improved if you created a center where he got to show that strength to peers?") (p. 8).

Reflect on a child you know who has prolonged displays of challenging emotions and/or behaviors. What labels are used to describe this child? These labels should be revisited, especially given how much growth occurs during these early years. As described previously, revisit current assumptions by filling in the bracketed statements that follow and considering your contributing role in environmental redesign to set the child up for success:

> We assume [child] will always do [challenging behavior] during [time of day/activity]. But, I wonder what would happen if we [attempt alternative approach aligned with the behavior's function] that the key players in this setting could consistently try for ~2 weeks? (Edwards, 2017b)

Limited Time and Enthusiasm for Data Collection

Although early childhood programs across multiple states are increasingly interested in adapting schoolwide PBIS, educators involved in a statewide PBIS initiative across 47 early childhood sites experienced notable difficulty with data collection, entry, and analysis (Muscott, Pomerleau, & Szczesiul, 2009). In another state, multiple school teams had difficulty devising behavior plans informed by the behavior's function (Van Acker, Boreson, Gable, & Potterton, 2005). This dilemma is unfortunately not uncommon across settings. To implement a multitiered PBIS framework, providers must *embrace* and have the resources to adequately support data collection. Ideally, birth–5 providers should be eager and curious to do each of the following:

- Step back and look objectively at what is occurring.

- Detect patterns (e.g., identify when the behavior is observed and not observed).

- Identify the behavior's function or purpose (see Chapter 3).

- Establish a baseline to ultimately assess the intervention's success (e.g., if a child went from hitting five times a week before the intervention, to hitting five to six times a week after the intervention, can we say this was a successful intervention?).

Recall from preceding chapters what is wrong with framing a child's challenging behaviors imprecisely or simplistically, as follows: "Hannah always misbehaves." First, *misbehaves* is a vague, nonmeasurable descriptor. If someone were helping you collect data, what specifically would you want this person to observe? As previously explained, describe *exactly* what the child does in objective/measurable terms. Second, *always* is an inaccurate descriptor. No child *always* misbehaves. Step back to complete objective data collection, which will help the team see when concerns are more/less likely to occur. Paying closer attention to when concerns do not occur may provide important clues as to how to proceed. For example, objective data collection might reveal patterns and result in insights such as these:

- She does not throw things when working one-on-one with Mr. Jones. What is it about that relationship that we could apply to interactions with other adults?

- The data suggest she is calmer in the mornings and does not usually hit and start crying until after lunch. Let's revisit the schedule and complete A-B-C charts.

- She is calm when we maintain a predictable routine. What can we do to help her when there are last minute changes to the schedule?

As noted earlier, I collected anonymous survey data from providers in a birth–5 northeastern center-based program after the staff attended a PBIS workshop and completed data forms on a student with prolonged concerns. The surveyed teachers' responses aligned with the typical patterns described in the research literature cited previously. Fifty-seven percent of this sample commented on how constraints impeded data collection. Table 5.1 presents specific comments teachers made about the strengths they saw in this data-collection approach and the concerns they had about implementing it (Edwards, 2014c).

Can you relate to any of the comments in Table 5.1? Which ones? Reflect on your own experience with and views on data collection. What might make the process more manageable and enjoyable for providers in your particular setting?

Table 5.1. Teacher comments when surveyed about PBIS and data collection

Sampling of strengths teachers noted about PBIS	Sampling of concerns and/or challenges teachers noted about PBIS
"Easy to implement"	"Trying to keep track of a specific child's daily behavior—as their moods change on a daily basis"
"Data collection to enhance understanding of behaviors"	
"I liked the ABC analysis chart—I think this will prove to be helpful in supporting positive behavior with our kids."	"Getting everything filled out during the chaos of a typical day with 14 children"
"Seeing the patterns that emerged"	"Having time to fill it out"
"Becoming more aware of classroom situations"	"Finding time to do it, [and] not forgetting to bring [forms] with us"
"Understanding the student's behavior and when it most frequently occurred and what prompted it"	"Finding time to complete it"
"The data exercise helped with staff collaboration in a way that the workshop did not."	"Finding time to record the data over time while trying to focus on all the other children in the class"
"[It will help us] work as a team on situations that may arise."	"It's not that difficult but way too time consuming. . . ."
"It was a joint effort to think critically and observe the child together. My co-teachers and I answered the questionnaire and charts together."	"[I]t was overwhelming to complete the [forms]. . . ."
"We worked together to really find out what happens before, how we react, and the consequences."	

Reponses are from survey data found in Edwards (2014c).
Key: PBIS, positive behavior interventions and supports.

Not Using Tailored Reinforcers or Reinforcement Schedules

Regardless of setting, a potentially useful, data-driven behavior plan may have limited success if the providers implementing it are not using tailored reinforcers and the correct reinforcement schedule with fading over time (Davis et al., 2014). These aspects of behavioral intervention are defined and described next.

Tailored Reinforcers   A *tailored reinforcer* is one that is chosen based on knowledge of what a particular child finds most rewarding. To reinforce a new, functionally equivalent, more adaptive behavior, it can be tempting to try a one-size-fits-all reinforcer (e.g., a stamp or verbal praise). Of course, children do not respond in the same way to the same type of reinforcement. One might respond most to food rewards such as a piece of chocolate; another to being rewarded with play experiences such as a bubble party; still another to being rewarded with a new toy or trinket; and another to being rewarded with extra storytime or other one-to-one time with an adult. In addition to concrete or tangible rewards, older children may respond well to being rewarded on a point system or with tickets. (In my experience, this statement broadly applies to children who are developmentally at age 4.5 years old and older. For example, my 5-year-old son enthusiastically responded to the use of a checkmark system to reinforce his staying in his own bed through the night, saying, "I get a 'super check' for sleeping in my bed the whole night!" After a short period of his getting a "super check" for each successful night of sleep, we switched to giving him this reward randomly; for example, only a few times a week. When he earned 10 "super checks," he got to pick a movie for movie night.)

Closely watch and document what the child enjoys during natural play choices. For example, notice if, when presented with two objects, a baby stares at and/or reaches toward the rattle during free play; notice if a toddler is often found playing with the bucket of toy cars; notice if a preschooler is always eager to jump around and dance when music is played. Paying attention to individual children's preferences will help you tailor reinforcements to the child so that the reinforcement and the selected intervention are more effective.

Reinforcement Schedules and Fading

In addition to the type of reinforcer, providers must not overlook the importance of how often to give the reinforcement; that is, the importance of having a well-thought-out *reinforcement schedule* (see Parry & Douglas, 1983; Rogers, 2000; Shearer & Shearer, 1972; Vargo, Heal, Epperley, & Kooistra, 2014). For example, suppose a toddler is being toilet trained. Using the toilet correctly is an adaptive replacement behavior that will replace the toddler's wetting or soiling himself because he did not visit the bathroom to use the toilet. Let's say the designated reinforcement (tailored to the child's preferences) is for the child to receive a piece of chocolate every time he uses the toilet. The child's care providers have many options for planning a reinforcement schedule. They might reinforce the child with chocolate every time he visits the bathroom to use the toilet, or every two times he does so. They might present this reinforcement at the end of lunchtime if the child successfully used the bathroom throughout the morning, or at dismissal if he did so throughout the day. Perhaps they might present this reinforcement only once a week on Fridays. If so, they would need to decide in advance how many times the child needs to engage in the adaptive behavior (compared with using his diaper) to receive the reinforcement.

There are no hard-and-fast guidelines for how frequently providers should reinforce an adaptive behavior, although it may be useful to err on the side of more frequent reinforcement when first introducing new expectations. The subjective opinions of teachers and other key players in a child's life are likely to affect the reinforcement schedule because they may or may not agree with the practice of frequent reinforcement. As one anonymous birth–5 provider shared via a written response prior to a PBIS workshop, "I feel that we recognize positive behavior but rewards shouldn't be given each time someone does something good" (Edwards, 2014c). As a result of providers' subjective views on this topic, the time interval between a child's engaging in the adaptive replacement behavior and receiving reinforcement may be too spread out and arguably set the child up for failure. For instance, suppose the child in the previous example earns a reward on Friday only if he uses the adaptive replacement behavior from Monday through Thursday. The effectiveness of this reinforcement schedule may depend on whether the child has the cognitive, executive functioning, and social/emotional skills needed to:

- Understand and remember that engaging in the adaptive behavior all week long will result in a reward at the end of the week.

- Set a goal (attaining the reward) and keep this goal in mind all week when making day-to-day behavioral choices (e.g., remembering to ask to use the bathroom as soon as the child senses the need).

Figure 5.3. These sample self-management charts include a tailored reinforcer that will be provided if the child does what is expected.

- Delay gratification by choosing to work toward the end-of-week reward rather than doing what is immediately gratifying (e.g., the child might occasionally need to interrupt his playtime to ask to be taken to the bathroom).

If a child does not yet have these skills because of where the child is developmentally, starting with a weekly reinforcement schedule may be less likely to be effective in fostering the adaptive behavior. Researchers have found, for example, that in a sample of preschool children, their ability to delay gratification (i.e., wait to receive a reward) correlated with their appropriate use of temporal terms (e.g., soon, later, yesterday, tomorrow) in their vocabulary (Kumst & Scarf, 2015). Although more research is needed to understand how reward frequency may need to be adjusted based on age, behavior, setting, and/or type of reinforcer, it is advisable to reward more frequently at first, as shown in the examples in Figure 5.3.

The same developmental consideration applies when home-based service providers or family members reinforce adaptive behaviors at home. Older children may be able to handle less frequent reinforcement schedules, like an end-of-week special movie night for good behavior. Younger children may need more frequent reinforcement. As a home-based example, Honaker and Meltzer (2014, p. 337) share the following for a child who has difficulty staying in his bed at night:

> With the Bedtime Pass intervention, one or more bedtime passes (e.g., notecard or token) are given to young children at bedtime, with instructions that each pass can be exchanged for a request or parental visit (e.g. drink of water, brief visit from parent). When the passes are gone, parents ignore additional requests. However, if the child still has passes left in the morning they can be exchanged for immediate small rewards. The number of passes allowed a child each night can be gradually reduced. [Other] studies have found the Bedtime Pass effective . . . leading to reductions in bedtime resistance in 3–6 year olds, with gains maintained at 3 months.

To minimize dependency, it is essential that providers gradually and systematically *fade* prompts and reinforcers over time (Wheeler & Richey, 2014). Once you and your team see that the selected reinforcer and reinforcement schedule are helping the child consistently engage in the alternate, functionally equivalent behavior for a predetermined period of time, you should then begin to incorporate fading. Using the previous example, perhaps the child would, for the first 2 weeks, earn chocolate each time he uses the bathroom. Then, over the next 1 to 2 weeks, the providers would gradually decrease the frequency of the reinforcement until the child is earning a piece of chocolate at lunch and dismissal. Next, they might continue decreasing the frequency of reinforcement until the child is earning chocolate at the end of the week only, and so on. Also, consider whether you want to use a *continuous reinforcement schedule* or an *intermittent reinforcement schedule*. A continuous reinforcement schedule involves providing reinforcement after each time you see the desired behavior and is more commonly used when teaching a novel replacement behavior, whereas an intermittent reinforcement schedule involves providing reinforcement only some of the time after seeing the desired behavior and is often used to maintain previously learned behaviors (Cooper, Heron, & Heward, 2007; also see Gavin Cosgrave's article "Schedules of Reinforcement," available at the Educate Autism web site). There are four types of intermittent reinforcement schedules:

- Fixed interval schedule: Emma is reinforced by being told, "I like how you are sitting!" when she sits in her chair for a full minute.

- Variable interval schedule: On average, Emma is reinforced when she stays seated for approximately 60 seconds (however, the interval length will vary).

- Fixed ratio schedule: Gene receives a "Good job" stamp on his paper after every third problem he completes.

- Variable ratio schedule: Gene receives a "Good job" stamp for successive questions answered during the day; he receives a stamp for every 2, 4, 6, or 8 questions answered.

Based on these examples, take a moment to try to discern the difference between each of these types of schedules.

Notice how each of these reinforcement schedules is classified as either fixed or variable. In a *fixed reinforcement schedule*, the pattern of reward is regular, or fixed, and therefore predictable (e.g., the child receives a piece of chocolate if he successfully uses the toilet three times). In a *variable reinforcement schedule*, the pattern of reward is irregular and consequently unpredictable (e.g., the child sometimes gets a piece of chocolate after using the toilet just once, sometimes gets a piece of chocolate after using the toilet three times, and sometimes gets a piece of chocolate only at dismissal after successfully using the toilet throughout the day). Consider whether you want the child to know when he or she will receive reinforcement for engaging in the adaptive behavior; if so, a fixed schedule is better, and if not, a variable schedule is better. (Note: For variable schedules, do not tell the child when he or she will next be reinforced.) These examples also highlight how both fixed and variable reinforcement schedules are based on *intervals* (periods of time) or *ratios* (average number of responses). Either one of these can be manipulated within a fixed or variable reward schedule. Reflect on the extent to which you have seen each of these four types of intermittent schedules of reinforcement used in your field placement or work experience.

Interested readers are encouraged to review literature highlighting noteworthy research on conditioning and learning in children and infants (see Fitzgerald

& Porges, 1971). A study of five 6- to 8-year-old children with moderate to profound hearing impairment suggested that although both fixed ratio and variable ratio schedules improved attentiveness and behavior, performance was better when using a variable ratio schedule (Houten & Nau, 1980). At the same time, to the best of my knowledge, there is a dearth of applied studies comparing the effectiveness of variable versus fixed schedules (Orlando & Bijou, 1960).

As mentioned previously, data collection must continue after the selected intervention and reinforcement schedule are in place. This will help determine what is working well and what may need to be tweaked. For a more in-depth review of reinforcement schedules and other applied behavior analysis concepts such as latency, differential reinforcement, and reinforcement magnitude, see Hanley and Tiger (2011).

Throughout Chapter 5, I have presented potential roadblocks that might stand in the way of an educational team's successfully implementing PBIS. The remaining chapters of this book will address ways to overcome such roadblocks. Take a moment to recall the two key elements that must be present in order to successfully implement a PBIS program for fostering children's healthy social-emotional development and use of adaptive behaviors:

- Strong lines of communication among the adults who play a key role in a child's world, including teachers, other service providers, and family members

- Consistency in how these adults implement recommended strategies within the guiding PBIS framework or Pyramid Model for fostering the child's social-emotional growth

To ensure these two key elements are present, it is essential to establish meaningful family–provider communication and partnerships in the bottom level of the pyramid or guiding framework for families of *all* young children, as emphasized in Chapters 2 and 3. This remains true for families of children with prolonged social-emotional concerns. The roadblocks to implementing PBIS that were described throughout this chapter can certainly affect family–provider exchanges in that they may hinder understanding or effective communication of key aspects of the framework. The ways that potential issues in family–provider relationships might impact communication and consistency, and therefore may weaken the effectiveness of the supports and interventions being used with a child, are summarized in the Collaborating With Families discussion about potential roadblocks. It is important for providers always to be aware of these potential issues.

Collaborating With Families: Potential Roadblocks

The following are potential issues in collaborating with families for providers to keep in mind: limited caregiver involvement; limited communication and variable use of culturally responsive practice; limited control over environmental redesign; awareness of complex family dynamics; not establishing a positive, trusting rapport; and recommending strategies that lack validity.

Limited Caregiver Involvement

Sometimes providers may not fully appreciate the importance of family involvement by offering *diverse* ways for them to participate, finding out what strategies work at home, and/or showing them strategies providers use to support the child. Recall that perceived and actual constraints may limit parent or primary caregiver participation.

One study found parental involvement in their child's Head Start program was positively associated with level of education and negatively linked to perceived economic stress and neighborhood social disorder (Waanders, Mendez, & Downer, 2007). Another study found that primary caregivers of children receiving EI across 22 states were minimally involved when services were provided entirely or partially outside a family's home (Dunst et al., 2014). Yet another study found that caregiver participation in an inclusive early childhood setting for children with disabilities was influenced by the school's beliefs about inclusion, perceived receptivity to parents, and willingness to make changes (Soodak & Erwin, 2000). Moreover, as Ingersoll and Dvortcsak (2006, p. 79) explain, "few public school programs include parent training as part of the early childhood special education (ECSE) curriculum." Providers may have only limited time to communicate with families. It is important to be mindful of family-centered practice and make a conscious effort to connect with caregivers, enhance their sensitivity to unique considerations, and partner across settings (Christian, 2006; Division for Early Childhood, 2014; Espinosa, 1995; Green, 2003; Swick & Williams, 2006).

Limited Communication and Variable Use of Culturally Responsive Practice

Communication with diverse families may also be limited. Within centers, verbal exchanges may consist of brief greetings and infrequent parent–teacher conferences. This can lead to erroneous assumptions and missed opportunities for providers and families to meaningfully connect with and support each other. The need for improved family–provider communication, particularly regarding children's social-emotional needs, is well documented (Minke & Anderson, 2005; Smith & Hubbard, 1988; Swartz & Easterbrooks, 2014; Webster-Stratton, 2015). A poor connection may partially stem from inconsistent views on the extent to which a behavior concern exists and/or from lack of cultural congruence regarding belief systems and/or strategies being used (Fallon, O'Keefe, & Sugai, 2012; Lansford et al., 2014; Schim & Doorenbos, 2010). *Cultural congruence* refers to commonalities between "cultural norms of child-rearing practices within families and the institution of schooling" (Masko & Bosiwah, 2016, p. 538). If they are not well aligned, there can be *cultural dissonance,* whereby providers will struggle to effectively partner with diverse caregivers (LaRocque, 2013). Unfortunately, many providers have insufficient academic training in how to connect with diverse families (Banerjee & Luckner, 2014). Without concerted effort to understand and respect diverse caregiver beliefs, values, and cultural norms, and to tailor outreach/suggestions accordingly, it will be difficult to reach common ground or optimally support each child (Edwards, 2012).

Limited Control Over Environmental Redesign

When a provider works with a child in that child's home, both the provider and the caregiver may feel uneasy about partially relinquishing control and privacy. It may at times be unclear if the provider's recommendations will be well received or viewed as offensive. For example, if a family's home environment is crowded with many expensive and/or fragile items, it will likely constrain a child's options for play. Yet a provider might not feel comfortable explaining this to the parents and asking them to modify the environment to be more developmentally appropriate. This may be especially true early on in the relationship while still developing a trusting rapport and not yet knowing other considerations related to a family's lifestyle, financial resources, cultural values, priorities, and/or comfort with home-based service delivery and external feedback.

Awareness of Complex Family Dynamics

Particularly in home-based settings, providers may feel concern when they encounter potentially unresolved, ever-changing, complex family dynamics. This concern may be especially likely to arise if the family must continually cope with a variety of stressors that, in addition, may impact their ability to implement a provider's recommendations. Readers are likely familiar with Maslow's (1987) Hierarchy of Needs, wherein fundamental needs (e.g., water, food, shelter, safety) must be met before higher-level needs can be addressed (see a detailed overview by Poston, 2009). As explained by Dunst, Leet, and Trivette (1988), "a family's failure to adhere to a professionally prescribed regimen may not be because its members are resistant, uncooperative, or noncompliant, but because the family's circumstances steer behavior in other, more pressing, directions" (p. 110). Certainly, families in Part C (IDEA) EI have free access to a service coordinator, a professional who coordinates services, provides access to a range of holistic resources (e.g., information on earning a graduate equivalency diploma [GED]; transportation options; local food banks), and ensures families' rights (for more information, see the online companion materials for this chapter). Nevertheless, if the family is currently confronted by non–child-related stressors, providers may experience added stress in empathizing with the family's situation and/or not feeling the family is receptive to new strategies, etc. In a focus group I conducted (Edwards, 2018), one home-based EI provider commented, "Given some of the problems that some of these . . . families face . . . the services are not there for them." Another noted, "We can't do it alone but we don't want to have blinders on and not deal with the rest of the social issues that are going on in the home too."

Not Establishing a Positive, Trusting Rapport Before Sharing Social-Emotional Concerns

The Pyramid Model and PBIS framework emphasize establishing a positive rapport with families from the beginning. If a level of trust, mutual respect, and comfort with one another is not yet reached when a provider asks to discuss social-emotional concerns, caregivers may understandably feel defensive or upset (Knopf & Swick, 2007). For example, a caregiver might think, "His teacher only calls to tell me something is wrong. The teacher must think I'm a terrible mom" or "The therapist is okay . . . but I can tell he doesn't like how I talk to my daughter . . . always telling me what I should do differently." Consider also how families receiving both center- and home-based services may have mixed levels of trust in their respective providers. In a focus group I conducted (Edwards, 2018), one EI provider commented, "There may be sensory or behavioral issues that, you know, obviously the [child] care is seeing, but the family doesn't want them to know that they're being addressed." Another pointed out that "If the primary caregiver does not feel supported, it is often difficult for them to be consistent enough to effect changes."

For these reasons, it is crucial to establish a positive, trusting rapport with families long before discussing social-emotional concerns or possible intervention strategies.

Recommended Strategies Lack Ecological or Social Validity

Sometimes the recommendations providers make for a particular family may simply not be a good fit, given that family's circumstances. For example, a single parent of a child in Head Start with no local support once complained about how hard it was to go food shopping with her 3-year-old son due to his behavior. When asked what the program's behavior consultant recommended, the mother replied, "Oh, she just suggested I go food shopping when he's asleep; but it's just me, so I can't do that" (Edwards, 2010).

Such recommendations lack ecological or social validity, or both. *Ecological validity* is the "degree of agreement between the subject's and the investigator's respective perceptions of environment" (Bernal & Saez-Santiago, 2006, p. 126). *Social validity* refers to "use of evaluative feedback from consumers to guide program planning and evaluation" (Schwartz & Baer, 1991, p. 189). For multilevel social-emotional supports to be well received and used by families when providers are not there, it is important to account for the ecological and social validity of what is being proposed (see Carr et al., 2002; Fallon et al., 2012). Suggesting ideas that are not useful or appropriate may happen regardless of setting, especially without adequate trust, communication, and/or sensitivity to cultural differences.

This chapter discussed potential roadblocks to successful implementation of PBIS that can occur across birth–5 settings and should be addressed. In the remaining two chapters, we will discuss ways of supporting family–provider collaboration and partnership (Chapter 6) and next steps toward widespread, sustainable improvements in diverse stakeholders' shared accountability in early emotional development (Chapter 7).

QUESTIONS FOR REFLECTION

1. Think about early childhood settings in which you have worked or volunteered. Identify one positive feature and one negative feature for each of these settings. If you have not worked in diverse settings, what do you anticipate to be possible pros and cons?

2. Recall this chapter's description of how a vision therapist, Juan, helped a special instructor, Valerie, understand why Bharavi was coloring on the table rather than the paper and then helped her devise a solution to the problem that she otherwise would not have considered. Reflect on a time that another provider or supervisor helped enhance your skill set in this way. What was the situation in which this occurred? What insights or solutions resulted from the peer support you received?

3. Suppose you work with a child named Brandon, age 3, who receives intervention services in his home. Brandon has autism spectrum disorder (ASD) and is mostly nonverbal. He lives with his mother, Andrea, who is a single parent. Usually, Andrea remains present in the room while you work with Brandon. Today, you plan to begin teaching him to communicate his emotions using an emotion chart with faces representing different feelings. When you arrive, Andrea says, "While you are working with Brandon, is it okay if I go wash the kitchen floor? I never have any time to do that when it's just us." What would concern you most about this request? How would you respond? In what ways could you support Andrea while ensuring Brandon's needs and the intent of family-centered services are met?

4. Review the earlier vignette, Varying Part C EI Service Models: Effects on Team Communication, that contrasted José, a special instructor under a traditional model of Part C EI service delivery, and Darrell, a special instructor under a PSP service model. For each service model, list two strengths and two concerns you would have about it. Search online to see which model is followed by the Part C EI program in your state.

5. Do you feel adequately supported in addressing and responding to children's social-emotional concerns? Which practices might need to be added or changed to foster a more supportive climate among providers and family members in your current placement or setting?

SUPPLEMENTAL EXERCISE: REFLECTING ON COMMUNICATION

As a professional, you should have a clear rationale or objective for how you choose to initiate and respond during these exchanges. Complete the following activities designed to help you be more mindful of remarks made in front of children and families.

1. With site permission, use your phone or another device to record 15 to 20 minutes of audio during a selected portion of your day or session. Replay the recording for yourself when you are home (or in a scheduled follow-up meeting with your supervisor). Focus on word choice during exchanges between you and another adult, and during exchanges between you and one or more children.

2. Document what you notice, using pseudonyms or initials. Respond to the following questions:

    • If another adult is talking with you in the recording, how would you describe the recorded interaction? Were the remarks you exchanged positive, helpful, and supportive? Describe the tone and content.

    • Were there any missed opportunities during the conversation (e.g., things you wish you had better stated or explained)? Please explain.

    • How would you describe the remarks made directly to the child(ren)? Were positive/supportive comments made to the child(ren)?

    • Did you, or other adults, say things that may have embarrassed, frustrated, or ridiculed a child? Was sarcasm used? Were children's requests ignored?

    • Is there anything that, in hindsight, you wish you had said differently? Please explain.

3. Conclude this reflection exercise by responding to the following questions:

    • What insights did you gain from doing this exercise?

    • How do the exchanges you recorded compare with what you typically say or hear others say to children and adults?

    • What could have been done to explicitly teach/model/reinforce new skills?

ONLINE RESOURCES

See the online companion materials for Chapter 5, available at www.brookespublishing.com/edwards/materials to learn more about the following topics:

• Defining Concerning Behavior

• Mental Health Supports for Providers

• Peer Coaching Among Adults

• Recommended Practices

• Reinforcement Inventories

• Reinforcement Schedules

• Service Delivery

6

Effective
Family-Provider Communication

To foster a child's social-emotional development and use of adaptive behaviors, it is crucial for the most important adults involved in that child's life to communicate well with each other and implement teaching and intervention strategies consistently. Chapter 5 discussed possible roadblocks that may arise for providers trying to implement positive behavior interventions and supports (PBIS) within a variety of settings. Overcoming these obstacles also requires effective interpersonal skills, including strong communication between care providers and families. Chapter 6 will focus on how to establish and maintain this effective communication. This chapter includes practical recommendations and strategies to nurture and strengthen caregiver–provider relations. Topics that will be addressed include how to identify questions to ask families proactively, and, when facing social-emotional concerns, how to distinguish between subjective and objective ways of documenting and sharing concerns, and other recommendations for ensuring respectful, supportive, and tailored communication.

EARLY SOCIAL-EMOTIONAL
DEVELOPMENT AND THE TRANSACTIONAL MODEL

"Grownups are like a role model for little kids.... Why would someone hit or yell?
[Instead of yelling] they can say, 'Can you stop please?' [They] can take a deep breath instead of hitting the desk. Sometimes when someone does something bad to me, I forgive them, so mommies and daddies and teachers should do the same" (my son, Jacob, at age 5).

This 5 year old's comment illustrates a core truth of early social-emotional development: All of the influences in a child's life, including that of caregivers at home, come together to shape that child's growth. Recall from Section I how challenging emotional displays and behaviors in the early years of development may possibly affect early schooling and later social and academic outcomes in the absence of proper intervention (Raver & Knitzer, 2002). Addressing problematic behaviors—and proactively teaching adaptive behaviors—requires that early childhood (EC) providers make a concerted effort to not only get to know each child's primary caregiver(s) but to also be more transparent by communicating how their child is progressing across each of the developmental milestones and why they are using particular multitiered strategies to support emerging skills. Although various potential roadblocks can certainly make things more complicated, providers and administrators must work with diverse primary caregivers to facilitate meaningful partnerships and collaboration that optimize child outcomes. Both proactively and in response to prolonged concerns, EC providers should prioritize building a positive, trusting rapport with all families and embracing the notion of shared accountability in emerging emotional development. Given that providers *and* caregivers contribute to early emotional development, both should be made to feel highly vested in engaging in tailored discourse and using recommended practices to support each child. Caregivers should collaborate with providers in being accountable for child outcomes (Brotherson, 2001).

One guiding theoretical framework to inform readers' understanding of the pivotal interplay between caregivers and providers is Sameroff and Chandler's (1975) *transactional model.* To help understand what is meant by *transactions,* or reciprocal interactions between two or more individuals, consider the places in which you typically find yourself (e.g., work, gym, college course, grocery store) and think of specific people in these settings with whom you regularly interact. As Sameroff (2009, p. 3) explains,

> Everyone in the universe is affecting another or is being affected by another. . . . The development of the child is a product of the continuous dynamic interactions of the child and the experience provided by his or her social settings. . . . Transactions are easiest to describe in the relationships between parents and children, but children and their parents are involved in many ecological settings that are also changing and being changed by their participants. Explaining developmental outcomes requires attention to these multiple sources of influence as well as the parent–child dyad.

With this transactional model in mind, let's examine three ways in which the choices providers make about communicating with families can influence these transactions and ultimately influence the child's development: choices about questioning caregivers, choices about how to convey concerns to caregivers, and choices about the other ways in which the provider engages supportively with the family.

EFFECTIVE QUESTIONING

Let's say you are getting ready to meet a new child on your caseload or in your classroom. To what extent do you *personally* anticipate that questioning this child's caregiver will yield highly valuable insights? How providers use questioning as part of family–provider communication may depend in part on the providers' perceptions of how much information the family can offer. Within the early childhood education (ECE) field in general, practitioners' views about this have fortunately shifted. A growing body of research supports the need for a reciprocal or two-way exchange of information between family members and providers to move away from expert-led behavior interventions and supports (Carr et al., 2002, p. 8; see also NAEYC's *Effective Family Engagement Principles,* 2017). It is antiquated and misguided to think of caregivers as simply recipients of providers' expertise; family-centered principles move beyond this way of thinking. As indicated in a resource created by Whipple et al. (2012, p. 5),

> Family-Centered Principles are a set of interconnected beliefs and attitudes that shape directions of program philosophy and behavior of personnel as they organize and deliver

services to children and families. Core to family-centered services is sensitivity and respect for the culture and values of individual family members and each family's ecology, as members define the people, activities and beliefs important to them. The purpose of early intervention is to achieve family outcomes as well as child outcomes. Preschool special education services must include family involvement as well as accomplish child outcomes.

In recent decades, there has been a noteworthy philosophical shift in acknowledging caregiver priorities and embracing a more family-centered, strength-based, competency-focused, and consumer-driven model for both service delivery and social-emotional interventions (e.g., Dunst & Trivette, 2009; Jacobson, 2000; Powell, Batsche, Ferro, Fox, & Dunlap, 1997).

In keeping with the reflective practices discussed in previous chapters, providers should be thoughtful in which questions they ask caregivers, why these questions are being asked, and how they anticipate using the disclosed information. Regardless of the setting in which they work, providers will gain valuable insights from asking the following sampling of questions over the course of multiple exchanges with the family. These questions address several fundamental topics: aspects of the family unit, child and family strengths and preferences, the extent to which challenging displays of emotion or behaviors occur across contexts or settings, and what works or does not work across settings.

Aspects of the family unit: Questions to ask about this topic may include, "Who are important key players in [Child's] life outside of child care?" and "Which other key players might you want at some of our sessions, so they can also see and get help with practicing ways of supporting [Child]?"

Child and family strengths and preferences: Questions to ask about this topic include: "What are some things you and your child love to do at home?" and "Some families may say their biggest strength is resiliency, resourcefulness, access to resources, good communication, or loyalty. What positive words might you use to describe your own family's strengths?"

Extent to which challenging displays of emotion/behavior occur across contexts or settings: The following questions may be useful to ask: "We have been seeing [behavior] when switching from one activity to another. Have you seen similar behavior at home?" and "I see that [Child] prefers to stand when eating, instead of sitting at the table. Do you think you should ask [Child's] child care if they have seen any similar concerns during lunchtime or snack?"

What works/does not work across settings: Questions to ask primary caregivers pertaining to this topic may include: "If you see [specific behavior] at home, can you share some things that seem to work? What have you tried that maybe we can try as well?" and "I notice [Child] covers her eyes during feeding. How do you respond when she does that with you? Can we brainstorm other strategies?"

Some providers or administrators may feel hesitant to ask families such questions. Failure to value caregiver insights or engage families in a meaningful partnership may result in missing key information or pieces of the puzzle regarding social-emotional concerns and possible interventions (and any other concerns). It can also result in missed opportunities for caregiver empowerment and capacity building and, ultimately, less influence over promoting positive child outcomes.

The exchange of ideas will likely be much more comfortable and candid if, starting with the *earliest* encounter, the provider strives to develop a positive rapport with caregivers and reinforce the importance of shared accountability in their child's development. As explained in the state of Maine's Part C Early Intervention (EI) document (2007, p. 17),

> [The process of] gathering family priorities, concerns, and resources should be as conversational as possible. To do this, the person asking for the information should create a climate in which the family feels free to talk about their child and family. This individual must have sufficient training in conducting interviews, including rapport-building, active listening and use of appropriate and effective questions. Using conversations to learn about the child's and family's background, strengths and needs, as well as their interests and activities in which they participate, is imperative. For some children, it is also important to learn about the child's early care and education settings. During this exchange, the family is given the opportunity to share their story, including their experiences with their child as well as previous medical, health, or developmental evaluation information, and to describe their concerns, priorities and information about their child's development. It is important that families be asked to provide information about their child's day, including what is working and what is challenging....

CONVEYING CONCERNS EFFECTIVELY

Administrators and providers, particularly in center-based settings, may feel unclear as to how much or how often to share with families. Some may take the perspective that it is best not to share everything with families and that families only need to know about concerns if and when those concerns escalate. Others may believe sharing all social-emotional strengths and concerns with families is essential, and that there needs to be complete transparency with families to facilitate trust and best support each child. Consider the following remarks from two different ECE professionals within a focus group I conducted (Edwards, 2017a). One administrator expressed the first perspective:

> ... I'm not sure it's really necessary to communicate every single time a child has a minor altercation with another child . . . one time I had a mom in tears saying "I hate to pick my child up because I know I'm going to hear something negative" . . . and the negative was something minor. And so I looked at the teachers and said pick your battles. We don't need . . . this is a child being a child. If it goes beyond that . . . if it's something that needs to be addressed. Sometimes there are things that we as professionals can deal with . . . These parents are working all day, they're tired. They don't necessarily want to hear every little [concern].

Another respondent took the second perspective, relating it to her own experiences as a parent:

> You know as a parent how impactful you are. . . . If I say to [my child], "We're going to have a good day. We're going to keep our hands to our belly and I'm going to check with the teacher to make sure you are using a personal bubble and gentle hands," [there is a] likely chance that [challenging] behavior is not going to be seen [at school] and he knows Mommy is going to follow-up. You can curtail concerns sooner if you get everyone on board.

Readers are encouraged to reflect on these two views. Although some may firmly align themselves with either perspective, others acknowledge a gray area, with decisions about how to express concerns depending on the context and/or family dynamics.

Reciprocal, Responsive, Respectful Communication

Leading organizations within the field of ECE recommend specific practices for effective provider–family communication. For example, the following three practices are recommended by the Division for Early Childhood (DEC, 2014, p. 10):

1. *Practitioners build trusting and respectful partnerships with the family through interactions that are sensitive and responsive to cultural, linguistic, and socioeconomic diversity* (DEC Family Recommended Practice, #1). For example, suppose a provider recommends that a parent read a particular storybook with the child and discuss how the main character behaved. This recommendation might seem straightforward, but the parent's ability to act on it could potentially be affected by barriers such as low literacy levels, limited knowledge of English, and/or having no money to spend on nonessentials and no easy access to a public library.

2. *Practitioners provide the family with up-to-date, comprehensive and unbiased information in a way that the family can understand and use to make informed choices and decisions* (DEC Family Recommended Practice, #2). For example, suppose a general educator has a toddler in his center-based setting whom he suspects of having a significant delay or disability. It would not be appropriate to give the family his opinion of a suspected diagnosis, state exactly which intervention(s) would be best, and/or assure the family that the child will outgrow concerns. Instead, his role would be to share a clear, easy-to-understand overview of where the child should be developmentally (e.g., sharing a milestone checklist), and respectfully and objectively identify specific areas where the child does not seem to be making progress (e.g., "By this age, he should be following two-step directions and doing pretend play alongside the other children; but here's what happened when we tried to encourage him to pretend a block was a flying bird.... This is similar to how he reacted when we ..."). The provider would encourage the toddler's primary caregiver to bring this information to the family's pediatrician and/or a developmental neurologist (or other pediatric specialist, depending on the concern). It would also be helpful to provide the family with specific contact information for options in the local area (e.g., Part C EI contact information to get a free developmental screening). The educator would assure the family that the child may not qualify, and there may not be anything wrong, but it's best to have all the information so they can be well informed.

3. *Practitioners are responsive to the family's concerns, priorities, and changing life circumstances* (DEC Family Recommended Practice, #3). For example, suppose Michael's mother recently passed away. The provider may help by consulting online resources for potential approaches to this topic to share or discuss with Michael's father, such as the "Dealing With Death" section of Fred Rogers' web site (The Fred Rogers Company, 2017). The provider might also share developmentally appropriate books on loss and offer to connect the family with program or community resources. When approaching the annual Mother's Day art project (e.g., making a card or breakfast in a bag), the provider and the program director might decide first to talk with Michael's father in private about different options that may work best for Michael. They should also be supportive when seeing Michael display unusual externalizing behaviors.

Similarly, the National Association for the Education of Young Children (NAEYC) web site lists several family-focused principles of effective practice (2017), which include the following:

1. *Programs invite families to participate in decision making and goal setting for their child* (NAEYC, Principle 1). For example, the family of Eli, a child in the infant room, may be concerned that other same-aged children are starting to transition to the young toddler room before him. To offset any frustration, the

director and infant room providers would initiate meeting with Eli's family. They would explain what milestones they would like to see him achieve before moving to the young toddler room (e.g., walking and holding his sippy cup independently), agree to the parents' request that he still have daily scheduled time to interact with his same-aged peers, and plan to check in weekly to revisit his readiness to transition.

2. *Teachers and programs engage families in two-way communication* (NAEYC, Principle 2). For example, in addition to sending home written materials and sharing brief progress updates at dismissal, the provider should also prioritize encouraging families to share progress updates, concerns, and/or ask questions via a preferred mode of communication (e.g., phone call, in person, shared notebook).

3. *Programs and teachers engage families in ways that are truly reciprocal* (NAEYC, Principle 3). For example, during the iterative process of programmatic changes being proposed and implemented, programs should maintain transparency, seek anonymous family feedback, and communicate how specific improvements validate and address families' concerns. Moreover, families may potentially feel blindsided or defensive if they perceive that social-emotional concerns are not being openly shared or communicated in a timely or thoughtful manner.

Consider this dilemma when reading about how the teachers providing care for Alex, age 2, chose to share a recent behavioral concern with Alex's parents.

Sharing Concerns via E-mail: The Importance of Communicating Concerns Promptly

Alex is a 2-year-old boy who lives with his mom, dad, and 7-year-old sister. Because his mom and dad both work full-time, they often take turns picking up Alex from the local child care center. He has attended this setting full-time for the past year. During dismissal on Friday, Alex greeted his dad at the door with a big hug and waved good-bye to his teacher. As they walked to the car, his dad quickly glanced at the daily progress paper the teacher had put in Alex's cubby. It noted the times his diaper was changed, the times he tried using the bathroom, whether he ate all or some of his food, a specific activity he enjoyed (music class), and whether the center staff needed more wipes/diapers. During that particular week, nothing else was noted on the daily paper or shared with Alex's parents during arrival or dismissal. His parents were therefore surprised when they received the following e-mail from Alex's teacher a little after 5:00 p.m. on Friday:

> "I wanted to make you aware that Alex has been crying—sometimes even closer to whining—quite a bit during class the last week. Many of the times appear to be random, and when we try to ask him to use words, or why he is crying, he has been unable to help us understand the situation. Usually in the classroom we are able to redirect his attention and he is fine for a while. Today, however, Alex wouldn't stop crying. I'm wondering if you might have any suggestions for us to help him calm down. Usually when he uses his words to let us know why he is upset, we are successful at making him happy. Do you have any ideas as to why he has been so sad the past few days? Please let me know if you have any suggestions to either help him calm down or any information about why he has been so sad. I truly want him to enjoy coming to school. Let me know your thoughts. Enjoy the weekend."

Alex's parents talked about the e-mail with one another, but were not sure how to respond. On the one hand, they were glad that the child care provider valued their opinion enough to seek their ideas on how to help Alex. On the other hand, they wondered why she hadn't mentioned this to them in the daily progress note left in Alex's cubby and hadn't said anything about it during arrival/dismissal at any time during the past week. Also, the tone of the e-mail felt to them as if the teacher suspected something was going on at home—with no mention of what might also be occurring at school. This made Alex's parents feel somewhat defensive.

In reflecting on this vignette, consider how you might have felt if you were one of Alex's parents and how you might respond to the teacher. As a teacher, can you think of any reasons why it would make sense to wait until the end of the week to tell the parents this information in an e-mail? Consider what communication strengths this teacher demonstrates in her e-mail and what information seems to be missing or incomplete. Consider also how the information might have been communicated in a more effective way. For example, perhaps the daily progress note left in Alex's cubby could be modified to include information about his behavior, or even a 0- to 5-point scale to rate his overall behavior for a given school day; that way, Alex's family could choose to follow-up and request details if they noticed lower ratings over a period of a few days.

Objective Descriptions, Supported by Behavioral Data

Ideally, let's suppose early childhood/early childhood special education (EC/ECSE) providers do all of the following. They work toward establishing a positive, trusting rapport with families starting with their first encounter. They assure caregivers that their child is truly valued. They readily communicate not only areas in need of improvement, but also each child's many strengths, interests, and signs of progress. They embrace the family's shared role in development and in explicitly teaching/reinforcing skills. Finally, they keep primary caregivers or guardians informed of noteworthy progress and possible concerns on a timely, ongoing basis.

Once the first three components are in place, what specific wording should be used to convey a particular behavioral issue? Recall from previous chapters the importance of using objective wording and defining issues precisely when conveying social-emotional concerns. Providers should take care to *avoid* using subjective red-flag terms or describing behaviors in ways that are not objective or measurable, such as the following: "Jen misbehaved during free play"; "Monika was very emotional this week"; "Charles was aggressive during music and defiant during gym." The language used within these sentences is problematic for two reasons: 1) terms like *misbehaved, very emotional, aggressive*, and *defiant* are red-flag words that can easily come across as pejorative, and 2) these terms do not convey much information about what each child actually did. How might you react if you were a parent and someone made these comments about your child? Because the comments do not effectively communicate exactly what happened, would you know what to do to address the problem?

Now consider how communication in the previous examples could be made more effective if the child care provider used more objective language and more detailed, precise descriptions of each child's behavior, such as the following: "Jen pressed her hands over her face when asked to clean up"; "Monika has been crying for 1 to 2 minutes at a time and sometimes pushing her peers"; "Charles pulled a classmate's hair during music and needed five verbal reminders before coming to line up at the end of gym." These statements more effectively communicate exactly what happened without using charged language that might make a caregiver feel anxious or defensive. Communicating about the behaviors in this way makes it easier for the provider and family to discuss the behavior calmly and begin planning ways to address it.

In a study I conducted, early childhood providers were guided in using multitiered PBIS over the course of 4 months (Edwards, 2017b). At the end of the study, participating teachers were asked, "If a first-year teacher came to you after 2 months of teaching and shared frustration about a 4-year-old child with concerning behavior, what would you recommend?" Here was one response from a teacher in a mid-Atlantic preschool program:

> You know, I'd say, "Write everything down . . . keep a journal, track everything, everything you do, write it all down. Everything you say, everything he does, or she does, and write it all down, [then] read it tomorrow or tonight—not when you're at school. Not when you're emotional. Read everything, you know, do it for a week . . . and then try to find the behavior. And then, try different strategies. Well, you know what you're doing now is not working, try something different—try this . . . try it this way or that way . . . Have a conversation with the parents in saying, "I've been noticing this behavior in your child . . . have you been noticing this at home as well? I'm concerned and I want to help this child be part of the classroom in a meaningful way . . . and to have a successful year. Let's work together."

Notice how this respondent expressed appreciation for objectively collecting data, partnering with caregivers, and making systematic changes. To use objective details to convey concerns, a multitude of data collection forms can be used (e.g., environmental checklists, running records, frequency/duration recordings, weekly scatterplots, antecedent-behavior-consequence charts, functional analysis screening tools, interview forms, preference assessments). (Many of these are available online. See the online companion materials for Chapter 3, available at www.brookespublishing.com/edwards/materials, for examples.)

Let's look at how data collection efforts may inform caregiver–provider dialogue. The examples that follow refer to data from an antecedent-behavior-consequence (ABC) chart (see Barbetta, Norona, & Bicard, 2005) and a weekly scatterplot (see Symons, McDonald, & Wehby, 1998). The first sample communication addresses the data shown in the ABC chart in Figure 6.1, and the second addresses the scatterplot data shown in Figure 6.2. Note that the sample communications here and in Figure 6.1 refer to a practice called Stop and Think, which can be used in lieu of time-out. I first saw this being used when student teaching in a private school that embraced a Responsive Classroom approach (see Elliot, 1995; Rimm-Kaufman et al., 2014).

1.   "Hi, [Caregiver's name]. I would like to show you a form I completed today to better understand something I observed. Jen was building a block tower during free play. She always makes such impressive towers! I reminded the class there were 2 minutes left to build. Then, as we sang the clean-up song, Jen stopped building, pressed her hands over her face, and did not help clean up. We guided her to Stop and Think on a nearby chair, and she sat there for 10 minutes before nodding that she was ready to help us put her blocks in the bin. Is this similar to how she responds when it's time to clean up at home? What have you tried? What seems to work at home?"

Day/time: Mon., 9:30 a.m.

Activity: Free play

Who was present: Two teachers, nine children

Antecedent (Right before the behavior)	Behavior (Objective/measurable)	Consequence (Right after the behavior)
Jen sitting on the floor next to three peers, stacking 10 foam blocks independently. Teacher B clapped her hands and announced 2 more minutes before clean-up.	When timer went off 2 minutes later and we began singing our clean-up song, Jen stopped building and covered her face with her hands.	Ignored Jen's behavior, praised others for cleaning up. After ~2 minutes, guided Jen to Stop and Think. After 10 minutes, she nodded when asked, "Are you ready to help clean up?"

Figure 6.1. Sample antecedent-behavior-consequence chart to share with vested stakeholders.

2. "Hi, [Caregiver's name]. It has been so nice getting to know Monika over the past 2 months! She seems much more comfortable with the adults, although still a bit uncomfortable with other children. I would like to show you a form I filled out to understand when certain behavior happens and how best to help her. The X's show times Monika started crying. This seems to occur around other children

Child: Monika

Behavior X: Crying

Behavior Y: Pushing with one or both hands

	Monday	Tuesday	Wednesday	Thursday	Friday
9:30–10:00 a.m. Free play	X/Y	X/Y		X	X
10:00–10:30 a.m. Art/snack					
10:30–11:00 a.m. Circle time					
11:00–11:30 a.m. Centers		X	X		
11:30–12:00 p.m. Specials (music, gym)					
12:00–12:30 p.m. Lunch					
12:30–1:00 p.m. Recess	X/Y	X	X		X/Y
1:00–1:30 p.m. Centers					
1:30–2:00 p.m. Story/dismissal					

Figure 6.2. Sample weekly scatterplot to share with vested stakeholders.

during less structured activities, like free play or recess. A few times, her crying was combined with using hands to push a child. On a positive note, this doesn't happen all the time, and the data suggest a pattern as to when the crying/pushing happens and doesn't happen. Is this similar to what you're seeing at home? What have you tried? What works at home that we could try at school? We also want to take a look at the reason behind the behavior, our review of expectations before free play and recess, and how staff responds to the crying and pushing. If she is doing this to get away from peers, we can give her a better way of communicating this to others. If she is doing this for attention, we can instead give her attention and reinforcement for behaving more appropriately during free play and recess. I hope we can work together to brainstorm ways to set her up for success. What are your thoughts?"

Previously we discussed how using red-flag words such as *misbehaved* or *very emotional* to describe Jen's and Monika's behavior might put their caregivers on the defensive, without actually conveying useful information about what is happening at school. Now consider how you might feel if you were Jen's or Monika's caregiver and providers communicated with you as described in these examples. How might you respond to seeing the data forms and hearing the provider's remarks? What do you like about each provider's approach and/or wording that you might try in future caregiver–provider exchanges?

In these examples, the description of each child's challenging behavior is worded in a neutral way and supported by objective data, and the provider approaches the caregiver as a partner in addressing the issue. Such dialogue may feel awkward, with possibly heightened caregiver defensiveness *if* this were the first time the provider was making an effort to discuss development and/or concerns. However, working toward establishing mutual respect and a trusting, positive rapport, beginning with the first encounter, will likely make such conversations well received. As noted in an Office of Head Start document (OHS, 2011, p. 7):

> All families want to know how their child is doing and how they can help, and data is a powerful tool for partnering with families. Teachers and other early childhood staff can use assessment information to help families understand their child's progress and explore new ideas for supporting their child's learning and development at home and in the community. When early childhood staff share information with families, families are better prepared to partner with programs to improve child outcomes.

SUPPORTIVE ENGAGEMENT

As emphasized in Section I of this book, providers and caregivers influence a child's emotion knowledge, emotion expression, and emotion regulation via their shared role in teaching and modeling (Wilson, Havighurst, & Harley, 2012). Administrators and providers should embrace families as "essential partners" in providing multitiered learning opportunities to develop and reinforce new skills (Fox, Carta, Strain, Dunlap, & Hemmeter, 2010, p. 7). Rather than use the term *involvement*, it is recommended that we focus on achieving *family engagement* involving meaningful, two-way, respectful communication and collaboration (Halgunseth, 2009; Lightfoot, 2004). Ferlazzo (2011, p. 10) effectively clarifies the key difference between these two terms: "One of the dictionary definitions of *involve* is 'to enfold or envelope,' whereas one of the meanings of *engage* is 'to come together and interlock.' Thus, involvement implies *doing to*; in contrast, engagement implies *doing with*."

Tailoring Outreach to Support Diverse Caregivers

A key underlying component to effective family–provider engagement is the extent to which your information sharing and communication is individualized, or tailored, to meet families where they are and align with current needs. Although many likely agree this implicitly makes sense, some providers may feel this can be difficult to achieve in practice, as illustrated by these remarks from ECE administrators I surveyed (Edwards, 2017a):

- "To come up and figure out who needs what is very, very hard when you get some parents who want every detail and others [who don't]."

- "I definitely think parent communication is critical and very important and how we get the value of what we are doing across and I think it's obvious that maybe [we should] be doing it more and in a different way than what we are."

Available research literature highlights the importance of assessing families' satisfaction with services and family–professional partnerships (LaForett & Mendez, 2010; Summers et al., 2005). In one midwestern sample, for example, satisfaction with family–professional partnerships partially mediated the link between service adequacy ratings and family quality of life (Summers et al., 2007). This emphasis aligns with the family-centered, capacity-building coaching model widely practiced and recommended in EI literature (see Friedman, Woods, & Salisbury, 2012). Despite the need for collaborative engagement, however, providers may feel underprepared in knowing how to involve and partner with primary caregivers (see Chavkin & Williams, 1988; Epstein & Sanders, 2006; Greenwood & Hickman, 1991; Murray & Mandell, 2006).

Professional development on teacher–caregiver communication can bolster teachers' self-efficacy and improve their attitudes toward families (Hoover-Dempsey, Walker, Jones, & Reed, 2002). To optimize respectful, supportive family–provider engagement, providers' efforts must be effectively *tailored* for each family unit (see Pianta, Kraft-Sayre, Rimm-Kaufman, Gercke, & Higgins, 2001). *Tailored*, in this context, means providers must be aware of, and carefully consider, several specific, unique attributes or characteristics of caregivers when interacting with them, and that providers' communication and collaboration efforts should be informed by their awareness of these characteristics. This final section highlights a sampling of caregiver-related factors that warrant thoughtful consideration. These include sensitivity to culture; understanding of caregivers' baseline knowledge, experience, and expertise; awareness of unique family stressors; and consideration of the caregivers' preferred mode of outreach.

Cultivating Sensitivity to Culture

To establish meaningful partnerships with diverse families, providers must enhance their knowledge base about other cultures and examine potential cultural biases (Dennis & Giangreco, 1996). Administrators and providers should also be sensitive to how families wish to be addressed (e.g., by their first or last name), and when a language other than English is spoken in the home, they should learn simple words in the family's language and translate information into the caregivers' primary language (Hyun & Fowler, 1995). Researchers recommend various strategies professionals can use to support diverse caregivers, including a strategy some have called "Skilled Dialogue" (i.e., a model for interactions that honors cultural beliefs and values; see Barrera,

Corso, & Macpherson, 2003). The developer of this model explained how the focus must shift from "How do I interact with people from this culture or that culture?" to "When I'm interacting with others who believe or behave in ways I find difficult to understand or accept, how can I best craft interactions that are respectful (honor their identity as well as mine), reciprocal (honor their voice as well as mine), and responsive (honor the fact that all behavior, no matter how diverse, is connected)?" (Barrera & Kramer, 2009).

It is helpful to view family members' caregiving techniques and values through the lens of each individual's culture. Families and child care providers are both deeply involved in the child's socialization. Bear in mind that "successful socialization involves learning a broad set of rules which govern accepted cultural normative behavior and provides the foundation for interaction with other children, caregivers, adults, neighbors and others in their social group" (Shulman, 2016, p. 43). These rules vary across cultures. Consider the following examples:

- Looking down when someone is speaking can be taught as a sign of respect in one culture and seen as a sign of disrespect in another culture (Akechi et al., 2013).

- Individuals from one culture may highly value autonomy and independence, which can conflict with another culture's emphasis on interdependence (Kalyanpur & Harry, 2012).

- Caregivers from one culture may have more or less permissive views toward using physical force, such as spanking, when raising a child (Kim & Hong, 2007; Straus, 2000).

- Cultural norms vary as to whether individuals endorse "masculine norms" on whether it is deemed appropriate for boys to cry and men to ask others for help (Vogel, Heimerdinger-Edwards, Hammer, & Hubbard, 2011).

- Cultural attitudes on gender vary, which can determine whether gender stereotypes affect what is acceptable for children's play; for example, whether it is desirable for girls to play with trucks and boys to play with dolls (Endendijk et al., 2014; Kane, 2006).

In one sample, when early childhood teachers/supervisors and families from different cultural backgrounds were interviewed, researchers found a lack of congruence in educational and social-emotional goals and what was considered "proper" child rearing (Bernhard, Lefebvre, Murphy Kilbride, Chud, & Lange, 1998).

Other barriers to collaboration were emphasized in a literature review by Harry (2008). For example, it is best to avoid having a deficit view of families. That is, when there are problems with achievement or behavior, it is limiting and counterproductive to believe the underlying cause resides within the child, family, and community. Through professional development, it is possible for educators to reframe such negative views and see families instead from a strength-based perspective (Garcia & Guerra, 2004). Readers must also be wary of potential cross-cultural misunderstanding of disability (Frye & Kagawa-Singer, 1994). Historically, some cultural groups have differed in the extent to which they view disability as a "gift" or "punishment," and in whether they seek to integrate individuals with disabilities into society or see rehabilitation services as worthwhile (Ingstad, 1990). Expectations for what someone with a disability can achieve may also vary among individuals from a Western culture, compared to individuals from an Eastern culture (Weller & Aminaday, 1989). There may also be cross-cultural differences in the extent to which a caregiver values goal setting (e.g., transition goals) (Harry, 2008). Such potential differences are important to keep in mind when talking with caregivers from diverse cultural groups about the emotional development of their child with or without special needs.

Along these same lines, providers should be sensitive to the ways caregivers from diverse cultural and linguistic groups may potentially vary in how they view their role in early development. For example, in one sample, European-American mothers were more interested in fostering their preschool child's social skills and self-esteem, compared with Chinese mothers who voiced more concern with academics and school success (Chao, 1996). In rural Africa, caregivers are discouraged from talking to their babies; Weber, Fernald, and Diop (2016) shared promising results of a caregiver-focused intervention to challenge this cultural norm. Reflect for a moment on your own upbringing as you read the following excerpt (Rubin, 1998, p. 612):

> If a given behavior is viewed as acceptable, then parents (and significant others) will attempt to encourage its development; if the behavior is perceived as maladaptive or abnormal, then parents (and significant others) will attempt to discourage its growth and development. Of course, the very means by which people go about encouraging or discouraging the given behavior may be culturally determined and defined. Thus, in some cultures, the response to an aggressive act may be to explain to the child why the behavior is unacceptable; in others, physical discipline may be the accepted norm; in yet others, aggression may be ignored or perhaps even reinforced.

As emphasized throughout this book, recommended practices include a collaborative approach to working with families (instead of an expert-led mindset) and engaging in ongoing professional development activities to reflect on and reassess assumptions. These practices are recommended to minimize such potential barriers. The intent of cross-cultural dialogue is not to identify who is right or wrong, but rather to suspend judgment, respect and appreciate strengths in each other's perspectives, find areas of commonality and shared goals (e.g., helping the child reach his or her full potential), and work toward establishing common ground.

Years ago, for example, I worked with a young toddler who would throw toys, scream, and knock things off shelves while laughing. During arrival and dismissal, the child would ignore his mother's request to pick up his coat or bag, so the mother would quickly pick up the fallen items for him. When I spoke with the mother about setting clear limits and natural consequences (e.g., using hand-over-hand prompting to help guide him to pick up something if initial prompts are ignored), the mother refused to consider using these techniques. She explained that in her culture, men needed to be seen as dominant. While I viewed the toddler's behavior as a concern, the mother saw it as a strength. Therefore, I had to be mindful of our different cultural perspectives when planning how to address the behavior and how to involve the child's mother.

Over the next few weeks, our rapport and trust developed. For example, I recall intentionally making note of positive things he said or did to share with his mom at dismissal. I invited her to a special family celebration so she and other caregivers could see a sampling of our class activities (which also helped her see how other same-age toddlers were able to play calmly and follow requests). With assistance from a bilingual service coordinator, I also sent home reading materials in Spanish on developmental milestones and recommendations on limit setting. At a follow-up meeting with myself and the bilingual service coordinator a few weeks later, the toddler's mother appeared much more comfortable talking openly about her desired goals and her concerns with her son's externalizing behavior and expressive language. Together, we brainstormed ways to help him gain the autonomy and confidence his mother valued via choice making within developmentally appropriate parameters and expectations set across settings.

In addition to learning more about and respecting others' cultural mores, beliefs, and values, it is also essential to account for *within-group variability* and avoid stereotypes. That is, "each family is different, and culture-specific information cannot be assumed to apply in every situation" (Hyun & Fowler, 1995, p. 28). One example is the variation among families who have emigrated to the United States. An online resource on immigrant families suggests, "Some immigrant parents are overwhelmed by adapting to the new culture and don't have the means or extra time to participate in school partnerships; others are able and eager to become leaders in their children's school, once they have a sense of how they could best contribute" (Sobel & Kugler, 2007, p. 64). Rather than narrowly looking at immigrant and nonimmigrant families, for example, there are noteworthy patterns and variations within each subgroup that should be acknowledged and embraced (DeFeyter & Winsler, 2009). To help reinforce this point, think of a person you identify as being in the same cultural group as you and consider ways in which your beliefs (and parenting practices, if applicable) are the same and/or different.

Considering Caregivers' Baseline Knowledge, Experience, and Expertise

Just as birth–5 providers vary in their training, qualifications, dispositions, and support, caregivers differ in ways that may influence family–provider collaborations. For example, a caregiver's experience with child rearing, or the number of children being raised by the caregiver, may potentially influence provider–family collaboration. Among a sample of 114 urban Head Start mothers, I found that, compared with mothers raising two or more children, mothers raising only one preschool child were significantly less supportive of the suggested role of mothers in the literature and less receptive to parent-focused behavior support (see Edwards, 2014b). Some participants with multiple children alluded to having persistent concerns with their oldest child and to how they would be more receptive to trying different strategies with their youngest child.

Another variable to consider is caregiver expertise. In addition to caregivers' unique insights into and knowledge about their child, caregivers range in the extent to which they have intradisciplinary and interdisciplinary expertise that may be beneficial and informative (Runswick-Cole, 2007). Avoid devaluing caregiver knowledge over professional knowledge, or assuming all caregivers have the same expertise, skills, and/or passion for advocacy, both of which are attitudes that can negatively affect partnerships (Adler & Adler, 1996; Hodge & Runswick-Cole, 2008; Ryan & Cole, 2009).

Still another variable is each caregiver's own childhood experiences. For example, a history of childhood abuse has been associated with later negative parenting outcomes (see Bailey, DeOliveira, Wolfe, Evans, & Hartwick, 2012; Marcenko, Kemp, & Larson, 2000). When assessing 434 low-income couples when the baby was in utero and again when the baby was 6 months old, researchers found, "Mother involvement during childhood was related to more parenting involvement, parenting positive experiences, and parenting sense of competence. History of being spanked as a child related to less time spent caregiving and less positive life change from being a parent" (Kershaw et al., 2014, p. 197).

Recognizing Unique Family Stressors

Think about a parent or primary caregiver you personally know who is experiencing high stress. What type of stressors might this person be experiencing? Caregivers with greater self-reported parenting stress may show less sensitivity toward their infants, with parenting stress mediating the link between maternal maltreatment during childhood and current parenting behavior (Pereira et al., 2012). In another study that included 203 Head Start caregivers, those who were sometimes or chronically depressed (nearly 40% of their sample) were less involved in home and/or school activities, had less parent–teacher interaction, and were less satisfied with the teacher, compared to parents who were never depressed (LaForett & Mendez, 2010). LaForett and Mendez recommended "teacher training to recognize unique needs involved in working to establish a home–school connection with [caregivers] experiencing depression" (p. 517). Although this can be difficult, there are specific things ECE/ECSE providers can do if they recognize that caregivers are experiencing prolonged depression or other unique family stressors, such as the following:

- Making families aware of available mental health services online and/or in the community (e.g., consider having a resource bulletin board and/or sharing handouts of updated resources with all families in their primary language so no one feels singled out)

- Forming partnerships with community mental health agencies to educate staff on warning signs for depression, strategies for engaging parents with mental health needs, and ways of navigating potentially stressful parent–provider exchanges

- Offering staff training on multiple ways in which we can broaden the notion of parent involvement opportunities (e.g., not just helping in the classroom)

- Providing workshops for families on the importance of parent engagement

- Increasing family–provider communication strategies (as highlighted in this book) (see Duch, 2005; LaForett & Mendez, 2010)

Considering Caregivers' Preferred Mode of Outreach

Suppose an ECE administrator shared the following comment: "We have a very small percentage of people come to [family–teacher] conferences; very small." Which of the following statements best aligns with your *initial* reaction? Would you think, "How frustrating that more families aren't coming. . . . They must not care about their child's education. If they cared, they would sign up for a conference" or would you think, "How frustrating that more options aren't available to families. . . . We need to brainstorm other ways of connecting with them that might be more well received"?

Providers may find themselves making assumptions or judgments about a family based on the level of communication and participation the family engages in with the provider or center. However, it is important to keep in mind that families vary in their preferred modes for this engagement. I began to look closely at this topic when conducting my doctoral dissertation research. Several measures were administered to 114 urban Northeastern Head Start mothers (over 60% of whom were African American, at or below age 30, had a high school education, raised two or more children, and resided in two-parent homes). As part of the analysis, each participating caregiver was asked to rate which of the following avenues or modes of behavior-related information and support would be most preferred. Different modes of communication and support were ranked as follows. For each mode, the number in parentheses shows the percentage of caregivers who ranked it as most preferred (Edwards, 2010):

- Small parent group (37.72%)
- One-on-one in the family's home (21.93%)
- Written information sent home (14.91%)
- One-on-one via phone (14.04%)
- Large lecture/workshop (5.26%)
- Video sent home (5.26%)
- None (0.98%)

Reflect on these results. Are you surprised that having advice shared within smaller caregiver groups was the most preferred option for nearly 38% of the sample? Is that what you would have most preferred if you were one of the caregivers filling out the survey? Notice the within-group variability in preferring a one-on-one context, group context, or less personal context. A total of 36% preferred one-on-one communication (in person or via phone), 43% preferred group communication (small or large group), and 20% preferred less personal communication (written material or videos sent home). Especially given that frequency of family–provider communication positively correlates with both child care quality (Ghazvini & Readdick, 1994) and children's social and academic competencies (McWayne, Fantuzzo, Cohen, & Sekino, 2004), tapping into families' preferred mode to enhance communication is essential. As explained by Reedy and McGrath (2010, p. 347), ECE/ECSE programs need to "focus more on the process of how information is provided and conveyed to, received by, and accepted by/from families. Communication between staff and family can be viewed as a theoretical model that contains three primary components: (1) The communication process is ongoing and continuous; (2) there is open, bi-directional communication; and (3) support of parents is provided through education."

In addition, the following remarks from women in the preceding sample of Head Start maternal caregivers highlights within-group variability in needs and preferences (Edwards, 2010, 2012):

- "Support needs to be more advertised to people; a lot of frustrated parents out there—a lot of single young mothers thrown into motherhood and don't know what to do, and not a lot of support."
- "There needs to be more support with issues on behavior—small parenting groups in the area to say this is normal..."
- "The community should advertise—commercials, billboards [saying] 'you are not alone'—or offer more programs. A lot of parents are very stressed and may not even realize it; [they] may feel depressed or all alone—not enough awareness of parenting classes... [Many] wouldn't know how to go about getting help."
- "[My interest in support] depends especially on location—that makes a difference (in whether I'd be interested). If it's not far, I will go and give it 100%."
- "[I] lean more towards definitely [interested]—all that interests me, even if I'm not concerned about his behavior right now. I like to help, learn what I can."

- "My mom did that—got other people involved and you felt your privacy was being invaded."

- "I hate to feel like I'm being taught how to raise her."

Although some caregivers expressed a desire for more support and resources, others were concerned about loss of privacy or having their role as caregiver diminished. Thus, it is important for providers to be aware of caregiver expectations about outreach and of the ways these expectations might vary among different caregivers in the same community.

In addition to a possible mismatch in expectations, caregiver–provider interactions can be negatively affected by unstated assumptions regarding communication (Chu, 2014). As explained in my dissertation research (Edwards, 2010, p. 182),

> Perhaps during large-group orientation meetings or individual intake sessions, early childhood programs could ask parents to disclose preferred avenues by which they might like to acquire information on their role in promoting emotional competence ["Please select from the following choices so we know the best way to share information with you"].... Parents may appreciate this relatively quick and simple gesture of having their child's [child]care or school accommodate what works best for [caregivers] (via private, group, or one-on-one methods), instead of expecting them to conform to a one-size-fits-all approach.

To minimize miscommunication or feeling singled out, providers may wish to emphasize that the information is being shared with *all* families. Multiple modes will likely be best to reach diverse families (e.g., general information sent home and shared in person/via phone, with follow-up opportunities to join small-group discussions and/or a workshop).

Understanding Characteristics of Adult Learners

In addition to respecting caregivers' choices about preferred mode of communication whenever possible, readers are encouraged to reflect on adult learning principles. For any adult learning situation, such as coaching family members to use a different approach or strategy to support early emotional development, consider this core set of principles (Knowles, 1984; Knowles, Holton, & Swanson, 1998):

- The learner's need to know: Ask yourself, "What do I want to recommend? Why does the caregiver need to know this?"

- The self-concept of the learner: Ask yourself, "Is the caregiver self-directed and able to do this independently?"

- The prior experience of the learner: Ask yourself, "What experiences, skills, and/or resources does this caregiver already have to inform use of this new recommended approach?"

- The learner's readiness to learn: Ask yourself, "Is the timing right for the caregiver to focus his or her attention on this new recommended approach?"

- The learner's orientation to learning: Ask yourself, "How might this caregiver learn best? Am I effectively showing him or her how the approach fits within the context of the family's existing schedule?"

- *The learner's motivation to learn:* Ask yourself, "Is the caregiver equally concerned about the child's emotions and behavior and intrinsically motivated and willing to try this approach?"

See a more detailed discussion of these principles in Knowles, Holton, and Swanson (2014, p. 6). Aligned with these principles, "adult learners draw on their own experiences, are self-directed and internally motivated, and learn best when they have a need to know or a problem to solve" (Bokony, Whiteside-Mansell, Swindle, & Waliski, 2013, p. 51).

Tailoring Content for Particular Needs

Recognizing the shared role of providers and family members in emotional development across settings, readers are strongly encouraged to do the following, especially because most programs will not have access to an on-site behavior specialist. First, they should become familiar with early emotional development (see Section I). Second, they should learn about and model using multitiered social-emotional strategies (see Section II). Third, they should willingly initiate and co-lead varying modes of information sharing for interested families (e.g., aligned with tailored preferences, cultural considerations, and adult learning principles discussed in this chapter). Finally, they should compile a list of online resources and local community options for families seeking additional social-emotional strategies and/or mental health supports (see Chapter 7).

Talking With Caregivers About Practices to Use or Avoid

Caregiver–provider communication has been viewed as "the mechanism" to enhance child-rearing practices (Bokony et al., 2013, p. 49). Building on the multilevel strategies for center- and home-based providers discussed earlier in this book, the remaining portion of this chapter highlights a few examples of how information about child-rearing practices might be conveyed to and received by diverse families.

Consider how diverse families may communicate different behavioral expectations to their child, compared with the expectations communicated by a provider or communicated at a child care center. This inconsistency might lead a provider to be concerned that the child is receiving mixed messages. For example, the provider might decide: "I don't think this family realizes that some of what they allow in the home and what we expect in the classroom results in mixed messages. I want to talk with them to understand what they expect at home, why we can't allow certain things in the classroom, and how young children may do better when there is more consistency in expectations across learning environments. They may not agree, but I at least want to initiate the conversation and will respect what they say either way."

Caregivers may respond in different ways when a provider initiates this kind of conversation. For example, suppose a provider talks with one family about how their child, Peter, is climbing on chairs in the classroom. The caregiver might have the following response:

"The teacher shared concerns about Peter climbing on chairs in the classroom. I acknowledged that I allow him to climb on the chairs and couch in the home. I hadn't really thought about it, but I agree with the teacher that it must be confusing for him. Being more consistent with what is allowed across settings may help him learn more quickly what the teacher expects." In this instance, the caregiver quickly saw the value of changing expectations at home to align with those at school. However, not all caregivers will respond this way in every situation.

Consider another example, in which a teacher communicates with a caregiver about having the child, Maria, speak more quietly when indoors. The caregiver might have the following response: "I appreciate that the teacher wants Maria to use a 'quiet, indoor voice' in the classroom, but I don't think it's necessary to have her be so quiet when she's home. Before drop-off, I'll remind Maria how we use softer voices in the classroom, just as we do in the library, and I'll verbally praise her at the end of the day when I get a good report from the teacher. But, I am fine with her using a louder voice with me. She'll learn that I care about her following teachers' rules during the school day, but that not every school rule needs to apply when she's home, just as not every home rule will be used at school." In this instance, the caregiver sees the value of teaching the child what the behavioral expectation is at school, but does not find it necessary to completely change rules at home to align with those at school.

Certainly, both responses from these caregivers are valid and must be respected. How do you suspect you would have responded had you been the caregiver in the previous scenarios? Asking family members to revisit certain child-rearing practices can understandably be a difficult conversation that may result in defensiveness or distrust. Caregivers may value certain practices based on their own culture or childhood upbringing (see Bögels, Lehtonen, & Restifo, 2010). There may be more receptiveness to revisiting child-rearing practices if there is an ongoing, concerted effort to establish a trusting, positive rapport and if the provider incorporates the following considerations: 1) the provider should share evidence-based practices that link to short- and long-term child outcomes, and 2) the provider should empower caregivers with feasible, effective alternatives (e.g., not just saying "Don't spank," but actually coaching caregivers to see firsthand how alternative responses can be used). Each of these considerations is discussed next.

Sharing Evidence-Based Practices With Caregivers   When discussing child-rearing recommendations with caregivers, it is important for providers to share evidence-based practices. Keep in mind that caregivers may not be familiar with the available research and evidence base concerning certain child-rearing practices and, in some instances, caregivers' preferred practices may be directly at odds with recommended evidence-based practices. Consider the following examples of caregivers' beliefs regarding three child-rearing practices: whether to use corporal punishment, how children should be socialized to discuss their emotions, and whether to expect that children's behavior will improve over time without adult intervention.

Regarding the first practice, corporal punishment, caregivers may use it even though evidence does not support it. Data from one study, conducted with a large sample of 1,366 caregivers (74.34% non–Hispanic Caucasian, 12.9% African American, 6.09% Hispanic, and 6.82% otherwise classified; 24% living in poverty), showed that parental use of corporal punishment correlated with negative behavioral adjustment among children at age 3 and age 6, with more notable effects at age 3 in children with difficult temperaments. The authors explained, "reduc[ing] the use of this parenting behavior would potentially increase children's mental health and decrease the incidence of children's behavior problems" (Mulvaney & Mebert, 2007, p. 389). Given that roughly 90% of children in the United States experience some degree of corporal punishment (Straus, 2001), caregivers are likely to need more information and support on this topic.

Regarding the second practice, caregivers may benefit from information about teaching children to discuss their emotions. It seems that there may be gender differences in how boys and girls are socialized by caregivers to discuss emotions; for example, placing emotions in a more interpersonal context for girls than for boys (Fivush, Brotman, Buckner, & Goodman, 2000). In addition, Dunn, Brown, and Beardsall (1991) found notable differences in the amount of emotion-related discourse in a sample of caregiver–preschooler dyads, which correlated with different child outcomes 3 years later. In two other studies, parents talking with 18-month-old children about others' emotions when reading a picture book resulted in positive child outcomes. More specifically, children of caregivers who asked their child to label and explain emotions depicted in the pictures were more likely to share with and help others. Rather than just label and explain emotions for the child, children may have greater prosocial behavior at age 2 if caregivers ask the young child to talk about the depicted emotions (Brownell, Svetlova, Anderson, Nichols, & Drummond, 2013). Informed by this research and Figure 6.3, consider the benefits children likely gain from repeatedly hearing and talking about emotions with caregivers and providers.

Regarding the third practice, caregivers may not address children's challenging behaviors proactively because they believe such behaviors will "naturally" go away over time. Nearly half of Head Start mothers in my dissertation research felt the preschool child's behavior would likely get better with age (i.e., improve as the child matures), with this belief significantly linked to not being as interested in caregiver-focused support (Edwards, 2010, 2012). Similarly, in a study comparing cross-cultural perceptions, Thai parents were more likely than American parents to rate problem behaviors such as shyness, disobedience, and fighting as less worrisome and more likely to improve over time (Weisz et al., 1988). However, available research literature emphasizes the *persistence* of social-emotional concerns over time (Kimonis et al., 2006) and how intervening early is one of the best ways to alter a child's developmental trajectory (Smith, Calkins, Keane, Anastopoulos, & Shelton, 2004).

Figure 6.3. Use varying modes to engage young children in meaningful conversation about emotions.

Empowering Caregivers With Feasible, Effective Alternatives   When working with children, PBIS involves actively helping children to learn and consistently use adaptive, functionally equivalent behaviors, rather than merely telling them what *not* to do. Although working with adults is obviously different, the same principle applies here: It is not enough to simply tell caregivers what child-rearing practices to avoid; instead, providers must coach them to see firsthand how alternative responses can be used. As indicated in the following vignette, the provider should not just list alternate evidence-based recommendations. Instead, the provider should offer meaningful suggestions (e.g., suggestions that are well aligned with family-specific considerations and cultural beliefs), observe as the caregiver attempts to practice this new approach, provide verbal reinforcement and opportunities for reflection, and arrange periodic check-ins to evaluate progress, satisfaction with the recommended strategy, and next steps across settings.

Seeing Is Believing: Learning to Embrace Setting Limits

You have been a provider in the Garcia family's home for the past 5 months. Twenty-seven-month-old Kevin is sitting at the table with a new container of blocks he received from his grandparents. While Kevin's father, Paul, sits with Kevin at the table looking at the blocks, you sit at the far end, intent on coaching Kevin's dad if behavior concerns arise. Paul follows your suggestion to offer specific verbal praise when he likes what Kevin is doing (e.g., "Wow, great job putting the blocks together! Can I have a block? Thank you for sharing! You are making the tower go so high!"). Paul glances up to give you a relieved smile. After 4 minutes of nice exchanges, Kevin smiles to himself, looks at the floor, and starts to throw the blocks, one by one—making a crashing sound on the wood floor. "Stop throwing those! Hey, knock it off, I said!" exclaims Paul. You quickly suggest, in a low voice, to ignore what Kevin is doing.

"But he's making a mess! I don't want him to think this is okay!" Paul responds.

You nod and say you understand, but assure Paul, "He's just testing—if you respond right now, you're giving him attention he's craving. He needs to see that this isn't going to work." Paul motions for you to say something to Kevin. Paul is visibly irritated and clearly doubts what you have told him.

As Kevin continues to throw each block, and then looks to see if there is any response from his dad, you state, "Kevin, the blocks must stay on the table. Throwing blocks is not a choice." Kevin ignores you and continues throwing them, while laughing. You then ask, "Kevin, do we need to go to Stop and Think? Let's count to three. If you don't help me pick up the blocks and put them nicely on the table, you are telling me you need to go to Stop and Think . . . 1 . . . 2 . . . 3." Kevin pauses, but then resumes throwing the blocks.

Next, you approach Kevin and bend down to say, "Kevin, because you are not cleaning up the blocks, you are telling us you need to Stop and Think. Let's go to the bottom step and count to 10." Paul follows your lead by taking his son's hand and calmly walking with him to the bottom of the stairs. Kevin begins to cry, but does not resist walking with his dad. You say, "Kevin, you need to calm your body and take deep breaths to show us you're ready . . . let's count to 10: 1 . . . 2 . . . 3 . . ." You take an exaggerated breath, modeling for him, as you continue counting, "4 . . . 5 . . . 6 . . ." Seeing Kevin start to follow your lead, you comment, "Good calming down, Kevin!" and then finish counting, "7 . . . 8 . . . 9 . . . 10." Kevin is still whimpering, although he is now sitting calmly. You tell Kevin, "Daddy and I will be over here. You can sit as long as you need to. Tell us when you're ready to help us clean up the blocks."

Paul is intrigued at this point, not sure if your approach will work. Paul has previously admitted to screaming at his son, but he agrees this does not teach Kevin how to do the right thing when Paul is not there. Soon Kevin is very quiet on the steps, and you and Paul approach him. "Are you ready to talk about what just happened?" you ask. Kevin nods. You motion toward Kevin's dad to encourage him to take over.

Paul bends down to Kevin's level. "Was I happy when you were throwing the blocks?" Paul asks. Kevin shakes his head. "What could happen if we throw things?"

Kevin responds, "Boo boos?"

Paul replies, "That's right, someone could get hurt. If you want to use the blocks, you need to play nicely. Can you do that?" Kevin nods. "Okay," says Paul, "Go show me how you clean up the blocks." Kevin proceeds to quickly return each fallen block to the container on the table.

"Great job cleaning up! You're making a good choice!" you exclaim.

"Yes," adds Paul, "I'm proud of you!" You leave their home, content that Kevin's father saw firsthand the effectiveness of one of your recommendations. You are eager to follow-up with them, via e-mail this week and in person next week, to see if Paul has any questions and whether he now feels empowered to use this response to behavior when you are not in the home.

When providers are respectful and supportive toward caregivers, and tailor communication and collaboration efforts to be appropriate for a particular family, caregivers may be very receptive to providers' suggestions. For example, at the conclusion of the study I conducted with Head Start mothers, I shared with participants a brief, caregiver-friendly packet on how they could support their child's early emotional development (see Edwards, 2012). Any informational handout or packet shared with families can be made caregiver-friendly by doing such things as using straightforward language that will likely be understood regardless of education or literacy levels (e.g., "When child does X, it is helpful to do Y"), having nonacademic jargon (e.g., "look at" instead of "assess"), writing out acronyms (e.g., "individualized education program" instead of "IEP"), avoiding long blocks of unbroken text, and using a respectful tone. After receiving this packet, one mother responded, "[This was] helpful . . . makes you realize the things you're doing that's not right as far as disciplining them . . . I'll maybe start to talk to him more about his feelings." Another said, "Support is available, but the way it's getting to parents isn't effective enough . . . [there] should be more of a connection between the teachers and the parents . . . teachers may be concerned that it will be taken the wrong way, especially with behavior; personally, [I feel] it will only get better if we communicate and we get involved."

This chapter discussed ways that providers can effectively communicate and partner with caregivers to ensure positive child outcomes. Aligned with the bioecological systems framework that informs this book, Chapter 7 will look beyond caregiver–provider exchanges to the larger social context in which the child develops. Chapter 7 examines what steps can be taken toward shared accountability and sustainability for *all* vested stakeholders to support early emotional development and optimize child and family outcomes.

QUESTIONS FOR REFLECTION

1. Early in this chapter, the section titled "Effective Questioning" presented examples of questions providers might ask caregivers about the following topics: 1) aspects of the family unit, 2) child and family strengths and preferences, 3) the extent to which challenging emotions/behavior occur across settings, and 4) what approaches work/don't work with the child across settings. Reflect on similar questions you have asked (or could ask) caregivers on these topics. What questions do you typically ask when you are getting to know caregivers and establishing rapport? What questions have you found to be especially valuable? What questions could you add?

2. Reflect on an example from your own experience when you or another provider communicated objectively worded social-emotional concerns to a caregiver. What was the concern and how did you word it? How did the caregiver respond? Did the exchange lead to positive change and, if so, how? Consider how the results might have been different if the social-emotional concern had been communicated differently.

3. Do you agree with the practitioners quoted in this chapter who expressed a need for more professional development on the topic of how to involve caregivers and partner with them? To what extent have previous coursework and/or workshops prepared you to partner with and support diverse families? What specific topics would you like to learn more about, and why?

4. Review the different modes of communication and outreach described in the section of this chapter titled, "Preferred Mode of Outreach." Which of these modes might you most prefer if you were a young child's caregiver? As a provider, which of these modes would you prefer to share information with caregivers? What advantages and disadvantages do you see in each of these modes?

5. Review the vignette about Kevin and Paul titled "Seeing Is Believing: Learning to Embrace Setting Limits." Have you had a similar experience, in which the caregiver seemed appreciative of your advice and showed a willingness to try out the recommended techniques? If so, what do you think you did effectively in your communication to ensure the caregiver felt supported, respected, and empowered?

6. Alternatively, have you encountered any families who have not been receptive to your suggestions? If so, why do you think the families were not receptive? What approaches may have helped in these cases?

SUPPLEMENTAL EXERCISE: PRACTICING ACTIVE LISTENING

In the "Effective Questioning" section of this chapter, the importance of active listening was briefly highlighted. What does this mean to you? To gain practice with this important skill, interview a familiar peer (e.g., co-worker, classmate, or friend) on an open-ended topic of your choice (e.g., their family, biggest accomplishment, future career aspirations, views on the education field, etc.). Allow your peer to do most of the talking for 10 to 15 minutes, asking only clarifying or probing questions as needed that directly align with their remarks. Without recording specific names, take notes at the end of the conversation to capture what was shared. Then go through the same process with someone you don't know as well (e.g., someone assigned by the program director, faculty professor, or someone you know indirectly via a personal contact). Compare and contrast your experience. What insights did you gain? For which person was this active listening exercise harder? Why?

SUPPLEMENTAL EXERCISE: DETERMINING HOW MUCH TO SHARE WITH FAMILIES

The section "Conveying Concerns Effectively" in this chapter highlighted two conflicting views on the extent and frequency of sharing behavior concerns with families when they occur in a center-based setting. For this exercise, informally ask/interview five fellow educators (teacher candidates and/or current providers) whom you personally know. Share with them the two previous views and ask them to select the one with which their own views about sharing behavior concerns most closely align. Also, ask why they feel this way and record their open-ended responses. Summarize and reflect on the results. Do all five individuals agree with each other? How do your own views compare to what the others shared? Let's suppose you are assigned to work with a co-teacher who feels differently than you about the extent to which details about challenging behavior should be shared with families. Reflect on why this could be a concern and brainstorm options to address this situation.

ONLINE RESOURCES

See the online companion materials for Chapter 6, available at www.brookes publishing.com/edwards/materials to learn more about the following topics:

- Family Partnerships: General Resources and Advice
- Culturally Diverse Families
- Social-Emotional Resources to Share With Families

7

Next Steps for
Sustaining Healthy
Social–Emotional Development

Section III of this book addresses possible roadblocks that may arise for providers as they work to implement a positive behavior interventions and supports (PBIS) framework, along with ways to overcome these obstacles. Chapter 6 discussed how to establish strong communication and a respectful, supportive partnership between birth–5 providers and families. This kind of relationship between the key players in a young child's social-emotional development—caregivers in the family and professional care or service providers—helps to ensure consistency and positive long-term outcomes.

This final chapter of Section III reinforces the notion of shared accountability by closely looking at informal and formal support systems and diverse key stakeholders within and across settings. More specifically, readers will better understand 1) family dynamics, such as mental health and key player awareness and implementation of tailored supports; and 2) birth–5 program staff dynamics that may influence use of recommended strategies such as teamwork and receptiveness to professional development. Topics discussed will include how providers, caregivers, and other stakeholders and agencies must work together to ensure the following:

- Caregiver awareness of available mental health resources
- Caregiver awareness of the importance of strategy use across family members
- Early childhood/early childhood special education (EC/ECSE) teamwork that includes strong communication and consistency among providers, including communication about, and consistency in, strategy use
- Ongoing professional development
- Effective information sharing across stakeholders and agencies

OVERVIEW: SHARED
ACCOUNTABILITY ACROSS SUPPORT NETWORKS

Recall that per Bronfenbrenner's ecological systems theory, a child's social and emotional development occurs in the context of many different interlocking social systems, with direct and indirect levels of influence (see Chapter 2). To reinforce the important role we each play in the lives of young children and their families, take a moment to read the following excerpt from Bronfenbrenner and Ceci (1994, p. 576), authors of a peer-reviewed article titled, "Nature-Nurture Reconceptualized in Developmental Perspective: A Bioecological Model":

> [O]nly those genetic predispositions of the individual can find realization for which the necessary opportunity structures exist, or are provided, in the particular immediate settings in which that person lives . . . For parents to further their children's learning and skill typically requires knowledge, know-how, and materials that, at some point, originated in the external world and, in effect, had to be imported into the family from the outside. Families who live in environmental contexts that contain such needed resources are therefore placed at an advantage. . . .

This quotation emphasizes "opportunity structures" that influence a family unit. What does this mean to you? The term *opportunity structures* refers to key people or resources to help facilitate growth and learning at opportune times in development. For example, Paige was born with an ability to play piano by ear. This talent, however, was not recognized until after her parents decided to purchase a piano. It was then that they noticed young Paige gravitating toward their piano and spontaneously playing familiar tunes without sheet music. Her mother praised her efforts and arranged for her to begin piano lessons. The first teacher dismissed Paige's natural talent, saying she must maintain focus on the sheet music (which she had already memorized) and play the exact notes at the same tempo each time. Paige quickly grew bored. Her mother recognized this teacher was not the right fit. Soon after, Paige began taking lessons from a family friend, a pianist in the community who was classically trained but similarly played by ear. This wonderful teacher inspired Paige to memorize longer melodies, playfully practice embellishing with varying chord compositions and tempos, and also gain confidence in reading sheet music. Consider what might have happened if Paige did not have access to a piano, had caregivers who were unable to afford lessons or unwilling to allow her to practice, and/or had not had a family with access to a local, knowledgeable piano teacher who was able and willing to optimize her talent. Reflect on a similar example from your own life—a natural skill or talent that would have never fully materialized in yourself or someone you know had it not been for a specific person and/or resource.

Who should be responsible for creating such structures and providing resources? Recall the shared role of a child's providers and primary caregivers. Thinking more broadly, who else has shared accountability in early emotional development? Consider those individuals who *directly* support and influence a child on a daily/weekly basis in an ECE/ECSE setting, such as a lead or co-teacher, assistant or aide, therapist, student worker, and support staff, as well as those who do so in a home/community setting, such as parents or guardians, siblings, extended family, babysitters, family friends, neighbors, or home-based Part C early intervention (EI) providers. Recall that as noted in previous chapters, embedding an emotion-centered curriculum and using emotion socialization across settings is advantageous for young children, and both practices are supported in the research literature (Denham, Zoller, & Couchoud, 1994; Hyson, 2004). Think about what opportunities arise across settings for the individuals listed previously to engage in this kind of teaching about, and socialization in using, adaptive emotional responses.

There are also many individuals who *indirectly* support children's emotional development by mentoring, educating, and/or empowering direct key players. These include administrators, supervisors, consultants, pediatricians, faculty and senior physicians who train and/or mentor pediatricians, faculty in teacher preparation programs, senior staff in community-based and parenting organizations, and researchers who share evidence-based information at regional, state, national, and/or international conferences. For example, pediatricians "can help to strengthen families and promote safe, stable, nurturing relationships with the aim of preventing maltreatment" (Flaherty & Stirling, 2010, p. 833). Others note the importance of considering the extent to which faculty embed content on social-emotional development and challenging behavior into early childhood coursework (Hemmeter, Santos, & Ostrosky, 2008). Furthermore, Fox and Hemmeter (2009) stressed how program administrators play a critical role in advocating for and committing resources to implement the Pyramid Model (see Chapter 3).

We will first look at the role of diverse key players in the home-based setting, followed by complex team dynamics that may influence attitudes and behaviors in center-based settings.

DYNAMICS WITHIN THE HOME

In this section, we will discuss family members' mental health and managing of their own emotions, and the need for more communication about, and carryover of, recommended, tailored social-emotional strategies across key players in the child's life.

Caregivers' Mental Health and Managing of Emotions

Sections I and II of this book emphasized assessing and supporting children's growth across domains and their social and emotional well-being, and Chapter 5 highlighted the importance of providers' own dispositions and emotional competencies in influencing how they work with children. Similarly, readers should be sensitive to the role that managing one's own emotions plays for caregivers, including possible mental health needs among key players in the home environment.

Mental Health Concerns   Unmet mental health needs are a prevalent issue in the United States and globally, with a continuum in the severity and extent to which individuals face episodic or lifelong concerns (Schaefer et al., 2017; van Randenborgh et al., 2012). In terms of prevalence estimates, the National Institute of Mental Health (NIMH) web site (2017) states, "In 2015, an estimated 16.1 million adults aged 18 or older in the United States had at least one major depressive episode in the past year. This number represented 6.7% of all U.S. adults." Based on a 2014 national survey conducted by the Substance Abuse and Mental Health Services Administration (SAMHSA, 2016), "an estimated 43.6 million (18.1%) Americans ages 18 and up experienced some form of mental illness [and] 20.2 million adults (8.4%) had a substance use disorder [in the previous year]." In addition, childhood trauma is widely prevalent (e.g., abuse, neglect, traumatic grief, domestic violence; see various types of trauma discussed at the web site of the National Childhood Traumatic Stress Network [2017]). The posttraumatic stress disorder fact sheet available from the SIDRAN Institute for Traumatic Stress Education and Advocacy (2016) estimates that "70 percent of adults in the United States have experienced a traumatic event at least once in their lives and up to 20 percent of these people go on to develop posttraumatic stress disorder, or PTSD." At the same time, researchers caution that prevalence estimates may vary widely based on global geographic and economic factors (see Viola et al., 2016).

Readers should be mindful that additional variables, such as raising a child with a disability, may enhance risk of mental health concerns in some families. Da Paz and Wallander (2017, p. 1) explained, "[w]ith convincing evidence that parenting a child with [autism spectrum disorder] is associated with elevated distress and mental health problems, researchers have begun to investigate treatments that directly target parents' psychological well-being."

Readers might be unclear of their role in caregivers' potential mental health concerns. In my own professional experience, I fondly recall working as an EI special instructor in an urban center-based setting and in families' homes. I once worked with a toddler and her mother in their home on a weekly basis. The mother repeatedly spent time disclosing personal details of her own psychiatric illness, leaving less time to discuss or practice recommended strategies to help her daughter. Although it was a positive sign that she felt comfortable sharing personal information, I recall feeling unsure of how best to respond. Certainly, the educator's role is not to diagnose or treat such concerns. Rather, we can get suggestions from our colleagues and supervisors, establish clearer expectations for the intent of the session or meeting time, serve as liaisons by sharing referral and outreach information, and encourage families to connect with community partners. Especially for those with depression, substance abuse, and/or trauma exposure, it is beneficial to refer them to both parenting *and* mental health services, with caregiver mental health affecting use of recommended child-rearing practices (Rogers, 2016).

In addition, birth–5 providers and administrators should spend quality time searching credible, evidence-based resources online and/or talking with mental health professionals to bolster understanding of, and empathy for, conditions that key adults in a child's life may experience and how these conditions may affect caregiver–child relations. For example, based on findings from a sample of fathers, caregivers with depression may be more withdrawn and less talkative during play interactions with their young infants (Sethna, Murray, Netsi, Psychogiou, & Ramchandani, 2015). Similarly, experiencing childhood trauma has been associated with physiological changes resulting in more neutral or negative affective expression during mother–infant interactions (Juul et al., 2016). Furthermore, consider how "substance misuse by parents was found in 40–80 percent of families who were identified for child welfare services" (National Council on Child Abuse and Family Violence, 2015; Renk et al., 2016, p. 1).

Such correlations do *not* suggest an absolute, definitive link, but it is important to be mindful that caregivers with varying personal stressors and mental health needs may be at greater risk. Rather than waiting for concerns to escalate, think proactively in terms of not ignoring red flags. Seek advice from colleagues, administrators, and community partners; set clear expectations for the shared role of the provider and caregiver during scheduled sessions; establish a positive rapport; and communicate tailored resource information on a broad array of holistic supports.

Self-Awareness and Self-Management   In addition to varying in mental health, individuals vary to the extent in which they reflect on their own modeling of emotions and their repertoire, or "bag of tricks," for coping with stressors. Some may be highly negative in how they express themselves in front of others. For example, based on the following small sampling of the 40 items in the *Self-Expressiveness in the Family Questionnaire* (Halberstadt, Cassidy, Stifter, Parke, & Fox, 1995, p. 95), consider how likely you are to "[express] anger at someone else's carelessness," "[show] contempt for another's actions," "spontaneously [hug] a family member," or "[express] deep affection or love for someone."

Simply saying "Be less negative" or "Show more positive emotions" to a parent or other caregiver is likely insufficient without proper intervention to facilitate personal growth. Although additional research on altering one's affect is warranted, it may be helpful for the parent to receive repeated, proper scaffolding from others he or she trusts; for example, watching the provider bend down to the child's eye level and model verbally praising the child's efforts, or hearing other caregivers sharing advice informally or at small parenting groups. It may also be helpful for the parent to have an opportunity to discuss and practice suggestions from resources such as online parenting web sites.

Keep in mind that a caregiver's ability to manage negative emotions in a constructive, adaptive way has implications for whether a child will learn to do so. Not surprisingly, those who have "ignored their own emotions [and/or] who find them unpleasant and difficult, are not [typically] willing participants in their child's negative emotions. Children who have not shared negative emotions constructively with another may not develop an emotion language others are able to share with them" (Hooven, Gottman, & Katz, 1995, p. 21).

Caregivers' *awareness* of early development and whether they need additional support in managing emotions and coping with stressors are positive first steps (e.g., see results from the 2015 National Caregiver Survey titled *Tuning In: Parents of Young Children Tell Us What They Think, Know, and Need* [ZERO TO THREE, 2016]). Consider the following remarks from one sample of urban Head Start mothers when discussing their role in emotional development (Edwards, 2012):

- "I have a problem with my emotions and my behavior so if I get more info on it, I'd be open."

- "[I feel] isolated . . . [I get] a little bit of help over a long time—waiting lists, far away appointments . . . [I am] at my breaking point, sometimes where I just break down and cry—his behavior adds to it . . . I ain't got a whole lot of answers on how to cope and stuff."

- "It's hard growing up in this neighborhood—a lot of drugs, a lot of deaths . . . Support? Depends on people—it's getting people to want to open up, seek support and be honest with themselves. People put up barriers and hide behind their doors. The cry for help usually isn't as loud as it should be. If they open up, it can help their child more . . ."

At the same time, self-awareness does not necessarily equate with communicating concerns to others, knowing where to find appropriate resources, and/or willingly accepting receipt of certain resources if offered. Urban Head Start mothers in my previous research were asked questions to tap into their perceived role in early emotional development. This sample reported being "very willing" (54.39%) or "somewhat willing" (37.72%) to modify their parenting behavior (e.g., discuss feelings/emotions with their children, use alternatives to yelling) if encouraged by a parent educator (Edwards, 2010, 2012), but the extent to which these were socially desirable responses is unclear (i.e., if they would actually adjust their approach if participating in a caregiver-focused intervention). Willingness to address unconstructive parenting behavior, or heed referral information to support one's mental health or manage emotions, may be affected by a host of variables, which might include any of the following:

- Whether there is a trusting, positive rapport with the person sharing the information

- Sleep deprivation (e.g., demanding schedule; adjusting to a new routine with a newborn)
- One's sense of self-efficacy or self-worth as a caregiver
- The match between the child and caregiver's temperament and developmental needs
- The caregiver's perceived emotional and financial supports/resources
- Competing work and/or school-related scheduling conflicts and/or stressors

Two of these variables are worth looking at more closely: trust and rapport, and caregiver self-efficacy. Trusting, positive relationships with professionals can make a difference in whether caregivers are willing to make changes in their child-rearing practices and family relationships. According to Levac, McCay, Merka, and Reddon-D'Arcy (2008, p. 78),

> When parents feel accepted, supported, and not blamed by [professionals], they seem to be able to engage in self-reflection specifically related to their parenting styles. In turn, their ability to reflect [and] make sense of their own thoughts, feelings, and behaviors seems to have a positive influence on the process of change in themselves, their children, and in their relationships with their children and other family members.

The caregiver's sense of self-efficacy also influences his or her caretaking practices and emotional well-being. Feeling powerless may be associated with using harsh practices like spanking, whereas empowering caregivers with recommended practices can lessen their stress and enhance child outcomes (Martorell & Bugental, 2006).

Supporting Caregivers by Connecting Them With Resources and Strategies
To summarize, although birth–5 providers and administrators will likely not be fully privy to the varying stressors and/or mental health concerns facing many caregivers, they are strongly encouraged to do the following:

1. Heighten their own awareness of resources, specifically, accessible local and web-based resources on both caregiver mental health and child-specific behavior management techniques.

2. Disseminate viable options both proactively (e.g., to all families) and in response to family-specific concerns, making a concerted effort to tailor information sharing in ways that are respectful of diverse cultural values, lifestyles, and needs, and preferred modes of communication.

3. Reach out to interdisciplinary community partners to better understand mental health issues potentially impacting caregivers and, if warranted, offer caregivers referral information to support their mental health (LaForett & Mendez, 2010). A small sampling of potential partners includes school psychologists, physicians, occupational therapists, social workers, school nurses, and Part C (birth–3) EI service coordinators.

Bear in mind that in your role as an educator, you may be able to serve as the liaison connecting caregivers to available resources and useful strategies of which they otherwise would not be aware. Consider these remarks from two mothers with children in an urban Head Start program (Edwards, 2012). One commented, "I'm not sure what's out there [in terms of support]; I don't know if it's too early to say I need help [with my 3-year-old], if [his behavior] is normal or not normal—it's kind of difficult [to determine]. We don't know these things like you do." The other observed, "[T]eachers are more important than most people believe and if they do know things, [it would be nice] for them to pass that on . . . I'm a little disappointed that I don't know the steps they take [to support emotions/behavior in the classroom]. I need to ask questions. Can't always assume."

Supporting Caregivers by Encouraging Mindfulness   Some readers may have heard of or encouraged the use of mindfulness. *Mindful parenting* can positively shape caregiver–child interactions and improve caregiver and child outcomes by focusing on moment-to-moment awareness within the caregiver–child relationship (Bögels, Lehtonen, & Restifo, 2010; Duncan, Coatsworth, & Greenberg, 2009). This process not only involves being present and accepting, but also "cultivating emotional awareness and self-regulation in parenting" (Duncan et al., 2009, p. 255). Although more research is needed on diverse caregiver samples, mindfulness has been linked to caregivers' improved general health; decreased depression, anxiety, and parenting stress; as well as improved child outcomes (Da Paz & Wallander, 2017; Singh et al., 2007). *Mindfulness* is an evidence-based approach associated with long-term positive outcomes for individuals with stress, anxiety, depression, and other mental health concerns (Kabat-Zinn et al., 2016; Miller, Fletcher, & Kabat-Zinn, 1995; Williams & Kabat-Zinn, 2013). Researchers increasingly recommend that mindfulness be used by key adults in a child's life (see Benn, Akiva, Arel, & Roeser, 2012; Bögels, Hellemans, van Deursen, Römer, & van der Meulen, 2014; Coatsworth, Duncan, Greenberg, & Nix, 2010; Goodman et al., 2014).

As a birth–5 service provider or administrator there is much you can do to help caregivers cultivate mindfulness, such as sharing informational handouts and modeling key practices. Consider the following dimensions of mindful parenting (Crawford, 2013) and reflect on the extent to which you model and recommend doing each of them: "listening with full attention, nonjudgmental acceptance of self and child, emotional awareness, self-regulation in the parenting relationship," and "compassion for self and child" (p. 1). The following examples demonstrate what these mindfulness techniques look like in practice.

Listening with full attention: This involves paying close attention to the child's verbal communication and nonverbal behavioral cues. For example, Rita keenly observes that her son, Jordan, is quieter than usual and not as playful as he sits in the grocery store cart after a full day of preschool. When she asks about his day, he whispers that he didn't like gym. She pauses in one of the aisles to learn more.

Nonjudgmental acceptance of self and child: This refers to having realistic expectations, accepting the child's particular traits, and embracing a mix of child- and parent-oriented goals during the interaction. For example, Rita knows that Jordan sometimes needs extended wait time (silence) before he responds to a question. Although it can be frustrating, especially given that she likes to multitask and is hurrying to pick up a few items for dinner, she tries to be patient and ask one simplified question at a time about what happened in gym class. She slowly counts to 10 in her head before expecting him to answer. Rita also accepts that he won't likely share all the details in that moment. She knows from previous interactions that he will likely share more of what happened before bedtime.

Emotional awareness: This involves being responsive toward and nondismissive of the child's emotions. For example, when Rita learns that Jordan refused to participate in gym because another child took the ball he wanted, she validates and gives him words to help express his feelings, without trivializing the situation.

Self-regulation in the parenting relationship: This pertains to parenting based on one's goals and values, rather than overreacting, regardless of the child's emotions in that particular moment. For example, rather than yelling about the other child and/or reprimanding him for missing gym for something so "silly," Rita remains calm and focused on helping her son communicate his emotions. She focuses on helping him brainstorm adaptive ways to respond the next time someone takes something that he wants (e.g., telling the teacher, asking the child to switch balls after a few minutes, making another choice). Rita makes a mental note to follow-up with the teacher the next morning so they can be consistent in reinforcing use of similar strategies to help Jordan better handle such situations.

Compassion for self and for child: This can occur through maintaining positive affect and being forgiving toward oneself when one has not responded to or interacted with one's child as planned. For example, after Jordan is asleep, Rita rehashes how she grew a little impatient in the grocery store when Jordan continued to give vague responses to her questions. At the same time, she tries to focus on the positive effort she made to help her son by trying her best to stay focused in the moment and respond sensitively to her son's concern.

In Section I, we discussed how caregivers' prolonged negative emotions and harsh discipline correlate with negative child outcomes in many caregiver–child samples (Chang, Schwartz, Dodge, & McBride-Chang, 2003). Some well-intentioned caregivers may prefer to only discuss happy emotions with their child and dismiss and/or try to hide unpleasant emotions (Edwards, 2012), but it is instead recommended that trusted adults help children label and make sense of a broader range of emotions, including occasional sadness, frustration, and anger. Meaningfully talking with 2 to 5 year olds about negative emotions as well as positive emotions exposes them to a larger emotion vocabulary and more open-ended questioning (Lagattuta & Wellman, 2002). Furthermore, engaging young children in emotion coaching and developmentally appropriate conversations on a range of positive and negative emotions can improve emotion recognition (Dunn, Brown, & Beardsall, 1991).

In the following vignette, the mother of a 2-year-old and a 5-year-old tells one of the teachers, Ms. Lisa, about their morning.

Mommy Should Have Stayed Calm: Supporting Mindful Parenting

Ms. Lisa has known the Brussel family for the past 4 years. She taught Lucy a few years ago and was thrilled when the family's youngest daughter, Jenny, entered her class. Today at drop-off, she noticed that the girls' mother, Sharon Brussel, seemed particularly harried and upset. Ms. Lisa overheard Sharon tell Jenny, who was clinging to her leg, that she was running late to a meeting and couldn't do a long good-bye. Ms. Lisa, who was involved in a small-group activity at that moment, quietly asked her co-teacher to take over. She knew it wasn't an ideal time to ask Sharon if something was wrong, but she thought she could help Jenny more smoothly separate from her mother. "Jenny, I need your help!" she called. "Our class guinea pig needs a new toy and I'm not sure which one to give her." Jenny stood up with a smile, always eager to help their class pet. Sharon exchanged a knowing smile with Ms. Lisa and waved good-bye as she hurried out the door.

Ms. Lisa continued to worry about Sharon after she left. She decided to e-mail her to let Sharon know how well Jenny was doing and ask if Sharon was okay. In her message, Ms. Lisa mentioned that she would have a little downtime during her break from 12:30 to 1:00 p.m. if Sharon wanted to chat. As she wrapped up her meeting and noticed Ms. Lisa's e-mail, Sharon felt appreciative that Ms. Lisa thought enough of her to reach out. Sharon decided to call, because the problem from the morning was still weighing on her. In the midday phone conversation, she shared the following with Ms. Lisa:

> "I feel so guilty about what happened this morning. It was a little after 7:30 a.m. I had to leave the house by 8:00 to drop the kids off and make it on time to my 8:30 a.m. meeting. I still needed to find my belt, put on Lucy's shoes, finish packing both of their lunches, and butter their waffles. All the while, Lucy was asking me random questions like, "We're mammals, right Mommy? We played tennis yesterday—when did you learn how to play, Mommy?" Jenny began crying because her favorite TV show just ended. So, in a frenzied moment, I shut off the TV and yelled, "Stop! Stop talking, both of you! Sit quietly until Mommy calls you for breakfast! I still have a lot to do, I don't want to forget anything, and I can't be late to my meeting!" Jenny immediately started to cry and looked panicked. I took a few breaths and tried to ignore the crying while hurrying to get everything done, but felt very guilty when seeing that she wasn't calming down. I walked over to her and held her hand from behind the couch. I said, "It's okay . . . shhhh . . . Mommy is sorry. There is just a lot to do." Jenny still cried, squeezing my hand. I guided her to Stop and Think until she was ready to calm down, and so I could continue getting everything ready. Jenny sat in a nearby chair, as we had practiced, and started to calm down after a few minutes. When I announced that breakfast was ready, the girls quickly came to the table. As they were eating, I sat down and gently said, "Mommy is sorry. I was feeling frustrated. I should have taken a deep breath and used my words calmly instead of yelling. There's just a lot to do and I want to make sure to get you ready for a great day at school. No more yelling, okay?" Lucy nodded, smiling. Jenny said, "Okay, Mommy" and gave me a hug. I guess they're seeing that even Mommy gets frustrated sometimes and it's okay to talk about it. Do you think I did the right thing?"

Ms. Lisa took some brief notes on her end so she could let Sharon talk uninterrupted. She realized that Sharon had all of this bottled up and probably appreciated being able to vent. When Sharon asked if she did the right thing, Ms. Lisa assured her, "We've all been there." She went on to praise Sharon's efforts—juggling so many tasks at the same time, taking such good care of her girls, responding right away when Jenny started to cry, having worked on Stop and Think before that incident so Jenny knew exactly what to do, and so on. Ms. Lisa emphasized that she was most impressed by how, after everyone had calmed down, Sharon was willing to talk with the girls about her negative feelings and what she would try to do next time. "You're really showing the girls a wonderful model for how it's okay to feel and talk about a range of emotions," Ms. Lisa said, adding that Sharon shouldn't be so hard on herself—and how it's great to reflect on what we can do differently next time and helpful to focus on the positives. She admitted that teachers often need to remind themselves of that, too. After they hung up, Sharon took a deep breath. She appreciated Ms. Lisa's compassion and felt like a weight had been lifted from her shoulders.

The mother in this vignette was experiencing a hectic morning, as most adults do from time to time. Think about what you can do as a provider to support caregivers when they are experiencing this. Keep in mind that providers should make a concerted effort to recognize strengths and good efforts in others. Think about what you see as this mother's strengths. Identify something positive she did—and something positive the provider did to support her.

Consider, also, which of the previously mentioned dimensions of mindful parenting this caregiver might need additional guidance with or support in putting into practice. What might you suggest this caregiver try to reduce morning stress and have a calmer start to the day?

Effectively Conveying Strategies to Caregivers

Readers should now have a clearer understanding of a guiding social-emotional framework and recommended strategies that providers and families can use to support early emotional development across settings. Early-onset challenging behavior can be improved by families using PBIS (see Dishion et al., 2008). Recall how it is beneficial to respond with sensitivity and warmth rather than negativity and anger, and to scaffold using self-soothing techniques when distressed (Caspi et al., 2004; Chang et al., 2003; Kimonis et al., 2006). As children grow, caregivers can guide them to be aware of things that may have led to the behavior, thereby increasing understanding of situations that make them upset (Gilliom, Shaw, Beck, Schonberg, & Lukon, 2002); guide them to talk about how they and others may be feeling (Denham et al., 2003); and guide them to think of different ways to respond depending on the situation (Gilliom et al., 2002).

Although more research is needed on this topic, caregivers may be more likely to use such recommendations when alone with their child if they

- Acknowledge and agree with the notion of shared accountability and their contributing role in early emotional development

- Recognize that social-emotional concerns will not likely go away without intervention

- Understand and are able to articulate a clear rationale for why certain approaches or techniques may be problematic

- Receive the right amount of timely, pertinent information (i.e., meeting families where they are) to avoid possibly feeling overwhelmed by too much information at one time

- Feel supported by key players in their informal and formal support network

Table 7.1 presents examples of how you might talk to caregivers to articulate why certain approaches or techniques are problematic, so that caregivers, in turn, can understand and articulate these rationales themselves and make well-thought-out decisions about how they respond to problematic or concerning behaviors (Edwards, 2012).

Identifying Family Support Networks

The narrative to this point has emphasized caregiver–provider or family–provider communication and collaboration. Of course, caregivers are not the only people in a child's home and community life who influence his or her emotional development. (Reflect on which individuals, besides immediate family members, played an

Table 7.1. Helping caregivers use positive interventions

Step 1: Acknowledge caregivers' difficult emotions; review the value of positive intervention. For example, say,

"When your child misbehaves, you may feel any number of reactions: *frustration* ('I don't know what else to do'), *irritation* ('She knows that we don't do that; this needs to stop'), *anger* ('I have so much on my plate and I just can't handle his screaming right now'), or *concern* ('Maybe I need to talk with someone about this'). As frustrated, irritated, angry, or concerned as you may be, the research is clear: yelling, screaming, spanking, or other negative responses will not help your child in the long run learn better ways of controlling and expressing his or her emotions. This is a good time to teach or guide your child in ways that will help him or her better handle or cope with similar situations in the future."

This approach helps the caregiver understand and feel vested in using easy-to-implement, effective alternatives.

Step 2: Encourage caregivers to consider what a child is communicating through challenging behavior. For example, say,

"In your head, try 'putting words' to the behavior your child is showing. That is, think about what your child is trying to tell you. For example, screaming might communicate, 'I don't want to go to bed!' Crying might communicate, 'I can't do this by myself!' Kicking the table might communicate, 'I want someone to pay attention to me!'

Step 3: Discuss specific strategies the caregiver can use to communicate effectively with the child. For example, say,

"Help your child feel supported by staying calm, bending down to your child's eye level, and validating feelings by giving words that seem to fit the situation. For example, if your child is screaming at bedtime say, 'Are you telling me you don't want to go to bed?' If your child is crying while struggling to do something ask, 'Do you need help? Are you feeling frustrated?' If your child is kicking the table and seems to be asking for attention say, 'Who can show me how we sit nicely at the table? Oh, I love how you are sitting with your feet under your chair!'"

Step 4: Explain how the caregiver can model specific adaptive behaviors/self-regulation strategies for the child. For example, say,

"Help your child by modeling ways of calming down (but perhaps looking slightly away so as not to give attention for screaming)." It is helpful to offer useful tools to self-soothe and appropriately handle and express emotions when upset. You can try these techniques:

- Counting slowly to 10 ("1 . . . 2 . . . 3 . . . [take a deep breath and let it out slowly] . . . 4 . . . 5 . . . 6 . . . say, 'Good calming down' . . . 7 . . . 8 . . . 9 . . . 10."); repeat if needed.
- Dimming lights and/or playing soothing music in the background
- Slowly lifting your hands above your head while deeply breathing in; slowly lowering your hands back down to your side, while exhaling
- Calmly walking with your child to a room with less stimulation (to a quieter space, perhaps briefly away from the television or other people)
- Giving your child a comforting object or favorite toy to hold
- Gently encouraging your child to sit quietly in a chair or in the corner of the room, *not* as a punishment but to help him or her calm down. Calmly say something like, "I think we need to calm our bodies. Let's sit down. Tell me/show me when you are ready" and then look away (staying nearby but partially focusing your attention on something else)."

Step 5: Explain how the caregiver can discuss the situation with the child after the fact, in a developmentally appropriate way. For example, say,

"Only after your child has calmed down, and when you are calm, talk about what happened." Recommend age-appropriate ways the caregiver can do so with his or her child. For example, support a child that has calmed down after hitting someone on the arm.

1. For an older baby or toddler, recommend that the caregiver ask the child to "make nice" on the arm of the person who was hit. If the child doesn't yet understand, the caregiver can gently take his or her hand and place it on the arm of the person who was hit, while patting gently and saying, "Nice . . . good job making nice! We use gentle hands."

2. For a young preschooler, recommend that the caregiver ask, "Is it okay to hit someone? No . . . we do not hit. Hands are for clapping, blowing kisses, waving hi . . . but not for hitting. Go ask [person hit] if [he or she] is okay. Good asking if [he or she] is okay. Make nice on [his or her] arm. Thank you! That's a better choice. Are you ready to [get back to activity]? Remember, we need to use gentle hands!"

(continued)

Table 7.1.   *(continued)*

3. For an older preschooler, recommend that the caregiver ask, "Are you ready to talk about this?" and wait until the child nods and agrees. If necessary, have the child sit calmly until ready. Then ask, "Why did I ask you to calm your body?" [If child is verbal, wait for response; if child does not respond, calmly explain in simple terms what your child did.] "You hit [him] on the arm. Was that a good choice? Do we use our hands to hurt other people?" Encourage child to answer, if possible. [If appropriate, ask the person hit to tell the child how he or she felt ("You hurt me on my arm; it really hurts and I feel sad"). Ask what we can do to help this person feel better (e.g., pat nicely, get an ice pack). Ask your older child if he or she can tell you why he or she hit ("He wouldn't share the toy") and help him or her think of better ways to handle the situation ("I could have opened my hand and nicely asked to share; I could have waited my turn by playing with a different toy; I could have asked you for help").

influential role for any length of time during your own childhood.) To fully embrace shared roles in emotional development, next steps must include identifying families' *formal and informal support networks* (see Table 7.2) and all those who influence the child (Bronfenbrenner, 2001; Dunst, 2000). As Fox, Carta, Strain, Dunlap, and Hemmeter (2010, p.7) explained, "When children have persistent challenges, families and other persons involved with the child [should] form a collaborative team to develop and implement comprehensive interventions and supports that are applied in all of the child's routines and activities."

In a study with 114 mothers of children in an urban Head Start program (Edwards, 2010), one promising finding was that 96% reported approaching at least one source for behavior-related support. Table 7.3 (Edwards, 2010) highlights which members in their network were approached. (Note that this maternal sample was not as likely to ask educators for behavior advice, a finding that may inform your outreach efforts.)

Furthermore, an increasing number of caregivers are looking to social media and the Internet for child-related information and support. This may reflect "the weakened support many of today's parents experience from their own parents, relatives and friends" (Plantin & Daneback, 2009, p. 34). In a separate study (Edwards, 2018), I collected self-reported data from caregivers of children receiving home-based Part C EI services. Nearly half of the sample reported differences in who provides emotional support and who is very supportive of their family receiving EI. Also, simply knowing that someone lives in the same home or neighborhood does not necessarily mean this individual is a valued source of support.

One way to understand who is in a family's formal and informal support network, and the extent to which each member lives near and is supportive of the family unit, is to complete an *eco-map*. The eco-map, a tool used in interdisciplinary contexts, is a schematic designed as a web with interconnected circles. It visually represents the

Table 7.2.   Identify which key individuals are considered vested stakeholders in each family's formal and informal support network

Sampling of formal supports	Sampling of informal supports
Child care provider(s)	Extended family (e.g., siblings, aunts, uncles, grandparents, cousins)
Therapist(s)	
Pediatrician; medical specialist	Babysitter(s) or nanny
Service coordinator	Neighbor(s) or family friend(s)
Social worker	Member(s) of faith-based organization

Table 7.3. Formal and informal support networks

Mothers of Preschoolers with a diagnosed delay (n = 20)		Mothers of preschoolers without a delay (n = 94)	
Community members sought	%	Community members sought	%
Family	80%	Family	73%
Neighbor or friend	60%	Neighbor or friend	53%
Health care professionals	55%	Health care professionals	33%
Head Start staff	55%	Head Start staff	27%
Non–Head Start staff	30%	Non–Head Start staff	11%
Member of religious community	25%	Member of religious community	12%
Other	5%	Other	3%

This is one sample of Head Start mothers' formal and informal support networks, noting which people the mothers self-reported having asked for behavior-related advice in the past year (Edwards, 2010, 2012). The percentage of mothers surveyed who sought support from each group (family members, neighbors, etc.) is indicated.

various sources of support to whom a given family is connected, the proximity of these support sources, and the strength of the family's connection to each one. Eco-mapping offers "a visual means of facilitating discussions around the structure and strength of networks . . . [that captures] strategic data through symbols expressing relationships that may be inadequately portrayed in words" (Ray & Street, 2005, p. 545). A sample eco-map is shown in Figure 7.1.

Support Network Awareness and Use of Strategies After identifying key players in a family's support network, it is helpful to pinpoint which individuals play a

Use the following key to interpret the eco-map for Edgar's family.	
——	**Shorter line** = closer proximity to the family
————	**Longer line** = farther away from family
——	**Straighter line** = stronger connection
∿	**Crooked/zig-zag line** = weaker connection

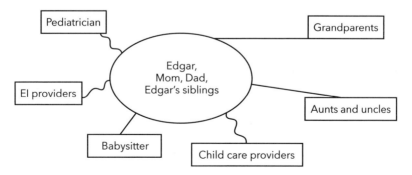

Figure 7.1. This eco-map provides a glimpse into dynamics unique to this family's informal and formal support network. What do you notice? (*Key:* EI, early intervention.)

direct role in watching or interacting with the child for any length of time. Ask yourself, "To what extent do other key players use recommended, tailored strategies when alone with this child?" Recall the importance of coaching others in the child's natural environment to consistently and meaningfully implement recommendations (see Rush, Shelden, & Hanft, 2003). If providers focus on relaying evidence-based, data-driven recommendations to only one caregiver, they cannot assume this will result in other key players being informed of and/or using these recommendations. For example, if a child frequently has tantrums, one parent might strive to consistently help the child calm down first and then guide her to make better choices; however, that parent's partner might insist on spanking the child. In surveying one EI caregiver sample, as part of a study currently under review for publication, I found that 86% of the caregivers reported asking one or more key players to use strategies when alone with the child, with little confidence that their requests were being heeded. Consider the following quotes:

- "My mother is [my child's] caretaker during work hours [but] I'm not confident that my mother uses all strategies consistently." Anonymous EI caregiver (Edwards, 2018)

- "Everyone tells me to beat them and that's not the right answer—[telling me to hit them] with belts, physically abuse them." Anonymous Head Start caregiver (Edwards, 2010)

- "You do try to get as many people in there because that is the child's day—and as many people can do whatever needs to be done, that's the best. If kid's in [child] care couple days a week, kid's with grandma couple days a week, it's best if all those people know what's going on and that they can add to it." Anonymous EI provider (Edwards, 2018)

We must move toward supporting caregivers' ability and willingness to discuss and promote strategy use and respond to possible criticism or indifference among key players not present during caregiver–provider interactions or home-based sessions (Hanft & Pilkington, 2000; McWilliam & Scott, 2001). More research is needed to understand and address these concerns.

PROGRAM STAFF DYNAMICS

In this final subsection, I will discuss the need for birth–5 providers to be consistent in using recommended practices, embrace ongoing professional development, and close the loop of information sharing across stakeholders.

Communication and Consistency Among Providers

Recall the importance of using emotion coaching with young children. To ensure its effectiveness, next steps must include promoting consistency in evidence-based, data-driven practices across providers within the same setting and over the course of multiple school years. In addition to understanding emerging developmental milestones, it can be helpful to consider emotion socialization and coaching as part of a *spiral curriculum*. This term refers to "an iterative revisiting of topics, subjects or themes . . . [it] is not simply the repetition of a topic taught. It requires also the deepening of it, with each successive encounter building on the previous one" (Bruner, 1960; Harden, 1999, p. 141).

Achieving this consistency takes effort and patience—and a willingness to revisit and reteach strategies when necessary. Perhaps you have heard colleagues make remarks such as, "The therapist already showed him ways to self-soothe last year, so I don't know why we have to keep going over it again!" or similar frustrations. What these remarks fail to take into account is that young children have to *continually* be reminded of rules, expectations, and adaptive ways of communicating and expressing emotions. For providers addressing difficult emotions or challenging behavior, it is vital to revisit concepts and reinforce increasingly more sophisticated skills over time as the child develops and experiences novel situations.

In terms of classroom-specific resources, lack of perceived support from fellow colleagues and administrators can make it more difficult for early childhood educators or early childhood special educators to use recommended practices (see Murray & Mandell, 2006). In a study of 400 co-teachers, general and special educator dyads who disagreed about their respective responsibilities had more difficulty providing a shared approach to teaching children with and without disabilities (Stefanidis & Strogilos, 2015). Furthermore, teachers who face inconsistencies between their specialized training and situations/resources in their birth–5 setting may experience heightened stress and emotional exhaustion (Stremmel, Benson, & Powell, 1993). A provider might worry, for instance, that her co-teacher responds to the children in ways that are very different from how the provider has been taught to respond. As highlighted in the following vignette, inconsistencies in how providers view and/ or respond to emotions can send young children mixed messages and potentially hinder progress. In a study of 63 early childhood providers, for example, researchers found they used different types of interaction styles (e.g., varying in how much they redirect behaviors), with cluster differences correlating with teacher sensitivity, classroom quality, and group–child engagement (de Kruif, McWilliam, Ridley, & Wakely, 2000).

The Other Teacher Ignores His Crying: Addressing Differences in Interaction Style

Ms. Iris and Ms. Ava have both been teaching for over 10 years and have worked together in the infant room for the past year. Ellen, a 9 month old, happily smiles and kicks her feet in the swing when she sees her father arrive at dismissal. "Hi, baby girl! I missed you! How was your day?" Ellen's father asks. Ms. Ava gives the father Ellen's food items, and Ms. Iris mentions how much fun they had visiting the park that day. Another infant, 10-month-old Jack, watches as Ellen and her father say their good-byes and leave. After they leave, only Jack remains in the room with the teachers. He clutches his blanket and cruises over to his family photo on the wall. Both teachers see Jack look at the photo, frown, and begin to cry.

Ms. Ava rolls her eyes and sharply says, "Oh, come on, can't we just have a day without one of these kids crying? I'm so tired . . . you know, there's a show on TV I want to watch later." She continues talking about the TV show while straightening up the room, ignoring Jack's cries.

Meanwhile, Ms. Iris kneels down next to Jack to get to his eye level. She knows it is important to help Jack label his emotions. "Jack, you look sad," she says. "Are you feeling sad? I understand. You want your Mommy and Daddy to come. I promise they'll be here soon." She tries to redirect his attention to the ball-drop toy on the other side of the room, but Jack refuses to leave the family photo on the wall. Instead of offering another toy, Ms. Iris follows his lead to talk about the photo. "Hmmm . . . I see a lot of things in that photo. Is that your dog, Wiggles? Look, I see your Mommy! What a pretty dress she is wearing! Oh, is that your older sister on Daddy's lap? Look at the pretty flowers in the grass! Let's pretend to smell the flowers!" Jack is very engaged by the teacher's comments. He smiles broadly, stares at the photo, and babbles excitedly.

Soon, a familiar voice calls from the doorway, "Hi, sweet boy!" Jack spins around and crawls excitedly to his mommy. As the teachers, parent, and Jack say their good-byes, Ms. Ava is subdued, while Ms. Iris is proud to have validated his emotions and helped him calm down before he reunited with his mother. Ms. Iris remains frustrated, though, by her co-teacher's dismissive, less responsive approach. Despite a recent emotion coaching workshop, and Ms. Iris modeling effective ways to respond each day, Ms. Ava does not seem to want to change.

What might you do if you were in a situation like Ms. Iris's? Ideally, this could be a good teachable moment for Ms. Iris to sit with her co-teacher after the children have left and spend a few minutes reflecting on the day—things that went well, things they might want to try differently tomorrow. During this exchange, Ms. Iris could ask Ms. Ava if she liked the way Ms. Iris responded when Jack started crying, to see if perhaps Ms. Ava would acknowledge that it did help him quickly calm down. This brief conversation would certainly be less awkward if it were something the co-teachers previously agreed to put in place at the end of *each* day. It would also be important for Ms. Iris to reflect on whether Ms. Ava's response is atypical (if she is usually personable and attentive) or if it is part of an increasingly troubling pattern in her interactions with parents and children. In addition, Ms. Iris should consider the severity of her co-teacher's response. A harsh response (e.g., yelling at, harming, or threatening to harm a child), even if it happens just once, must be immediately reported to the supervisor. Depending on Ms. Iris's overall assessment of the situation, she may also need to privately communicate less serious, but still important, concerns to her supervisor (i.e., detailing exactly what is happening). The administrator might choose to do any of several things, depending on the context and particular situation, which may include the following:

- Spending some time personally observing in the room during the times Ms. Ava is reportedly more negative or subdued

- Talking with Ms. Ava one-on-one to ask if something is wrong and if she is satisfied with her position/assigned age level

- At the next staff meeting, formally revisiting NAEYC and DEC recommended practices related to teacher–child interactions and key concepts from their recent emotion coaching workshop

- Asking Ms. Ava to complete an online follow-up training on emotion coaching

- Formally documenting/filing concerns and working with Ms. Ava to create an action plan for what the supervisor will expect to see moving forward

- Considering terminating Ms. Ava's employment with the child care center if she refuses to revisit her interaction style and make necessary changes

Again, whether Ms. Iris should involve a supervisor depends on the overall context for her concerns. For instance, if Ms. Ava is usually warm and attentive but was irritable and apathetic on one particular day, involving the supervisor might not be warranted. A conversation between the two co-teachers might suffice, especially if Ms. Ava acknowledges that her response to the child wasn't ideal and identifies strategies she can use to ensure she responds appropriately to children at the end of the day when she's feeling tired or stressed. In contrast, if this is an ongoing pattern of behavior, and/or if Ms. Ava doesn't see anything wrong with the way she responded and just gets defensive, then getting a supervisor involved might be the next step.

Embracing Professional Development

Practitioners in early childhood education can benefit from professional development addressing several key topics:

- Strategies for managing their own and others' emotions
- The major topics discussed in previous chapters of this book, including development across domains; emotion coaching; reflective practice and data collection; the multitiered PBIS framework; and culturally responsive, family-centered practices
- Provider–provider communication and teamwork, and interdisciplinary approaches

Early childhood educators who have a greater array of emotion-regulation strategies and are more accepting of others' emotions may have more supportive responses to children's negative emotions and less nonsupportive responses to children's positive emotions (Swartz & McElwain, 2012). All providers in direct contact with a child (e.g., therapists, lead teachers, co-teachers, aides, paraprofessionals, student workers) should be exposed to ongoing opportunities to reflect on and enhance knowledge and skills in areas such as development across domains, emotion coaching, reflective practice and data collection, the multitiered PBIS framework, and culturally responsive, family-centered practices.

In Part C EI, trainings are mandated under the federal provision for a comprehensive system of personnel development (see Edwards, 2017b; Evan, 1980). Historically, only 18 states required ECE teachers in center-based settings to have any preservice training (Ackerman, 2004) and child care programs follow in-service training guidelines under their state-specific quality rating system (see Barnard, Smith, Fiene, & Swanson, 2006). In a study of family child care providers, researchers found a "collaborative approach to evaluation and assessment that focused on a small number of specific items each month supported the continuous quality improvement process" (Lanigan, 2011, p. 399). Norris (2001) assessed quality indicators among 70 family child care providers from three groups: those who never participated in training, intermittently attended training, or continually participated in training during their career. It is noteworthy that those who continually participated had higher ratings for quality of care than the other two groups. In terms of type of in-service training, researchers who collected data from 255 preschool teachers from 26 states found that on-site training in participants' classrooms was more well received and effective (in terms of improving teaching practices) than either conference presentations or 1- to 3-day workshops (Dunst & Raab, 2010).

Another area warranting professional development is provider–provider communication and teamwork. Providers benefit from information sharing and ongoing conversations to improve carryover and collaboration within and across settings (Rush & Hanft, 2003). Especially to support children with disabilities, a *transdisciplinary team approach* is recommended, whereby individuals pool their interdisciplinary expertise and contribute unique knowledge and skills to optimize decision making and service delivery in the home and/or center-based setting (Bruder, 1998; Stayton, 2015). As Raver and Childress (2014, p. 50) explain,

> Early intervention provides a process that demands highly committed, professional, collaborative service providers who come together as a team to help families develop their own abilities in parenting their child. The quality of any early intervention program is determined by the quality of the disciplinary expertise, mutual respect, and communication skills of the team members. Effective teamwork permits interventionists to expand their individual knowledge as they offer support to parents who are learning ways to improve their child's development and learning.

Information Sharing Among Providers Within Programs

It is important to move toward collaborative information sharing among diverse birth–5 providers *within programs* to best support early emotional development. Previous research has examined the positive influence of mentor teachers and the provision of "colleague-support networks" (Odell, 1990). Others have found a promising connection between teacher–teacher collaboration and educational change (Butler & Schnellert, 2012). To begin to move in this direction, providers and administrators must reflect on the following critical questions:

- Does each member of the program or agency feel valued and respected?

- To what extent are providers receptive to changing/altering their current approach?

- Is time set aside (or is there compensation) to encourage regularly scheduled brainstorming and shared reflection among team members on social-emotional concerns, interpretation of data, use of recommended strategies, and progress monitoring?

- Are there ongoing opportunities for formal professional development?

- Is there follow-up to reinforce concepts/skills beyond each workshop or webinar?

- Is there informal resource sharing and support from a program supervisor?

- Is there a shared commitment to programwide use of PBIS and the Pyramid Model?

The relevance of each of these questions is further explored in the following text.

Question 1: Does each member of the program or agency feel valued and respected? A center-based provider once memorably remarked to me, "[I] need more input to deal with parents that are not open to working with teachers—they only consider [us] babysitters." Low wages and/or being referred to as "babysitters" are things that may shortchange our providers and make them feel less respected in society (Tuominen, 2003). If providers don't highly value their important and unique contribution to the individual agency/program or field as a whole, it is possible they will have lowered self-efficacy. This in turn has been linked with task disengagement and lower mastery of desired learning outcomes (Liem, Lau, & Nie, 2008). In other words, if you do not feel highly valued and do not think your contributions necessarily matter, you may not be as interested in learning more about emotional development and PBIS.

Question 2: To what extent are providers receptive to changing/altering their current approach? It is also important to consider the extent to which providers are open to change and committed to improvement. Although more research on ECE/ECSE providers' willingness to change is warranted, Sheridan, Edwards, Marvin, and Knoche (2009, p. 392) explain,

Motivation for change in the early childhood teacher likely affects the training and training/coaching/consultation process and efforts to guide positive growth. However, what motivates change in professional behaviors is not clear. It can be assumed that practitioners who are motivated and "ready" to change have an outlook or perspective that change in their own behaviors will result in positive outcomes for children.

Although research has not yet provided clear explanations for why some teachers are open to change while others are not, it may help to convey to teachers the rationale for the requested new strategies—specifically, how they are anticipated to support children's growth. Keep in mind that individual staff members may personally be motivated by different things, such as getting a paycheck, having a sense of belonging, doing challenging work, receiving verbal praise, or having access to opportunities to learn. Consider also each provider's approach to tasks and communication/interaction style.

Question 3: Is time set aside (or is there compensation) to encourage regularly scheduled brainstorming and shared reflection among team members on social-emotional concerns, interpretation of data, use of recommended strategies, and progress monitoring? When I conducted a focus group with Part C EI home-based providers working within a traditional model (Edwards, 2018), one provider commented, "[It] would be nice if there was a designated time during the week . . . to sit down and bounce [ideas] off of someone." This statement reflects what is also apparent in available research literature: Reflection is an important part of effective teaching practice. Sheridan et al. (2009, p. 392) explained, "practitioners' inclinations to reflect on personal experiences and practice may influence whether they achieve meaningful, lasting change." There are many ways for programs to accomplish this, including semi-structured staff meetings to discuss and reflect on preselected topics, and even use of approved recordings. For example, a study by Cherrington and Loveridge (2014) suggested early childhood teachers may benefit from collectively viewing and reflecting on recorded teaching samples to better understand each other's teaching practices. Additional research on this and other plausible ways to promote collaborative reflection is warranted. In cases where it is not feasible for staff to meet to engage in shared reflection (e.g., due to time or fiscal constraints), a notebook might be used to maintain ongoing reflective communication. Home-based providers who work with the same family might communicate using a notebook that stays at the family's home; alternatively, they might maintain a mass e-mail chain or request permission from their supervisor to access a password-protected remote site (e.g., documents stored in a Dropbox or Google Docs) to see team members' views and respond to particular threads of conversation about any of the previously mentioned topics.

Question 4: Are there ongoing opportunities for formal professional development? Early childhood practitioners need more explicit, embedded course instruction and hands-on experiences to enhance understanding of family-centered practice, teaming, PBIS, and emotion coaching at the preservice and in-service level. According to Epstein (2005, p. 125), "a chain of professional development events is needed . . . start[ing] with college courses and continu[ing] with inservice education, ongoing technical assistance and support, and external networking." Less formal professional development experiences may also have value. Opportunities for informal and formal professional development can include the following:

- Coursework or recommended readings
- Review of online professional resources

- In-service PBIS workshops
- Practitioner-focused sessions at annual conferences, such as the Division for Early Childhood, the National Association for the Education of Young Children, the National Head Start Association, the National Training Institute on Effective Practices, and ZERO TO THREE

Teachers who have access to these professional development opportunities may find them very valuable. Table 7.4 shows a sampling of unpublished, anonymous responses from teacher candidates and practicing teachers who completed my university-level positive behavior supports course and an in-service PBIS workshop, respectively.

Question 5: Is there follow-up to reinforce concepts and/or skills beyond each workshop or webinar? Available research literature recommends doing more than just a one-time training. In one study, for example, Head Start teaching staff randomly assigned to additional experiential practice after a 1-day behavior workshop had improved behavior management strategies compared to the group assigned to just the 1-day workshop (Fabiano et al., 2013). When I conducted a PBS workshop and used a devised follow-up data collection exercise on teacher-selected children in a birth–5 setting, providers appreciated being able to collaborate with fellow team members in a new way and acknowledged that the combination of the workshop and follow-up exercise promoted objective provider–supervisor communication about concerns.

Question 6: Is there informal resource sharing and support from a program supervisor? Providing immediate, relevant feedback and opportunities to debrief correlate

Table 7.4. Teacher responses to professional development opportunities related to positive behavior interventions and supports (PBIS)

Responses of teacher candidates taking a university-level course in positive behavior supports (PBS)

1. "Figure 2-1 on page 60 [Wheeler & Richey, 2014] is a point in the chapter that caught my attention. When I first read about the importance of positive 'alliances' with the students and families, I kind of blew it off, thinking that forming positive relationships was something you begin to learn in preschool. How different could it be? But I didn't quite think about what makes those alliances strong, positive and beneficial or how I could improve them, especially in cases with families that are not cooperative. Seeing a physical list of 8 different obligations that describe how to create a positive, professional and strong relationship opened my eyes to the fact that there is more than just simple communication and being friendly. It truly takes a lot of time and effort and cooperation with families to build a foundation that will benefit all parties."

2. "[I learned] it is important to work more closely with the adults and parents in students' lives by coaching them and skill building with them, rather than telling them what to do."

Responses of participants who completed an in-service PBIS workshop

1. "I liked learning about the different techniques to calm down an upset or misbehaving child."

2. "This workshop has motivated me to observe my children more close[ly]."

3. "I enjoyed learning about specific techniques to use to better the children's learning environment while incorporating all aspects, such as teaching style, the classroom setting, curriculum, and even home life."

4. "It got me thinking [about] what preceded target behavior, follows it, and time of day."

5. "It gave me some strategies to use to help me find the sources of behavior and address them. Focus on why and how to meet needs without unnecessary punishment."

6. "It helped me better understand that different children do the same behavior for different reasons . . . [I] want to learn more about it so that I can use different strategies in my classroom."

Quotes in the first portion are comprised of two anonymous responses from teacher candidates completing mini-reflection assignments as part of the author's university-level PBS course. The second portion is from an unpublished institutional review board-approved study whereby participants in part provided anonymous feedback following an in-service PBIS workshop (Edwards, 2014c).

with improved teacher and child outcomes (Landry, Anthony, Swank, & Monseque-Bailey, 2009). From my own teaching experience, I can fondly recall times a supervisor supported staff in various ways; for example, posting a sticky note on the back of the classroom door following random 15- to 20-minute observations, on which was written one observed strength and one suggestion; sharing copies of journal articles to bolster understanding of timely issues; and asking one or two teachers who attended a conference to share new information, handouts, and key insights with fellow staff members at the next scheduled staff meeting. The following vignette illustrates other ways a supervisor might support providers on an ongoing basis.

A Supervisor Lends a Helping Hand: Supporting Providers

As the program supervisor, Ms. Farrell likes to briefly stop by each classroom to warmly greet children and staff whenever possible. One morning, she peeked into a classroom to find three toddlers sitting on a small couch. The aide in the room had called in sick that day. It looked as if the children were being reprimanded by the lead teacher, Ms. Brandi, who was yelling, "These books are very old! You do not throw them!" A small boy, Ling, responded by smiling and laughing. The teacher sharply turned her attention to him, "Excuse me! Oh no, okay, you know what . . ." The teacher led Ling to sit in a nearby chair and sternly said, "You think it's funny that I almost tripped on the book? It was not funny, and I don't appreciate you laughing at me!" Ling continued smiling, and Ms. Brandi looked up to see Ms. Farrell by the door. She approached her supervisor and said in a quieter tone, "It's going to be one of those days . . . you know, I don't even feel well, but I had to come because I know we're short-staffed." This teacher then admitted, "I don't know what to do."

Ms. Farrell asked if perhaps she could make Ling the leader in returning books to the shelf. Ms. Brandi responded, "Maybe I can try that," but her voice trailed off. She looked like she needed a break. At that point, Ms. Farrell felt it was okay to intervene. "Oh no, look at all the books on the floor!" she said. "Let's make nice on our books. This is our room. Let's make it look nice! Kaleel, can you help me? Great job! Who else can help me?"

When Ling threw a book, Ms. Farrell ignored that behavior and said, "Ling, which book do you want to put back on the shelf, this one or this one?" Once Ling made his selection, he walked to the bookshelf and returned it nicely by himself. Ms. Farrell brought attention back to the lead teacher by asking her, in front of the children, if the others could help, too. The teacher gave her supervisor a knowing smile and said that would be fine. Together, Ms. Brandi and Ms. Farrell exclaimed, "Yay, look how clean you made our rug! Let's clap hands! Yay!" As Ms. Farrell walked toward the door, sensing a much more positive tone in the room, Ms. Brandi smiled at her and said quietly, "I owe you one. Thank you."

Consider what might have happened in this situation if the supervisor hadn't willingly offered to help. In addition, think about what steps might have occurred prior to this episode to make the teacher feel so comfortable admitting that she needed help. How does this provider–supervisor exchange compare to what you have personally observed or experienced?

Question 7: Is there a shared commitment to programwide use of PBIS and the Pyramid Model? Programwide implementation of the Pyramid Model has been associated with improved school climate, annual parent evaluations, and ratings of teacher satisfaction (Fox & Little, 2001). Variables that must be in place include commitment to the Pyramid Model by trusted administrators, ongoing training to enhance teacher competence, and involvement of a leadership team (e.g., to reflect on tailored, data-driven plans) (Fox & Hemmeter, 2009). Other researchers suggest well-defined behavior expectations, short- and long-term goals, and a data system for monitoring and evaluation (Wheeler & Richey, 2010).

Information Sharing Across Stakeholders and Agencies

In addition to moving toward a shared vision and meaningful collaboration within programs, we need to convey a consistent message and learn from other key stakeholders across programs, agencies, and community settings in a child's life. This includes understanding the connections among these key stakeholders; for example, educator–therapist, therapist–therapist, providers–family, and primary caregivers–key players in the caregivers' support network. Consider, for example, caregivers' potential confusion or frustration from receiving contradictory oral or written communication depending on the provider. As a program administrator acknowledged in Edwards (2017a), "I think who fills [out the daily note], their take on it, and just to have one person's take on it may be different than another person's take or the way they express it." Others call for more collaboration among EC/ECSE professional organizations, federal and state agencies, university faculty, and staff development providers (Stayton, 2015).

Still other researchers in the field refer to "closing the loop" with regard to a broad range of considerations that influence young children and their families, such as teachers receiving timely, collaborative, and useful feedback on evaluations (Butty et al., 2015); faculty studying assessment data to inform programmatic improvements (Blaich & Wise, 2011); and, even in the case of children receiving pediatric emergency care, providing follow-up information to families (Bucaro & Black, 2014) and other medical providers (Willig et al., 2013). Similarly, with regard to our shared role in early emotional development and adaptive behavior, it is essential to follow up with appropriate stakeholders after receiving questions, progress updates, or new recommendations from families, therapists, colleagues, and/or pediatricians. Providers and administrators should:

- Validate stakeholders' concerns and show how their information will inform next steps (Goodall, 2015)
- Let them know key aspects of what happened (as it pertains to their particular role and level of involvement)
- Enhance willingness for stakeholders to reconnect and continue to divulge useful, relevant concerns, questions, progress updates and/or recommendations in the future

It is my hope that this book has enhanced readers' understanding of shared roles in emotional development and recommended, tailored practices providers can use with children to lay a strong foundation in this area. Certainly, research limitations within the field need to be addressed. For example, researchers often mention the limitation of "unknown generalizability" or application of findings to groups not included in a particular study's sample. That is, results from a sample of urban Head Start mothers may not necessarily apply to Head Start fathers, Head Start programs in other geographic regions, or to caregivers of children not enrolled in Head Start. It's important for providers to continually stay updated with the extant literature by doing keyword searches to locate peer-reviewed journal articles. If you find that a certain strategy has not yet been assessed with a particular subgroup you are trying to reach, keep this in mind when weighing how best to proceed. Researchers and providers must work toward translating findings into practice (see Lowell, Carter, Godoy, Paulicin, & Briggs-Gowan, 2011). As Olsen, Astor, Booth-Miner, and Miner (2007, p. 1) noted:

> Now the field has a robust research base providing evidence about effective family-strengthening strategies and the professional development that educators need to effectively implement them. The research base forms a foundation for the early childhood field's increasingly intentional efforts to support families.

Readers are urged to embrace continuous opportunities to reflect on and assess current practices; stay informed of research on emotions, data-driven PBIS, and family/provider partnerships; as well as use coaching and active collaboration with stakeholders within and across settings. In closing, keep in mind the words of one anonymous birth–5 provider following a tailored PBIS workshop (Edwards, 2014c): "Remember how important we are and how we can make changes."

QUESTIONS FOR REFLECTION

1. This chapter discussed several variables that might affect a caregiver's willingness to address challenging behavior or heed referral information to support one's mental health or manage emotions. These include the degree of trust and rapport with the person sharing the information, sleep deprivation, the caregiver's sense of self-efficacy, the match between the child and caregiver's temperament and developmental needs, perceived emotional and financial supports/resources, and competing work- and/or school-related scheduling conflicts and/or stressors. Can you think of any additional variables that might affect a caregiver's willingness to adjust responses or seek help? What are they? How have they affected caregivers with whom you have worked?

2. Recall a time that you had mental health concerns about caregivers in a particular family. How did you respond? Which community partners and/or resources may have helped optimize supports for this family?

3. This chapter discussed five dimensions of mindful parenting: listening with full attention, nonjudgmental acceptance of self and child, emotional awareness, self-regulation in the parenting relationship, and compassion for self and for child. Think of a primary caregiver you know who has a young child (birth–5). On which of these five dimensions might this caregiver need additional guidance or support? What could you do to provide this support?

4. Review Table 7.3, which summarizes results from a study that included 114 mothers of children in an urban Head Start program (Edwards, 2010, 2012), indicating which members of their available support network these mothers sought out for support related specifically to their children's behavior. Were you surprised this maternal sample was not as likely to ask educators for behavior advice? Why or why not? How might this information inform your outreach efforts?

5. Review the vignette, "Communication and Consistency Among Providers," concerning Ms. Iris's and Ms. Ava's contrasting responses to the children in their care. Have you met any birth–5 providers who remind you of Ms. Ava? Why might

Ms. Ava not be as willing to use techniques shared in a recent workshop and repeatedly modeled by her co-teacher? How might you respond to Ms. Ava in this situation?

SUPPLEMENTAL EXERCISE: CREATING AN ECO-MAP

To complete this exercise, refer to the subsection, Effectively Conveying Strategies to Caregivers, which discusses the importance of eco-maps.

1. Using Figure 7.1 as an example, draw an eco-map of your own family's formal and informal support network.

2. Reflect on two or three new insights you gain from the eco-map (e.g., in terms of your network's proximity and perceived strength of the relationships).

3. If possible, exchange eco-maps with a peer. Pair-share on what the visual says (and doesn't say) about the types of supports available to each of you. Ask each other one or two probing questions, then practice listening attentively to better understand each other's family dynamics. Consider what recommendations/ suggestions you might make if this individual were a caregiver of a child on your caseload.

SUPPLEMENTAL EXERCISE: RESEARCHING MENTAL HEALTH ISSUES

To complete this exercise, refer to the subsection, Supporting Caregivers by Connecting Them With Resources and Strategies, which discussed reaching out to interdisciplinary community partners regarding potential mental health issues caregivers may experience.

1. Building on the brief descriptions of possible mental health concerns listed in this chapter, identify two or three concerns that you are most interested in learning more about.

2. Prepare a list of specific questions about each of the selected mental health concerns you would like to ask a mental health expert. Reflect on why you would be interested in asking each one.

3. If possible, bring these questions to a mental health consultant in your area either by setting up an appointment in person, by phone, or via e-mail (e.g., a school psychologist, a behavior specialist, an educational researcher with counseling expertise). Take notes on what is discussed. Which of the shared responses, if any, surprise you? Reflect on new insights gained from this experience.

ONLINE RESOURCES

See the online companion materials for Chapter 7, available at www.brookes publishing.com/edwards/materials to learn more about the following topics:

- Sampling of Resources to Share With Families
- Mental Health Resources for ECE/ECSE Professionals
- Sampling of Resources on Quality Interactions With Others

References

Ackerman, D. J. (2004). States' efforts in improving the qualifications of early care and education teachers. *Educational Policy, 18*(2), 311–337.

Adler, P. A., & Adler, P. (1996). Parent-as-researcher: The politics of researching in the personal life. *Qualitative Sociology, 19*(1), 35–58.

Akechi, H., Senju, A., Uibo, H., Kikuchi, Y., Hasegawa, T., & Hietanen, J. K. (2013). *Attention to eye contact in the west and east: Autonomic responses and evaluative ratings. PLoS ONE, 8*(3), e59312. Retrieved from http://doi.org/10.1371/journal.pone.0059312

Alink, L. R., Mesman, J., Van Zeijl, J., Stolk, M. N., Juffer, F., Koot, H. M., . . . & Van Ijzendoorn, M. H. (2006). The early childhood aggression curve: Development of physical aggression in 10- to 50-month-old children. *Child Development, 77*(4), 954–966.

Allegheny County Family Resource Guide. (2016). Early intervention and therapy for all ages and needs. Retrieved from http://www.familyresourceguide.org/early-intervention/types-therapies.aspx

Amato-Zech, N. A., Hoff, K. E., & Doepke, K. J. (2006). Increasing on-task behavior in the classroom: Extension of self-monitoring strategies. *Psychology in the Schools, 43*(2), 211–221.

Anderson (2015). *Why are so many preschoolers getting suspended?* Retrieved from http://www.theatlantic.com/education/archive/2015/12/why-are-so-many-preschoolers-getting-suspended/418932/

Applied Behavioral Strategies. (2018). *Getting to know ABA*. Retrieved from http://www.applied-behavioralstrategies.com/what-is-aba.html

Atance, C. M., & O'Neill, D. K. (2005). The emergence of episodic future thinking in humans. *Learning and Motivation, 36*(2), 126–144.

Avramidis, E., & Kalyva, E. (2007). The influence of teaching experience and professional development on Greek teachers' attitudes towards inclusion. *European Journal of Special Needs Education, 22*(4), 367–389.

Ayers, H., Clarke, D., & Murray, A. (2015). *Perspectives on behaviour: A practical guide to effective interventions for teachers*. New York, NY/London, UK: Routledge.

Bagnato, S. J. (2007). *Authentic assessment for early childhood intervention: Best practices*. New York, NY: Guilford Press.

Bailey, H. N., DeOliveira, C. A., Wolfe, V. V., Evans, E. M., & Hartwick, C. (2012). The impact of childhood maltreatment history on parenting: A comparison of maltreatment types and assessment methods. *Child Abuse & Neglect, 36*(3), 236–246.

Baker, J. A., Grant, S., & Morlock, L. (2008). The teacher-student relationship as a developmental context for children with internalizing or externalizing behavior problems. *School Psychology Quarterly, 23*(1), 3–15.

Bambara, L. M., Cole, C. L., & Koger, F. (1998). Translating self-determination concepts into support for adults with severe disabilities. *Journal of the Association for Persons with Severe Handicaps, 23*(1), 27–37.

Banerjee, R., & Luckner, J. (2014). Training needs of early childhood professionals who work with children and families who are culturally and linguistically diverse. *Infants & Young Children, 27*(1), 43–59.

Barbetta, P. M., Norona, K. L., & Bicard, D. F. (2005). Classroom behavior management: A dozen common mistakes and what to do instead. *Preventing School Failure: Alternative Education for Children and Youth, 49*(3), 11–19.

Barkley, S. G. (2010). *Quality teaching in a culture of coaching*. Lanham, MD: Rowman & Littlefield Education.

Barnard, W., Smith, W. E., Fiene, R., & Swanson, K. (2006). *Evaluation of Pennsylvania's Keystone STARS quality rating system in child care settings*. Harrisburg, PA: Pennsylvania Office of Child Development.

Barnhill, G. P. (2005). Functional behavioral assessment in schools. *Intervention in School and Clinic, 40*(3), 131–143.

Barrera, I., Corso, R. M., & Macpherson, D. (2003). *Skilled dialogue: Strategies for responding to cultural diversity in early childhood*. Baltimore, MD: Paul H. Brookes Publishing Co.

Barrera, I., & Kramer, L. (2009). *Using skilled dialogue to transform challenging interactions: Honoring identity, voice, and connection*. Baltimore, MD: Paul H. Brookes Publishing Co. [Excerpted online by the National Association for the Education of Young Children.] Retrieved from http://www.naeyc.org/files/naeyc/2012NAEYC_Ebook3.pdf

Barrish, K. (2013). How do children learn to regulate their emotions? The Blog [online]. *Huffington Post*. Retrieved from http://www.huffingtonpost.com/kenneth-barish-phd/how-do-children-learn-to-_b_3890461.html

Barton, E. E., & Smith, B. J. (2015). Advancing high-quality preschool inclusion: A discussion and recommendations for the field. *Topics in Early Childhood Special Education, 35*(2), 69–78.

Bayer, J. K., Hiscock, H., Ukoumunne, O. C., Price, A., & Wake, M. (2008). Early childhood aetiology of mental health problems: A longitudinal population-based study. *Journal of Child Psychology and Psychiatry, 49*(11), 1166–1174.

Begeny, J. C., & Martens, B. K. (2006). Assessing pre-service teachers' training in empirically-validated behavioral instruction practices. *School Psychology Quarterly, 21*(3), 262–285.

Benazzi, L., Horner, R. H., & Good, R. H. (2006). Effects of behavior support team composition on the technical adequacy and contextual fit of behavior support plans. *The Journal of Special Education, 40*(3), 160–170.

Benedict, E. A., Horner, R. H., & Squires, J. K. (2007). Assessment and implementation of positive behavior support in preschools. *Topics in Early Childhood Special Education, 27*(3), 174–192.

Benn, R., Akiva, T., Arel, S., & Roeser, R. W. (2012). Mindfulness training effects for parents and educators of children with special needs. *Developmental Psychology, 48*(5), 1476.

Berglund, E., Eriksson, M., & Johansson, I. (2001). Parental reports of spoken language skills in children with Down syndrome. *Journal of Speech, Language, and Hearing Research, 44*(1), 179–191.

Bernal, G., & Sáez-Santiago, E. (2006). Culturally centered psychosocial interventions. *Journal of Community Psychology, 34*(2), 121–132.

Bernhard, J. K., Lefebvre, M. L., Murphy Kilbride, K., Chud, G., & Lange, R. (1998). Troubled relationships in early childhood education: Parent-teacher interactions in ethnoculturally diverse child care settings. *Early Education and Development, 9*(1), 5–28.

Bevill, A. R., Gast, D. L., Maguire, A. M., & Vail, C. O. (2001). Increasing engagement of preschoolers with disabilities through correspondence training and picture cues. *Journal of Early Intervention, 24*(2), 129–145.

Bicard, S. C., Bicard, D. F., & the IRIS Center. (2012). *Defining behavior.* Retrieved from http://iris.peabody.vanderbilt.edu/wp-content/uploads/2013/05/ICS-015.pdf

Blaich, C. F., & Wise, K. S. (2011, January). *From gathering to using assessment results: Lessons from the Wabash national study* (NILOA Occasional Paper No. 8). Urbana: University of Illinois and Indiana University, National Institute for Learning Outcomes Assessment.

Blair, K. S. C., Fox, L., & Lentini, R. (2010). Use of positive behavior support to address the challenging behavior of young children within a community early childhood program. *Topics in Early Childhood Special Education, 30*(2), 68–79.

Blood, E., & Neel, R. S. (2007). From FBA to implementation: A look at what is actually being delivered. *Education and Treatment of Children, 30*(4), 67–80.

Bobeck, B. L. (2002). Teacher resiliency: A key to career longevity. *The Clearing House: A Journal of Educational Strategies, Issues and Ideas, 75*(4), 202–205.

Bögels, S. M., Hellemans, J., van Deursen, S., Römer, M., & van der Meulen, R. (2014). Mindful parenting in mental health care: Effects on parental and child psychopathology, parental stress, parenting, coparenting, and marital functioning. *Mindfulness, 5*(5), 536–551.

Bögels, S. M., Lehtonen, A., & Restifo, K. (2010). Mindful parenting in mental health care. *Mindfulness, 1*(2), 107–120.

Bokony, P., Whiteside-Mansell, L., Swindle, T., & Waliski, A. (2013). Increasing parent-teacher communication in private preschools. *NHSA Dialog, 16*(1), 45–64.

Bondy, A., & Frost, L. (2002). *A picture's worth: PECS and other visual communication strategies in autism.* Bethesda, MD: Woodbine House.

Bradshaw, C. P., Reinke, W. M., Brown, L. D., Bevans, K. B., & Leaf, P. J. (2008). Implementation of school-wide positive behavioral interventions and supports (PBIS) in elementary schools: Observations from a randomized trial. *Education and Treatment of Children, 31*(1), 1–26.

Branson, D., & Demchak, M. (2011). Toddler teachers' use of teaching pyramid practices. *Topics in Early Childhood Special Education, 30*(4), 196–208.

Briesch, A. M., & Chafouleas, S. M. (2009). Review and analysis of literature on self-management interventions to promote appropriate classroom behaviors (1988–2008). *School Psychology Quarterly, 24*(2), 106–118.

Briggs, R. D., Silver, E. J., Krug, L. M., Mason, Z. S., Schrag, R. D., Chinitz, S., & Racine, A. D. (2014). Healthy Steps as a moderator: The impact of maternal trauma on child social-emotional development. *Clinical Practice in Pediatric Psychology, 2*(2), 166–175.

Britsch, S. (2010). Photo-booklets for English language learning: Incorporating visual communication into early childhood teacher preparation. *Early Childhood Education Journal, 38*(3), 171–177.

Brody, L. R. (1985). Gender differences in emotional development: A review of theories and research. *Journal of Personality, 53*(2), 102–149.

Bronfenbrenner, U. (1979). *The ecology of human development: Experiments by nature and design.* Cambridge, MA: Harvard University Press.

Bronfenbrenner, U. (1986). Ecology of the family as a context for human development: Research perspectives. *Developmental Psychology, 22*(6), 723–742.

Bronfenbrenner, U. (2001). Human development, bioecological theory of. In N. J. Smelser & P. B. Baltes (Eds.), *International encyclopedia of the social and behavioral sciences* (pp. 6963–6970). Oxford, UK: Elsevier.

Bronfenbrenner, U. (2005). *Making human beings human: Bioecological perspectives on human development.* Thousand Oaks, CA: Sage Publications.

Bronfenbrenner, U., & Ceci, S. J. (1994). Nature-nurture reconceptualized in developmental perspective: A bioecological model. *Psychological Review, 101*(4), 568–586.

Bronfenbrenner, U., & Morris, P. A. (2006). The bioecological model of human development. In R. M. Lerner (Ed.), *Handbook of child psychology* (6th ed.). Volume 1: Theoretical models of human development (pp. 793–828). New York, NY: Wiley.

Bronson, M. (2000). *Self-regulation in early childhood: Nature and nurture*. New York, NY: Guilford Press.

Brotherson, M. J. (2001). The role of families in accountability. *Journal of Early Intervention, 24*(1), 22–24.

Brownell, C. A., Svetlova, M., Anderson, R., Nichols, S. R., & Drummond, J. (2013). Socialization of early prosocial behavior: Parents' talk about emotions is associated with sharing and helping in toddlers. *Infancy, 18*(1), 91–119.

Bruder, M. B. (1998). A collaborative model to increase the capacity of childcare providers to include young children with disabilities. *Journal of Early Intervention, 21*(2), 177–186.

Bruder, M. B. (2010). Early childhood intervention: A promise to children and families for their future. *Exceptional Children, 76*(3), 339–355.

Bruder, M. B., & Dunst, C. J. (2005). Personnel preparation in recommended early intervention practices degree of emphasis across disciplines. *Topics in Early Childhood Special Education, 25*(1), 25–33.

Bruner, J. S. (1960). *The process of education*. Cambridge, MA: Harvard University Press.

Bucaro, P. J., & Black, E. (2014). Facilitating a safe transition from the pediatric emergency department to home with a post-discharge phone call: A quality-improvement initiative to improve patient safety. *Journal of Emergency Nursing, 40*(3), 245–252.

Bugental, D. B., Blue, J., & Cruzcosa, M. (1989). Perceived control over caregiving outcomes: Implications for child abuse. *Developmental Psychology, 25*(4), 532.

Bullock, A., Coplan, R. J., & Bosacki, S. (2015). Exploring links between early childhood educators' psychological characteristics and classroom management self-efficacy beliefs. *Canadian Journal of Behavioural Science/Revue canadienne des sciences du comportement, 47*(2), 175–183.

Butler, D. L., & Schnellert, L. (2012). Collaborative inquiry in teacher professional development. *Teaching and Teacher Education, 28*(8), 1206–1220.

Butty, J. A. L. M., Wakiaga, L. A., McKie, B. K., Thomas, V. G., Green, R. D., Avasthi, N., & Swierzbin, C. L. (2015). Going full circle with teacher feedback. *SAGE Open, 5*(3), doi:10.1177/2158244015596207

Campbell, A. M., & Hibbard, R. (2014). More than words: The emotional maltreatment of children. *Pediatric Clinics of North America, 61*(5), 959–970.

Campbell, P. H., Milbourne, S. A., & Silverman, C. (2001). Strengths-based child portfolios: A professional development activity to alter perspectives of children with special needs. *Topics in Early Childhood Special Education, 21*(3), 152–161.

Campbell, P. H., & Sawyer, L. B. (2007). Supporting learning opportunities in natural settings through participation-based services. *Journal of Early Intervention, 29*(4), 287–305.

Campos, J. J., Campos, R. G., & Barrett, K. C. (1989). Emergent themes in the study of emotional development and emotion regulation. *Developmental Psychology, 25*(3), 394–402.

Campos, J. J., Sorce, J. F., Emde, R. N., & Svejda, M. (2013). Emotions as behavior regulators: Social referencing in infancy. *Emotions in Early Development, 2*, 57.

Carlson, J. S., Mackrain, M. A., Van Egeren, L. A., Brophy-Herb, H., Kirk, R. H., Marciniak, D., . . . & Tableman, B. (2012). Implementing a statewide early childhood mental health consultation approach to preventing childcare expulsion. *Infant Mental Health Journal, 33*(3), 265–273.

Carr, E. G. (1994). Emerging themes in the functional analysis of problem behavior. *Journal of Applied Behavior Analysis, 27*(2), 393–399.

Carr, E. G., Dunlap, G., Horner, R. H., Koegel, R. L., Turnbull, A. P., Sailor, W., . . . & Fox, L. (2002). Positive behavior support evolution of an applied science. *Journal of Positive Behavior Interventions, 4*(1), 4–16.

Carr, J. E., & Sidener, T. M. (2002). On the relation between applied behavior analysis and positive behavioral support. *The Behavior Analyst, 25*(2), 245–253.

Carter, C. M. (2001). Using choice with game play to increase language skills and interactive behaviors in children with autism. *Journal of Positive Behavior Interventions, 3*(3), 131–151.

Carter, D. R., & Pool, J. L. (2012). Appropriate social behavior: Teaching expectations to young children. *Early Childhood Education Journal, 40*(5), 315–321.

Casey, L. B., & Smith, J. B. (2014). Functional behavior assessments in evaluating individuals with autism spectrum disorders. In V. B. Patel, V. R. Preedy, & C. R. Martin (Eds.), *Comprehensive guide to autism* (pp. 487–501). New York, NY: Springer.

Caspi, A., Moffitt, T. E., Morgan, J., Rutter, M., Taylor, A., Arseneault, L., . . . & Polo-Tomas, M. (2004). Maternal expressed emotion predicts children's antisocial behavior problems: Using monozygotic-twin differences to identify environmental effects on behavioral development. *Developmental Psychology, 40*(2), 149–161.

Center on Social and Emotional Foundations for Early Learning at Vanderbilt University. (2003). *Pyramid Model for promoting social and emotional competence in infants and young children*. Nashville, TN: Author.

Chang, L., Schwartz, D., Dodge, K., & McBride-Chang, C. (2003). Harsh parenting in relation to child emotion regulation and aggression. *Journal of Family Psychology, 17*(4), 598–606.

Chao, R. K. (1996). Chinese and European American mothers' beliefs about the role of parenting in children's school success. *Journal of Cross-Cultural Psychology, 27*(4), 403–423.

Chaplin, T. M., & Aldao, A. (2013). Gender differences in emotion expression in children: A meta-analytic review. *Psychological Bulletin, 139*(4), 735–765.

Chaplin, T. M., Cole, P. M., & Zahn-Waxler, C. (2005). Parental socialization of emotion expression: Gender differences and relations to child adjustment. *Emotion, 5*(1), 80–88.

Chavkin, N. F., & Williams, D. L. (1988). Critical issues in teacher training for parent involvement. *Educational Horizons, 66*(2), 87–89.

Chazin, K. T., & Ledford, J. R. (2016). Preference assessments. In *Evidence-based instructional practices for young children with autism and other disabilities.* Retrieved from http://vkc.mc.vanderbilt.edu/ebip/preference-assessments

Cherrington, S., & Loveridge, J. (2014). Using video to promote early childhood teachers' thinking and reflection. *Teaching and Teacher Education, 41,* 42–51.

Cherry, K. (2017, May). *What is a schedule of reinforcement?* Retrieved from https://www.verywell.com/what-is-a-schedule-of-reinforcement-2794864#vdTrn

ChildHelp. *Child abuse statistics and facts.* ChildHelp. Retrieved from https://www.childhelp.org/child-abuse-statistics/

Christian, L. G. (2006). Understanding families: Applying family systems theory to early childhood practice. *Young Children, 61*(1), 12–20.

Chu, M. (2012). Observe, reflect, and apply: Ways to successfully mentor early childhood educators. *Dimensions of Early Childhood, 3*(40), 20–28. Retrieved from http://www.southernearlychildhood.org/upload/pdf/Dimensions_Vol40_3_Chu.pdf

Chu, S. Y. (2014). Perspectives of teachers and parents of Chinese American students with disabilities about their home–school communication. *Preventing School Failure: Alternative Education for Children and Youth, 58*(4), 237–248.

Clark, C., & McDonnell, A. P. (2008). Teaching choice making to children with visual impairments and multiple disabilities in preschool and kindergarten classrooms. *Journal of Visual Impairment & Blindness, 102*(7), 397.

Coatsworth, J. D., Duncan, L. G., Greenberg, M. T., & Nix, R. L. (2010). Changing parent's mindfulness, child management skills and relationship quality with their youth: Results from a randomized pilot intervention trial. *Journal of Child and Family Studies, 19*(2), 203–217.

Cole, C. L., Marder, T., & McCann, L. (2000). Self-monitoring. In E. S. Shapiro & T. R. Kratochwill (Eds.), *Conducting school-based assessments of child and adolescent behaviour* (pp. 121–149). New York, NY: Guilford Press.

Cole, P. M., Michel, M. K., & Teti, L. O. (1994). The development of emotion regulation and dysregulation: A clinical perspective. *Monographs of the Society for Research on Child Development, 59*(2–3, Serial No. 240), 73–100.

Coles, E. K., Owens, J. S., Serrano, V. J., Slavec, J., & Evans, S. W. (2015). From consultation to student outcomes: The role of teacher knowledge, skills, and beliefs in increasing integrity in classroom management strategies. *School Mental Health, 7*(1), 34–48.

Collaborative for Academic, Social and Emotional Learning (CASEL) (2014, February). [Web page]. Retrieved from www.casel.org

Contrerras, J. M., Kerns, K. A., Weimer, B. L., Gentzler, A. I., & Tomich, P. L. (2000). Emotion regulation as a mediator of associations between mother-child attachment and peer relations in middle childhood. *Journal of Family Psychology, 14,* 111–124.

Cooper, J., Heron, T., & Heward, W. (2007). *Applied behaviour analysis* (2nd ed.). Upper Saddle River, NJ: Pearson.

Cooper, J. L., Masi, R., & Vick, J. (2009). *Social-emotional development in early childhood: What every policymaker should know.* New York, NY: National Center for Children in Poverty. Retrieved from http://www.nccp.org/publications/pdf/text_882.pdf

Council for Exceptional Children. (2018). *Professional standards and practice policies and positions.* Retrieved from https://cec.sped.org/Standards/Professional-Policy-and-Positions

Council on Children and Families. (2017). *Career development resource guide: Exploring positions.* Retrieved from http://ccf.ny.gov/ and http://earlychildhood.org/cdrg/exp_positions.cfm

Crawford, J. (2013). *Mindful parenting for parents and caregivers.* Washington State University Extension Fact Sheet FS108E. Retrieved from https://www.gvsu.edu/cms4/asset/614589D9-D87D-F6884E9414B96B94C137/parents_and_caregiver_practices.pdf

Crone, D. A., Hawken, L. S., & Horner, R. H. (2015). *Building positive behavior support systems in schools: Functional behavioral assessment.* New York, NY: Guilford Press.

Crone, D. A., & Horner, R. H. (2003). *Building positive behavior support systems in schools: Functional behavior assessment.* New York, NY: Guilford Press.

Cullinan, D., & Sabornie, E. J. (2004). Characteristics of emotional disturbance in middle and high school students. *Journal of Emotional and Behavioral Disorders, 12*(3), 157–167.

Cummings, E. M., Davies, P. T., & Campbell, S. B. (2002). *Developmental psychopathology and family process: Theory, research, and clinical implications.* New York, NY: Guilford Press.

Cummins, L., & Asempapa, B. (2013). Fostering teacher candidate dispositions in teacher education programs. *Journal of the Scholarship of Teaching and Learning, 13*(3), 99–119.

Curby, T. W., Brown, C. A., Bassett, H. H., & Denham, S. A. (2016). Associations between preschoolers' social–emotional competence and preliteracy skills. *Infant and Child Development, 24*(5), 549–570.

Curran, F. C. (2016). Estimating the effect of state zero tolerance laws on exclusionary discipline, racial discipline gaps, and student behavior. *Educational Evaluation and Policy Analysis, 38*(4), 647–668.

Dadds, M. R., Sanders, M. R., Behrens, B. C., & James, J. E. (1987). Marital discord and child behavior problems: A description of family interactions during treatment. *Journal of Clinical Child Psychology, 16*(3), 192–203.

Da Paz, N. S., & Wallander, J. L. (2017). Interventions that target improvements in mental health for parents of children with autism spectrum disorders: A narrative review. *Clinical Psychology Review, 51*, 1–14.

Darling-Hammond, L. (2003). Keeping good teachers: Why it matters, what leaders can do. *Educational Leadership, 60*(8), 7–13.

Davis, E., Gilson, K. M., Christian, R., Waters, E., Mackinnon, A., Herrman, H., . . . & Marshall, B. (2015). Building the capacity of family day care educators to promote children's social and emotional wellbeing: Results of an exploratory cluster randomised-controlled trial. *Australasian Journal of Early Childhood, 40*(2), 57–67.

Davis, T. N., Dacus, S., Bankhead, J., Haupert, M., Fuentes, L., Zoch, T., . . . & Lang, R. (2014). A comparison of self-monitoring with and without reinforcement to improve on-task classroom behavior. *Journal of School Counseling, 12*(12), 1–23.

DeFeyter, J. J., & Winsler, A. (2009). The early developmental competencies and school readiness of low-income, immigrant children: Influences of generation, race/ethnicity, and national origins. *Early Childhood Research Quarterly, 24*(4), 411–431.

de Kruif, R. E., McWilliam, R. A., Ridley, S. M., & Wakely, M. B. (2000). Classification of teachers' interaction behaviors in early childhood classrooms. *Early Childhood Research Quarterly, 15*(2), 247–268.

Denham, S. A. (2006). Social-emotional competence as support for school readiness: What is it and how do we assess it? *Early Education and Development, 17*(1), 57–89.

Denham, S. A., Bassett, H. H., Brown, C., Way, E., & Steed, J. (2015). "I know how you feel": Preschoolers' emotion knowledge contributes to early school success. *Journal of Early Childhood Research, 13*(3), 252–262.

Denham, S. A., Bassett, H., Mincic, M., Kalb, S., Way, E., Wyatt, T., & Segal, Y. (2012). Social–emotional learning profiles of preschoolers' early school success: A person-centered approach. *Learning and Individual Differences, 22*(2), 178–189.

Denham, S. A., Bassett, H. H., & Zinsser, K. (2012). Early childhood teachers as socializers of young children's emotional competence. *Early Childhood Education Journal, 40*(3), 137–143.

Denham, S. A., Blair, K. A., DeMulder, E., Levitas, J., Sawyer, K., Auerbach–Major, S., & Queenan, P. (2003). Preschool emotional competence: Pathway to social competence? *Child Development, 74*(1), 238–256.

Denham, S. A., Wyatt, T. M., Bassett, H. H., Echeverria, D., & Knox, S. S. (2009). Assessing social-emotional development in children from a longitudinal perspective. *Journal of Epidemiology and Community Health, 63*(Suppl. 1), i37–i52.

Denham, S. A., Zoller, D., & Couchoud, E. A. (1994). Socialization of preschoolers' emotion understanding. *Developmental Psychology, 30*(6), 928–936.

Denmark, T., Atkinson, J., Campbell, R., & Swettenham, J. (2014). How do typically developing deaf children and deaf children with autism spectrum disorder use the face when comprehending emotional facial expressions in British sign language? *Journal of Autism and Developmental Disorders, 44*(10), 2584–2592.

Dennis, R. E., & Giangreco, M. F. (1996). Creating conversation: Reflections on cultural sensitivity in family interviewing. *Exceptional Children, 63*(1), 103–116.

Dennis, T. A., & Hajcak, G. (2009). The late positive potential: A neurophysiological marker for emotion regulation in children. *Journal of Child Psychology and Psychiatry, 50*(11), 1373–1383.

DeSimone, J. R. & Parmar, R. S. (2006). Middle school mathematics teachers' beliefs about inclusion of students with learning disabilities. *Learning Disabilities Research & Practice, 21*(2), 98–110.

Diamond, K. E., Justice, L. M., Siegler, R. S., & Snyder, P. A. (2013). *Synthesis of IES research on early intervention and early childhood education.* NCSER 2013–3001. National Center for Special Education Research.

Dingwall, R., Eekelaar, J., & Murray, T. (2014). *The protection of children: State intervention and family life* (Vol. 16). New Orleans, LA: Quid Pro Books.

Dishion, T. J., Shaw, D., Connell, A., Gardner, F., Weaver, C., & Wilson, M. (2008). The family check-up with high-risk indigent families: Preventing problem behavior by increasing parents' positive behavior support in early childhood. *Child Development, 79*(5), 1395–1414.

DiStefano, C., Greer, F. W., & Kamphaus, R. W. (2013). Multifactor modeling of emotional and behavioral risk of preschool-age children. *Psychological Assessment, 25*(2), 467–476.

Division for Early Childhood. (2014). *DEC Recommended Practices.* Retrieved from http://www.dec-sped.org/recommendedpractices

Dobbs, J. (2007). Teachers' ratings of preschool children's behavior: Inter-teacher agreement, correlation with observations, and the prediction of teacher behavior. *Dissertation Abstracts International: Section B: The Sciences and Engineering, 67*(11-B), 6734.

Dodge, D. T., Colker, L. J., Heroman, C., & Bickart, T. S. (2002). *The creative curriculum for preschool.* Washington, DC: Teaching Strategies.

Dooley, P., Wilczenski, F. L., & Torem, C. (2001). Using an activity schedule to smooth school transitions. *Journal of Positive Behavior Interventions, 3*(1), 57–61.

Doubet, S. L., & Ostrosky, M. M. (2015). The impact of challenging behavior on families: I don't know what to do. *Topics in Early Childhood Special Education, 34*(4), 223–233.

Dube, S. R., & Rishi, S. (2017). Utilizing the salutogenic paradigm to investigate well-being among adult survivors of childhood sexual abuse and other adversities. *Child Abuse & Neglect, 66*, 130–141.

Duch, H. (2005). Redefining parent involvement in Head Start: A two-generation approach. *Early Child Development and Care, 175*(1), 23–35.

Duncan, L. G., Coatsworth, J. D., & Greenberg, M. T. (2009). A model of mindful parenting:

Implications for parent–child relationships and prevention research. *Clinical Child and Family Psychology Review, 12*(3), 255–270.

Dunlap, G., & Fox, L. (2015). *The Pyramid Model: PBS in early childhood programs and its relation to school-wide PBS.* Tampa: Pyramid Model Consortium, University of South Florida and Florida Center for Inclusive Communities. Retrieved from http://challengingbehavior.fmhi.usf.edu/do/resources/documents/PBS%20and%20Pyramid%20Model.pdf

Dunlap, G., Strain, P. S., Fox, L., Carta, J. J., Conroy, M., Smith, B. J., . . . & Sailor, W. (2006). Prevention and intervention with young children's challenging behavior: Perspectives regarding current knowledge. *Behavioral Disorders, 32*(1), 29–45.

Dunn, J., Brown, J., & Beardsall, L. (1991). Family talk about feeling states and children's later understanding of others' emotions. *Developmental Psychology, 27*(3), 448.

Dunsmore, J. C., & Karn, M. A. (2001). Mothers' beliefs about feelings and children's emotional understanding. *Early Childhood and Development, 12*(1), 117–138.

Dunst, C. J. (2000). Revisiting "Rethinking Early Intervention." *Topics in Early Childhood Special Education, 20*(2), 95–104.

Dunst, C. J. (2007). Early intervention for infants and toddlers with developmental disabilities. In S. L. Odom, R. H. Horner, & M. E. Snell (Eds.), *Handbook of developmental disabilities* (pp. 161–180). New York, NY: Guilford Press.

Dunst, C. J., & Bruder, M. B. (2002). Valued outcomes of service coordination, early intervention, and natural environments. *Exceptional Children, 68*(3), 361–375.

Dunst, C. J., Bruder, M. B., & Espe-Sherwindt, M. (2014). Family capacity-building in early childhood intervention: Do context and setting matter? *School Community Journal, 24*(1), 37–48.

Dunst, C. J., Bruder, M. B., Trivette, C. M., & Hamby, D. W. (2006). Everyday activity settings, natural learning environments, and early intervention practices. *Journal of Policy and Practice in Intellectual Disabilities, 3*(1), 3–10.

Dunst, C. J., Bruder, M. B., Trivette, C. M., Hamby, D., Raab, M., & McLean, M. (2001). Characteristics and consequences of everyday natural learning opportunities. *Topics in Early Childhood Special Education, 21*(2), 68–92.

Dunst, C. J., Leet, H. E., & Trivette, C. M. (1988). Family resources, personal well-being, and early intervention. *The Journal of Special Education, 22*(1), 108–116.

Dunst, C. J., & Raab, M. (2010). Practitioners' self-evaluations of contrasting types of professional development. *Journal of Early Intervention, 32*(4), 239–254.

Dunst, C. J., & Trivette, C. M. (2009). Capacity-building family-systems intervention practices. *Journal of Family Social Work, 12*(2), 119–143.

Durand, V. M. (1990). *Severe behavior problems: A functional communication training approach.* New York, NY: Guilford Press.

Early Childhood Technical Assistance Center (ECTAC). (2015). State resources on service delivery approaches. Retrieved from http://ectacenter.org/topics/eiservices/stateresources.asp

Edwards, N. M. (2010). *The maternal role in promoting emotional competence: Predicting Head Start mothers' expressiveness, perceived role, and receptivity to support* (Unpublished doctoral dissertation). University of Maryland, College Park.

Edwards, N. M. (2012). Understanding emotional development: Helping early childhood providers better support families. *NHSA Dialog, 15*(4), 355–370.

Edwards, N. M. (2014a). Distinct factors associated with Head Start mothers' self-report of perceived low positive and high negative maternal expressiveness. *Early Education and Development, 25*(8), 1219–1247.

Edwards, N. M. (2014b). Number of children associated with mothers' perceived need for behavior support: Implications for parenting interventions. *Journal of Child and Family Studies, 23*(3), 527–536.

Edwards, N. M. (2014c). *Utility of a tailored positive behavior support workshop and follow-up data collection exercise for birth–five providers in an early childhood program.* Unpublished manuscript.

Edwards, N. M. (2017a, August). Family feedback and programmatic decision-making: Responsiveness of early childhood administrators. *Early Childhood Education Journal,* 1–11. doi:10.1007/s10643-017-0874-6

Edwards, N. M. (2017b). Teacher perceptions impeding child behavior assessment in an early childhood setting. *Preventing School Failure: Alternative Education for Children and Youth, 61*(3), 220–233.

Edwards, N. M. (2018). *Are we maximizing the role of caregivers' support networks in early intervention?* Manuscript submitted for publication.

Edwards, N. M., & Gallagher, P. A. (2016). Early intervention special instructors and service coordinators in one state: Characteristics, professional development, and needed lines of inquiry. *Infants & Young Children, 29*(4), 299–311.

Eisenberg, N., & Fabes, R. A. (1994). Mothers' reactions to children's negative emotions: Relations to children's temperament and anger behavior. *Merrill-Palmer Quarterly (1982–), 40*(1), 138–156.

Eisenberg, N., Fabes, R. A., Carlo, G., & Karbon, M. (1992). Emotional responsivity to others: Behavioral correlates and socialization antecedents. *New Directions for Child and Adolescent Development, 55*, 57–73.

Eisert, D., & Lamorey, S. (1996). Play as a window on child development: The relationship between play and other developmental domains. *Early Education and Development, 7*(3), 221–235.

Elliot, S. (1995). *The Responsive Classroom approach: Its effectiveness and acceptability.* Washington, DC: The Center for Systemic Educational Change, District of Columbia Public Schools.

Endendijk, J. J., Groeneveld, M. G., van der Pol, L. D., van Berkel, S. R., Hallers-Haalboom, E. T., Mesman, J., & Bakermans-Kranenburg, M. J. (2014). Boys don't play with dolls: Mothers' and fathers' gender talk during picture book reading. *Parenting, 14*(3–4), 141–161.

English, D., Thompson, R., White, C. R., & Wilson, D. (2015). Why should child welfare pay more attention to emotional maltreatment? *Children and Youth Services Review, 50*, 53–63.

Epstein, J. L. (2005). Links in a professional development chain: Preservice and inservice education for effective programs of school, family, and community partnerships. *The New Educator, 1*(2), 125–141.

Epstein, J. L., & Sanders, M. G. (2006). Prospects for change: Preparing educators for school, family, and community partnerships. *Peabody Journal of Education, 81*(2), 81–120.

Erickson, M. F., & Egeland, B. (2002). Child neglect. In J. E. B. Myers, L. Berliner, J. Briere, C. T. Hendrix, C. Jenny, & T. A. Reid (Eds.), *The APSAC handbook on child maltreatment* (2nd ed., pp. 3–20). Thousand Oaks, CA: Sage Publications.

Erwin, E. J., & Brown, F. (2003). From theory to practice: A contextual framework for understanding self-determination in early childhood environments. *Infants & Young Children, 16*(1), 77–87.

Espino, C. M., Sundstrom, S. M., Frick, H. L., Jacobs, M., & Peters, M. (2002). International business travel: Impact on families and travelers. *Occupational and Environmental Medicine, 59*(5), 309–322.

Espinosa, L. M. (1995). *Hispanic parent involvement in early childhood programs*. Urbana, IL: ERIC Clearinghouse on Elementary and Early Childhood Education, University of Illinois.

Evan, M. A. (1980). Comprehensive system of personnel development: The Oregon Experience. *Teacher Education and Special Education, 3*(1), 33–35.

Evans, G. W., & Marcynyszyn, L. A. (2004). Environmental justice, cumulative environmental risk, and health among low-and middle-income children in upstate New York. *American Journal of Public Health, 94*(11), 1942–1944.

Fabes, R. A., Eisenberg, N., Jones, S., Smith, M., Guthrie, I., Poulin, R., . . . & Friedman, J. (1999). Regulation, emotionality, and preschoolers' socially competent peer interactions. *Child Development, 70*(2), 432–442.

Fabiano, G. A., Vujnovic, R. K., Waschbusch, D. A., Yu, J., Mashtare, T., Pariseau, M. E., . . . & Smalls, K. J. (2013). A comparison of workshop training versus intensive, experiential training for improving behavior support skills in early educators. *Early Childhood Research Quarterly, 28*(2), 450–460.

Fallon, L. M., O'Keefe, B. V., & Sugai, G. (2012). Consideration of culture and context in school-wide positive behavior support: A review of current literature. *Journal of Positive Behavior Interventions, 4*(14), 209–219. doi:10.1177/1098300712442242

Farkas, M. S., Simonsen, B., Migdole, S., Donovan, M. E., Clemens, K., & Cicchese, V. (2012). Schoolwide positive behavior support in an alternative school setting: An evaluation of fidelity, outcomes, and social validity of tier 1 implementation. *Journal of Emotional and Behavioral Disorders, 20*(4), 275–288.

Ferlazzo, L. (2011). Involvement or engagement. *Educational Leadership, 68*(8), 10–14.

Fettig, A., Schultz, T. R., & Ostrosky, M. M. (2013). Collaborating with parents in using effective strategies to reduce children's challenging behaviors. *Young Exceptional Children, 1*(16), 30–41. doi:10.1177/1096250612473127

Fink, L. D. (2013). *Creating significant learning experiences: An integrated approach to designing college courses* (2nd ed.). Somerset, NJ: Jossey-Bass.

Fitzgerald, H., McKelvey, L., Schiffmen, R., & Montañez, M. (2006). Exposure of low income families and their children to neighborhood violence and paternal antisocial behavior. *Parenting, 6*(2), 243–258.

Fitzgerald, H. E., & Porges, S. W. (1971). A decade of infant conditioning and learning research. *Merrill-Palmer Quarterly of Behavior and Development, 17*(2), 79–117.

Fivush, R., Brotman, M. A., Buckner, J. P., & Goodman, S. H. (2000). Gender differences in parent–child emotion narratives. *Sex Roles, 42*(3–4), 233–253.

Flaherty, E. G., Stirling, J., & Committee on Child Abuse and Neglect. (2010). The pediatrician's role in child maltreatment prevention. *Pediatrics, 126*(4), 833–841. Retrieved from http://faceitabuse.org/wp-content/uploads/2013/06/Pediatrics-2010-the-pediatricians-role-in-child-maltreatment-prevention.pdf

Fletcher, S. (2012). *FBA: Prioritize concerns and describe behavior in observable terms* [Video file]. Retrieved from https://www.youtube.com/watch?v=SPjLZflC8r4

Folger, A. T., Putnam, K. T., Putnam, F. W., Peugh, J. L., Eismann, E. A., Sa, T., . . . & Ammerman, R. T. (2017). Maternal interpersonal trauma and child social-emotional development: An intergenerational effect. *Paediatric and Perinatal Epidemiology, 31*(2), 99–107.

Fox, L., Carta, J., Strain, P., Dunlap, G., & Hemmeter, M. L. (2009). *Response to intervention and the Pyramid Model*. Tampa: University of South Florida, Technical Assistance Center on Social Emotional Intervention for Young Children [PowerPoint presentation]. Retrieved from http://challengingbehavior.fmhi.usf.edu/do/resources/documents/rti_pyramid_web.pdf

Fox, L., Carta, J., Strain, P. S., Dunlap, G., & Hemmeter, M. L. (2010). Response to intervention and the Pyramid Model. *Infants & Young Children, 23*(1), 3–13.

Fox, L., Dunlap, G., Hemmeter, M. L., Joseph, G. E., & Strain, P. S. (2003). The teaching pyramid: A model for supporting social competence and preventing challenging behavior in young children. *Young Children, 58*(4), 48–52.

Fox, L., & Hemmeter, M. L. (2009). A program-wide model for supporting social emotional development and addressing challenging behavior in early childhood settings. In W. Sailor, G. Dunlap, G. Sugai, & R. Horner (Eds.), *Handbook of positive behavior support* (pp. 177–202). New York, NY: Springer.

Fox, L., Hemmeter, M. L., Snyder, P., Binder, D. P., & Clarke, S. (2011). Coaching early childhood special educators to implement a comprehensive model for promoting young children's social competence. *Topics in Early Childhood Special Education, 31*(3), 178–192.

Fox, L., & Lentini, R. H. (2006). *Teaching children a vocabulary for emotions: Beyond the journal.* Retrieved from https://www.naeyc.org/files/yc/file/200611/BTJFoxSupplementalActivities.pdf

Fox, L., & Little, N. (2001). Starting early: Developing school-wide positive behavior support in a community preschool. *Journal of Positive Behavior Interventions, 3*(4) 251–254.

Frank, K., & Esbensen, A. J. (2015). Fine motor and self-care milestones for individuals with Down syndrome using a retrospective chart review. *Journal of Intellectual Disability Research, 59*(8), 719–729.

Frey, A. J., Boyce, C. A., & Tarullo, L. B. (2009). Integrating positive behavior support in Head Start. In W. Sailor, G. Dunlap, G. Sugai, & H. F. Horner (Eds.), *Handbook of positive behavior support: Special issues in clinical child psychology* (pp. 125–148). New York, NY: Springer.

Friedman, I. A., & Farber, B. A. (1992). Professional self-concept as a predictor of teacher burnout. *The Journal of Educational Research, 86*(1), 28–35.

Friedman, M., Woods, J., & Salisbury, C. (2012). Caregiver coaching strategies for early intervention providers: Moving toward operational definitions. *Infants & Young Children, 25*(1), 62–82.

Frye, B. A., & Kagawa-Singer, M. (1994). Cross-cultural views of disability. *Rehabilitation Nursing, 19*(6), 362–365.

Fullerton, E. K., Conroy, M. A., & Correa, V. I. (2009). Early childhood teachers' use of specific praise statements with young children at risk for behavioral disorders. *Behavioral Disorders, 34*(3), 118–135.

Gable, R. A., Park, K. L., & Scott, T. M. (2014). Functional behavioral assessment and students at risk for or with emotional disabilities: Current issues and considerations. *Education and Treatment of Children, 37*(1), 111–135.

Garcia, M. (2014). *Assessment practices past and future: Alternative approaches and teacher perceptions.* Retrieved from http://digitalcommons.bryant.edu/honors_appliedpsychology/5/

Garcia, S. B., & Guerra, P. L. (2004). Deconstructing deficit thinking: Working with educators to create more equitable learning environments. *Education and Urban Society, 36*(2), 150–168.

Gardner, F., Shaw, D. S., Dishion, T. J., Burton, J., & Supplee, L. (2007). Randomized prevention trial for early conduct problems: Effects on —proactive parenting and links to toddler disruptive behavior. *Journal of Family Psychology, 21*(3), 398.

Garner, A. S., Shonkoff, J. P., Siegel, B. S., Dobbins, M. I., Earls, M. F., McGuinn, L., . . . & Wood, D. L. (2012). Early childhood adversity, toxic stress, and the role of the pediatrician: Translating developmental science into lifelong health. *Pediatrics, 129*(1), e224–e231.

Garner, P. W. (2006). Prediction of prosocial and emotional competence from maternal behavior in African American preschoolers. *Cultural Diversity and Ethnic Minority Psychology, 12*(2), 179–198.

Garner, P. W. (2010). Emotional competence and its influences on teaching and learning. *Educational Psychology Review, 22*(3), 297–321.

Garner, P. W., Dunsmore, J. C., & Southam-Gerrow, M. (2008). Mother–child conversations about emotions: Linkages to child aggression and prosocial behavior. *Social Development, 17*(2), 259–277.

Garner, P. W., Jones, D. C., Gaddy, G., & Rennie, K. M. (1997). Low income mothers' conversations about emotions and their children's emotional competence. *Social Development, 6*(1), 37–52.

Gerber, R. J., Wilks, T., & Erdie-Lalena, C. (2010). Developmental milestones: Motor development. *Pediatrics in Review, 31*(7), 267–277.

Gergely, G., & Watson, J. S. (1999). Early socio-emotional development: Contingency perception and the social-biofeedback model. *Early social cognition: Understanding others in the first months of life, 60*, 101–136.

Gershoff, E. T., & Font, S. A. (2016). Corporal punishment in U.S. public schools: Prevalence, disparities in use, and status in state and federal policy. *Social Policy Report, 30*(1). Retrieved from https://srcd.org/sites/default/files/documents/spr_30_1.pdf

Gershoff, E. T., Purtell, K. M., & Holas, I. (2015). Corporal punishment in U.S. public schools: Legal precedents, current practices, and future policy. *Springer Briefs in Psychology Series, Advances in Child and Family Policy and Practice Subseries, 1*, 1–105. doi:10.1007/978-3-319-14818-2

Gerstenblatt, P., Faulkner, M., Lee, A., Doan, L. T., & Travis, D. (2014). Not babysitting: Work stress and well-being for family child care providers. *Early Childhood Education Journal, 42*(1), 67–75.

Ghazvini, A. S., & Readdick, C. A. (1994). Parent-caregiver communication and quality of care in diverse child care settings. *Early Childhood Research Quarterly, 9*(2), 207–222.

Gilliam, W. S. (2005). *Prekindergarteners left behind: Expulsion rates in state prekindergarten systems.* New York, NY: Foundation for Child Development.

Gilliom, M., Shaw, D. S., Beck, J. E., Schonberg, M. A., & Lukon, J. L. (2002). Anger regulation in disadvantaged preschool boys: Strategies, antecedents, and the development of self-control. *Developmental Psychology, 38*(2), 222–235.

Goelman, H., & Guo, H. (1998). What we know and what we don't know about burnout among early childhood care providers. *Child and Youth Care Forum, 27*(3), 175–199.

Goldsmith, H. H., & Davidson, R. J. (2004). Disambiguating the components of emotion regulation. *Child Development, 75*(2), 361–365.

Gomez Paloma, F., D'Anna, C., & Agrillo, F. (2013). Social-educational evolution of crawling. *Journal of Human Sport and Exercise, 8*(Proc2), 1–12. Retrieved from http://rua.ua.es/dspace/bitstream/10045/27655/1/jhse_Vol_8_N_proc2_180-191.pdf

Goodall, J. (2015). *Leading Parent Partnership Award Recertification–Results.* University of Bath. Retrieved from http://opus.bath.ac.uk/42416/

Goodman, J. H., Guarino, A., Chenausky, K., Klein, L., Prager, J., Petersen, R., . . . & Freeman, M. (2014). CALM pregnancy: Results of a pilot study of mindfulness-based cognitive therapy for perinatal anxiety. *Archives of Women's Mental Health, 17*(5), 373–387.

Goodman, K., & Hooks, L. (2016). Encouraging family involvement through culturally relevant pedagogy. *SRATE Journal, 25*(2), 33–41.

Gottman, J. M., Katz, L. F., & Hooven, C. (1996). Parental meta-emotion philosophy and the emotional life of families: Theoretical models and preliminary data. *Journal of Family Psychology, 10*(3), 243–268.

Gray, C. (2018). *Carol Gray: Social Stories.* Retrieved from https://carolgraysocialstories.com.

Gray, D. E. (2002) "Everybody just freezes. Everybody is just embarrassed": Felt and enacted stigma among parents of children with high functioning autism. *Sociology of Health & Illness, 24*(6), 734–749.

Gray, D. E. (2009). Ten years on: A longitudinal study of families of children with autism. *Journal of Intellectual and Developmental Disability, 27*(3), 215–222.

Graziano, P. A., Reavis, R. D., Keane, S. P., & Calkins, S. D. (2007). The role of emotion regulation in children's early academic success. *Journal of School Psychology, 45*(1), 3–19.

Green, S. (2003). Reaching out to fathers: An examination of staff efforts that lead to greater father involvement in early childhood programs. *Early Childhood Research and Practice: An Internet Journal on the Development, Care, and Education of Young Children, 5*(2), 225–241.

Greenwood, G. E., & Hickman, C. W. (1991). Research and practice in parent involvement: Implications for teacher education. *The Elementary School Journal, 91*(3), 279–288.

Hadjikhani, N., Zürcher, N. R., Rogier, O., Ruest, T., Hippolyte, L., Ben-Ari, Y., & Lemonnier, E. (2015). Improving emotional face perception in autism with diuretic bumetanide: A proof-of-concept behavioral and functional brain imaging pilot study. *Autism, 19*(2), 149–157.

Halberstadt, A. G., Cassidy, J., Stifter, C. A., Parke, R. D., & Fox, N. A. (1995). Self-expressiveness within the family context: Psychometric support for a new measure. *Psychological Assessment, 7*(1), 93–103.

Halberstadt, A. G., Denham, S. A., & Dunsmore, J. C. (2001). Affective social competence. *Social Development, 10*(1), 79–119.

Halgunseth, L. (2009). Family engagement, diverse families, and early childhood education programs: An integrated review of the literature. *Young Children, 64*(5), 56–58.

Hallett, G., Strain, P. S., Smith, B. J., Barton, E. E., Steed, E. A., & Kranski, T. A. (2016). The Pyramid Plus Center: Scaling up and sustaining evidence-based practices for young children with challenging behavior. *Young Exceptional Children,* 1096250616674333.

Hanft, B. E., & Pilkington, K. O. (2000). Therapy in natural environments: The means or end goal for early intervention? *Infants & Young Children, 12*(4), 1–13.

Hanley, G. P., & Tiger, J. H. (2011). Differential reinforcement procedures. In W. W. Fisher, C. C. Piazza, & H. S. Roane (Eds.), *Handbook of applied behavior analysis* (pp. 229–249). New York, NY: Guilford Press.

Hanson, M. J., Lynch, E. W., & Poulsen, M. K. (2013). *Understanding families: Supportive approaches to diversity, disability, and risk.* Baltimore, MD: Paul H. Brookes Publishing Co.

Harden, R. M. (1999). What is a spiral curriculum? *Medical Teacher, 21*(2), 141–143.

Harden, B. J. (2004). Safety and stability for foster children: A developmental perspective. *The Future of Children, 14*(1), 30–47.

Harman, J. S., Childs, G. E., & Kelleher, K. J. (2000). Mental health care utilization and expenditures by children in foster care. *Archives of Pediatrics & Adolescent Medicine, 154*(11), 1114–1117.

Harms, T., Clifford, R. M., & Cryer, D. (2014). *Early childhood environment rating scale.* New York, NY: Teachers College Press.

Harris, N. B., Marques, S. S., Oh, D., Bucci, M., & Cloutier, M. (2017). Prevent, screen, heal: Collective action to fight the toxic effects of early life adversity. *Academic Pediatrics, 17*(7), S14–S15.

Harris, P. L. (1994). The child's understanding of emotion: Developmental change and the family environment. *Journal of Child Psychology and Psychiatry, 35*(1), 3–28.

Harris, P. (2000). Understanding emotions. In M. Lewis & J. Haviland-Jones (Eds.), *Handbook of emotions* (2nd ed., pp. 281–292). New York, NY: Guilford Press.

Harry, B. (2008). Collaboration with culturally and linguistically diverse families: Ideal versus reality. *Exceptional Children, 74*(3), 372–388.

Hart, B. M., Reynolds, N. J., Baer, D. M., Brawley, E. R., & Harris, F. R. (1968). Effect of contingent and non-contingent social reinforcement on the cooperative play of a preschool child. *Journal of Applied Behavior Analysis, 1*(1), 73–76.

Hastings, P. D., Nuselovici, J. N., Utendale, W. T., Coutya, J., McShane, K. E., & Sullivan, C. (2008). Applying the polyvagal theory to children's emotion regulation: Social context, socialization, and adjustment. *Biological Psychology, 79*(3), 299–306.

Hayes, G. R., Hirano, S., Marcu, G., Monibi, M., Nguyen, D. H., & Yeganyan, M. (2010). Interactive visual supports for children with autism. *Personal and Ubiquitous Computing, 14*(7), 663–680.

Head Start. (2017). Early Childhood Learning and Knowledge Center. *Early Head Start programs.* Retrieved from https://eclkc.ohs.acf.hhs.gov/hslc/tta-system/ehsnrc/about-ehs

Hemmeter, M. L., Fox, L., Jack, S., & Broyles, L. (2007). A program-wide model of positive behavior support in early childhood settings. *Journal of Early Intervention, 29*(4), 337–355.

Hemmeter, M. L., Fox, L., & Snyder, P. (2013). *Teaching Pyramid Observation Tool (TPOT™) for preschool classrooms set, research edition.* Baltimore, MD: Paul H. Brookes Publishing Co.

Hemmeter, M. L., Ostrosky, M., & Fox, L. (2006). Social and emotional foundations for early learning: A conceptual model for intervention. *School Psychology Review, 35*(4), 583–601.

Hemmeter, M. L., Santos, R. M., & Ostrosky, M. M. (2008). Preparing early childhood educators to address young children's social-emotional development and challenging behavior: A survey of higher education programs in nine states. *Journal of Early Intervention, 30*(4), 321–340.

Herndon, K. J., Bailey, C. S., Shewark, E. A., Denham, S. A., & Bassett, H. H. (2013). Preschoolers' emotion expression and regulation: Relations with school adjustment. *The Journal of Genetic Psychology, 174*(6), 642–663.

Herzenberg, S., Price, M., & Bradley, D. (2005). *Losing ground in early childhood education: Declining workforce qualifications in an expanding industry, 1979–2004: Summary*. Washington, DC: Economic Policy Institute.

Hildyard, K. L., & Wolfe, D. A. (2002). Child neglect: Developmental issues and outcomes. *Child Abuse & Neglect, 26*(6), 679–695.

Hodge, N., & Runswick-Cole, K. (2008). Problematising parent–professional partnerships in education. *Disability & Society, 23*(6), 637–647.

Hoeksma, J. B., Oosterlaan, J., & Schipper, E. M. (2004). Emotion regulation and the dynamics of feelings: A conceptual and methodological framework. *Child Development, 75*(2), 354–360.

Hoff, E. (2006). Language experience and language milestones during early childhood. In K. McCartney & D. Phillips (Eds.). *Handbook of early childhood development* (pp. 233–251). Malden, MA: Blackwell Publishing Ltd. doi:10.1002/9780470757703.ch12

Honaker, S. M., & Meltzer, L. J. (2014). Bedtime problems and night wakings in young children: An update of the evidence. *Paediatric Respiratory Reviews, 15*(4), 333–339.

Hooven, C., Gottman, J. M., & Katz, L. F. (1995). Parental meta-emotion structure predicts family and child outcomes. *Cognition & Emotion, 9*(2–3), 229–264.

Hoover-Dempsey, K. V., Walker, J. M., Jones, K. P., & Reed, R. P. (2002). Teachers involving parents (TIP): Results of an in-service teacher education program for enhancing parental involvement. *Teaching and Teacher Education, 18*(7), 843–867.

Horner, R. H. (2000). Positive behavior supports. *Focus on Autism and Other Developmental Disabilities, 15*(2), 97–105.

Horner, R. H., Carr, E. G., Halle, J., McGee, G., Odom, S., & Wolery, M. (2005). The use of single-subject research to identify evidence-based practice in special education. *Exceptional Children, 71*(2), 165–179.

Horner, R. H., & Sugai, G. (2015). School-wide PBIS: An example of applied behavior analysis implemented at a scale of social importance. *Behavior Analysis in Practice, 8*(1), 80–85.

Houten, R. V., & Nau, P. A. (1980). A comparison of the effects of fixed and variable ratio schedules of reinforcement on the behavior of deaf children. *Journal of Applied Behavior Analysis, 13*(1), 13–21.

Howlin, P. (1988). Living with impairment: The effects on children of having an autistic sibling. *Child: Care, Health and Development, 14*(6), 395–408.

Hutchinson, L. M., Hastings, R. P., Hunt, P. H., Bowler, C. L., Banks, M. E., & Totsika, V. (2014). Who's challenging who? Changing attitudes towards those whose behavior challenges. *Journal of Intellectual Disability Research, 58*(2), 99–109.

Hyson, M. (2004). *The emotional development of young children: Building an emotion-centered curriculum*. New York, NY: Teachers College Press.

Hyson, M. C., & Lee, K. M. (1996). Assessing early childhood teachers' beliefs about emotions: Content, contexts, and implications for practice. *Early Education and Development, 7*(1), 59–78.

Hyun, J. K., & Fowler, S. A. (1995). Respect, cultural sensitivity, and communication: Promoting participation by Asian families in the individualized family service plan. *Teaching Exceptional Children, 28*(1), 25–28.

Ingersoll, B., & Dvortcsak, A. (2006). Including parent training in the early childhood special education curriculum for children with autism spectrum disorders. *Journal of Positive Behavior Interventions, 8*(2), 79–87.

Ingram, D., Louis, K. S., & Schroeder, R. G. (2004). Accountability policies and teacher decision making: Barriers to the use of data to improve practice. *Teachers College Record, 106*(6), 1258–1287.

Ingstad, B. (1990). The disabled person in the community: Social and cultural aspects. *International Journal of Rehabilitation Research, 13*(3), 187–194.

Iversen, M. D., Shimmel, J. P., Ciacera, S. L., & Prabhakar, M. (2003). Creating a family-centered approach to early intervention services: Perceptions of parents and professionals. *Pediatric Physical Therapy, 15*(1), 23–31.

Iwaniec, D., Larkin, E., & Higgins, S. (2006). Research review: Risk and resilience in cases of emotional abuse. *Child & Family Social Work, 11*(1), 73–82.

Izard, C. E. (2013). *Human emotions*. New York, NY: Springer Science & Business Media.

Izard, C., Trentacosta, C., King, K., & Mostow, A. (2004). An emotion-based prevention program for Head Start children. *Early Education & Development, 15*(4), 407–422.

Jacobson, J. W. (2000). Early intensive behavioral intervention: Emergence of a consumer-driven service model. *The Behavior Analyst, 23*(2), 149–171.

Jantz, R. K., & Seefeldt, C. (1999). Early childhood social studies. In C. Seefeldt (Ed.), *The early childhood curriculum: Current findings in theory and practice* (3rd ed.) (pp. 159–179). New York, NY: Teachers College Press.

Jennings, P. A. (2015). Early childhood teachers' well-being, mindfulness, and self-compassion in relation to classroom quality and attitudes towards challenging students. *Mindfulness, 6*(4), 732–743.

Jennings, P. A., & Greenberg, M. T. (2009). The prosocial classroom: Teacher social and emotional competence in relation to student and classroom outcomes. *Review of Educational Research, 79*(1), 491–525.

Johnson, S. B., Riley, A. W., Granger, D. A., & Riis, J. (2013). The science of early life toxic stress for pediatric practice and advocacy. *Pediatrics, 131*(2), 319–327.

Jolivette, K., Stichter, J. P., Sibilsky, S., Scott, T. M., & Ridgley, R. (2002). Naturally occurring opportunities for preschool children with or without disabilities to make choices. *Education and Treatment of Children, 25*(4), 396–414.

Jones, D. E., Greenberg, M., & Crowley, M. (2015). Early social-emotional functioning and public health: The relationship between kindergarten social competence and future wellness. *American Journal of Public Health, 105*(11), 2283–2290.

Jussim, L. (1986). Self-fulfilling prophecies: A theoretical and integrative review. *Psychological Review, 93*(4), 429–445.

Juul, S. H., Hendrix, C., Robinson, B., Stowe, Z. N., Newport, D. J., Brennan, P. A., & Johnson, K. C. (2016). Maternal early-life trauma and affective parenting style: The mediating role of HPA-axis function. *Archives of Women's Mental Health, 19*(1), 17–23.

Kabat-Zinn, J., de Torrijos, F., Skillings, A. H., Blacker, M., Mumford, G. T., Alvares, D. L., . . . & Rosal, M. C. (2016). Delivery and effectiveness of a dual language (English/Spanish) mindfulness-based stress reduction (MBSR) program in the inner city: A seven-year experience: 1992–1999. *Mindfulness & Compassion, 1*(1), 2–13.

Kalyanpur, M., & Harry, B. (2012). *Cultural reciprocity in special education.* Baltimore, MD: Paul H. Brookes Publishing Co.

Kane, E. W. (2006). "No way my boys are going to be like that!" Parents' responses to children's gender nonconformity. *Gender & Society, 20*(2), 149–176.

Karkhaneh, M., Clark, B., Ospina, M. B., Seida, J. C., Smith, V., & Hartling, L. (2010). Social Stories™ to improve social skills in children with autism spectrum disorder: A systematic review. *Autism, 14*(6), 641–642. doi:10.1177/1362361310373057

Kaufman, J., & Zigler, E. (1989). The intergenerational transmission of child abuse. In D. Cicchetti & V. Carlson (Eds.), *Child maltreatment: Theory and research on the causes and consequences of child abuse and neglect.* Cambridge, MA: Cambridge University Press.

Kautz, T., Heckman, J. J., Diris, R., Ter Weel, B., & Borghans, L. (2014). *Fostering and measuring skills: Improving cognitive and non-cognitive skills to promote lifetime success* (No. w20749). National Bureau of Economic Research.

Kelm, J. L., & McIntosh, K. (2012). Effects of school-wide positive behavior support on teacher self-efficacy. *Psychology in the Schools, 49*(2), 137–147.

Kendall-Tackett, K. A., Williams, L. M., & Finkelhor, D. (1993). Impact of sexual abuse on children: A review and synthesis of recent empirical studies. *Psychological Bulletin, 113*(1), 164.

Keogh, B. K. (2003). *Temperament in the classroom: Understanding individual differences.* Baltimore, MD: Paul H. Brookes Publishing Co.

Kershaw, T., Murphy, A., Lewis, J., Divney, A., Albritton, T., Magriples, U., & Gordon, D. (2014). Family and relationship influences on parenting behaviors of young parents. *Journal of Adolescent Health, 54*(2), 197–203.

Killu, K. (2008). Developing effective behavior intervention plans: Suggestions for school personnel. *Intervention in School and Clinic, 43*(3), 140–149.

Kim, E., & Hong, S. (2007). First-generation Korean-American parents' perceptions of discipline. *Journal of Professional Nursing, 23*(1), 60–68.

Kim, H. K. (2011). Developmentally appropriate practice (DAP) as defined and interpreted by early childhood preservice teachers: Beliefs about DAP and influences of teacher education and field experience. *SRATE Journal, 20*(2), 12–22.

Kim, W. J. (2015, January). *Variation in child care policy across states and impact on the choice of child care.* In Society for Social Work and Research 19th Annual Conference: The Social and Behavioral Importance of Increased Longevity. Society for Social Work and Research.

Kimonis, E. R., Frick, P. J., Boris, N. W., Smyke, A. T., Cornell, A. H., Farrell, J. M., & Zeanah, C. H. (2006). Callous-unemotional features, behavioral inhibition, and parenting: independent predictors of aggression in a high-risk preschool sample. *Journal of Child and Family Studies, 15*(6), 741–752.

Kincaid, D., Knab, J. T., & Clark, H. B. (2005). Person-centered planning. *Encyclopedia of behavior modification and cognitive behavior therapy* (Vol. 1), 429.

Klinnert, M. D., Campos, J., Sorce, J., Emde, R. N., & Svejda, M. J. (1983). Social referencing: Emotional expressions as behavior regulators. In R. Plutchik & H. Kellerman (Eds.), *Emotion: Theory, research and experience: Vol. 2. Emotions in early development* (pp. 57–86). Orlando, FL: Academic Press.

Knight, V., Sartini, E., & Spriggs, A. D. (2015). Evaluating visual activity schedules as evidence-based practice for individuals with autism spectrum disorders. *Journal of Autism and Developmental Disorders, 45*(1), 157–178.

Knopf, H. T., & Swick, K. J. (2007). How parents feel about their child's teacher/school: Implications for early childhood professionals. *Early Childhood Education Journal, 34*(4), 291–296.

Knowles, M. S. (1984) Adult learning: Theory and practice. In L. Nadler (Ed.), *The handbook of human resource development* (pp. 6.1–6.23). New York, NY: Wiley-Interscience.

Knowles, M., Holton, E., & Swanson, R. (1998). *The adult learner: The definitive classic in adult learning and human resource development* (5th ed.). Woburn, MA: Butterworth-Heinneman.

Knowles, M. S., Holton III, E. F., & Swanson, R. A. (2014). *The adult learner: The definitive classic in adult education and human resource development.* New York, NY: Routledge.

Kochanska, G., Philibert, R. A., & Barry, R. A. (2009). Interplay of genes and early mother–child relationship in the development of self-regulation from toddler to preschool age. *Journal of Child Psychology and Psychiatry, 50*(11), 1331–1338.

Koplow, L. (Ed.). (1996). *Unsmiling faces: How preschools can heal.* New York, NY: Teachers College Press.

Kosko, K. W., & Wilkins, J. L. (2009). General educators' in-service training and their self-perceived ability to adapt instruction for students with IEPs. *The Professional Educator, 33*(2), 1–10.

Kremenitzer, J. P. (2005). The emotionally intelligent early childhood educator: Self-reflective journaling. *Early Childhood Education Journal, 33*(1), 3–9.

Kucirkova, N., Messer, D., & Sheehy, K. (2014). Reading personalized books with preschool children enhances their word acquisition. *First Language, 34*(3), 227–243.

Kuhn, M., & Marvin, C. (2015). "Dosage" decisions for early intervention services. *Young Exceptional Children.* Advance online publication. doi:1096250615576807

Kumst, S., & Scarf, D. (2015). Your wish is my command! The influence of symbolic modelling on preschool children's delay of gratification. *PeerJ, 3,* e774. Retrieved from https://peerj.com/articles/774/

LaForett, D. R., & Mendez, J. L. (2010). Parent involvement, parental depression, and program satisfaction among low-income parents participating in a two-generation early childhood education program. *Early Education and Development, 21*(4), 517–535.

Lagattuta, K. H., & Wellman, H. M. (2002). Differences in early parent-child conversations about negative versus positive emotions: Implications for the development of psychological understanding. *Developmental Psychology, 38*(4), 564–580.

Lamb-Parker, F., LeBuffe, P., Powell, G., & Halpern, E. (2008). A strength-based, systemic mental health approach to support children's social and emotional development. *Infants and Young Children, 21*(1), 45–55.

Landry, S. H., Anthony, J. L., Swank, P. R., & Monseque-Bailey, P. (2009). Effectiveness of comprehensive professional development for teachers of at-risk preschoolers. *Journal of Educational Psychology, 101*(2), 448–465.

Lane, J. D., Gast, D. L., Shepley, C., & Ledford, J. R. (2015). Including social opportunities during small group instruction of preschool children with social-communication delays. *Journal of Early Intervention, 37*(1), 3–22.

Lane, K. L., Stanton-Chapman, T., Jamison, K. R., & Phillips, A. (2007). Teacher and parent expectations of preschoolers' behavior: Social skills necessary for success. *Topics in Early Childhood Special Education, 27*(2), 86–97.

Lanigan, J. D. (2011). Family child care providers' perspectives regarding effective professional development and their role in the child care system: A qualitative study. *Early Childhood Education Journal, 38*(6), 399–409.

Lansford, J. E., Woodlief, D., Malone, P. S., Oburu, P., Pastorelli, C., Skinner, A. T., ... & Al-Hassan, S. M. (2014). A longitudinal examination of mothers' and fathers' social information processing biases and harsh discipline in nine countries. *Development and Psychopathology, 26*(3), 561–573.

LaRocque, M. (2013). Addressing cultural and linguistic dissonance between parents and schools. *Preventing School Failure: Alternative Education for Children and Youth, 57*(2), 111–117.

Laursen, E. K. (2000). Strength-based practice with children in trouble. *Reclaiming Children and Youth, 9*(2), 70–75.

Leaf, J. B., Oppenheim-Leaf, M. L., Leaf, R. B., Taubman, M., McEachin, J., Parker, T., ... & Mountjoy, T. (2015). What is the proof? A methodological review of studies that have utilized social stories. *Education and Training in Autism and Developmental Disabilities, 50*(2), 127–141.

LeCuyer, E. A., Christensen, J. J., Kearney, M. H., & Kitzman, H. J. (2011). African American mothers' self-described discipline strategies with young children. *Issues in Comprehensive Pediatric Nursing, 34*(3), 144–162.

Lequia, J., Machalicek, W., & Rispoli, M. J. (2012). Effects of activity schedules on challenging behavior exhibited in children with autism spectrum disorders: A systematic review. *Research in Autism Spectrum Disorders, 6*(1), 480–492.

Lerner, C. (2015). *Meet Charlie—A young child expelled in preschool* [Video file]. Retrieved from https://www.youtube.com/watch?v=38AGD4c4l9Y or https://youtu.be/38AGD4c4l9Y

Levac, A. M., McCay, E., Merka, P., & Reddon-D'Arcy, M. L. (2008). Exploring parent participation in a parent training program for children's aggression: Understanding and illuminating mechanisms of change. *Journal of Child and Adolescent Psychiatric Nursing, 21*(2), 78–88.

Lewis, M., & Feiring, C. (1981). Direct and indirect interactions in social relationships. In L. P. Lipsett (Ed.), *Advances in infancy research* (I, pp. 129–161). Norwood, NJ: Ablex.

Lewis, M., & Michalson, L. (1983). *Children's emotions and moods: Developmental theory and measurement.* New York, NY: Plenum.

Lewis, M., & Sullivan, M. W. (2014). *Emotional development in atypical children.* New York, NY: Psychology Press.

Lewis, M., Sullivan, M. W., Stanger, C., & Weiss, M. (1989). Self-development and self-conscious emotions. *Child Development,* 146–156.

Liem, A. D., Lau, S., & Nie, Y. (2008). The role of self-efficacy, task value, and achievement goals in predicting learning strategies, task disengagement, peer relationship, and achievement outcome. *Contemporary Educational Psychology, 33*(4), 486–512.

Lifter, K., Mason, E. J., & Barton, E. E. (2011). Children's play: Where we have been and where we could go. *Journal of Early Intervention, 33*(4), 281–297. doi:10.1177/1053815111429465

Lightfoot, D. (2004). "Some parents just don't care": Decoding the meanings of parental involvement in urban schools. *Urban Education, 39*(1), 91–107.

Liso, D. R. (2010). The effects of choice making on toy engagement in nonambulatory and partially ambulatory preschool students. *Topics in Early Childhood Special Education, 30*(2), 91–101.

Lochman, J. E., & Lenhart, L. A. (1993). Anger coping intervention for aggressive children: Conceptual models and outcome effects. *Clinical Psychology Review, 13*(8), 785–805.

Lowell, D. I., Carter, A. S., Godoy, L., Paulicin, B., & Briggs-Gowan, M. J. (2011). A randomized controlled trial of Child FIRST: A comprehensive home-based intervention translating research into early childhood practice. *Child Development, 82*(1), 193–208.

Lucyshyn, J. M., Dunlap, G., & Albin, R. W. (2002). *Families and positive behavior support: Addressing problem behavior in family contexts.* Baltimore, MD: Paul H. Brookes Publishing Co.

Macdonald, H., Rutter, M., Howlin, P., Rios, P., Conteur, A. L., Evered, C., & Folstein, S. (1989). Recognition and expression of emotional cues by autistic and normal adults. *Journal of Child Psychology and Psychiatry, 30*(6), 865–877.

Macks, R. J., & Reeve, R. E. (2007). The adjustment of non-disabled siblings of children with autism. *Journal of Autism and Developmental Disorders, 37*(6), 1060–1067.

Mahoney, G., Kaiser, A., Girolametto, L., MacDonald, J., Robinson, C., Safford, P., & Spiker, D. (1999). Parent education in early intervention: A call for a renewed focus. *Topics in Early Childhood Special Education, 19*(3), 131–140.

Main, M., & Goldwyn, R. (1984). Predicting rejection of her infant from mother's representation of her own experience: Implications for the abused-abusing intergenerational cycle. *Child Abuse & Neglect, 8*(2), 203–217.

Maine Department of Education (2007). *Guidance document: Early intervention process for infants, toddlers, and their families. Eligibility determination, IFSP development, intervention planning.* Retrieved from http://ectacenter.org/~pdfs/topics/families/me_guide_1_17_07final.pdf

Malak, M. S., Sharma, U., & Deppeler, J. M. (2015). "Can I really teach without my magic cane?" Teachers' responses to the banning of corporal punishment. *International Journal of Inclusive Education, 19*(12), 1325–1341.

Marcenko, M. O., Kemp, S. P., & Larson, N. C. (2000). Childhood experiences of abuse, later substance use, and parenting outcomes among low-income mothers. *American Journal of Orthopsychiatry, 70*(3), 316–326.

Markus, H. (1977). Self-schemata and processing information about the self. *Journal of Personality and Social Psychology, 35*(2), 63–78.

Marlow, L., & Inman, D. (2002). *Pro-social literacy: Are educators being prepared to teach social and emotional competence?* Paper presented at the Annual Meeting of the National Council of Teachers of English, Atlanta, GA.

Marshall, M. (2005). Discipline without stress, punishments, or rewards. *The Clearing House: A Journal of Educational Strategies, Issues and Ideas, 79*(1), 51–54.

Martorell, G. A., & Bugental, D. B. (2006). Maternal variations in stress reactivity: Implications for harsh parenting practices with very young children. *Journal of Family Psychology, 20*(4), 641–647.

Masko, A. L., & Bosiwah, L. (2016). Cultural congruence and unbalanced power between home and school in rural Ghana and the impact on school children. *Comparative Education, 52*(4), 538–555.

Maslow, A. H. (1954). *Hierarchy of needs.* New York, NY: Harper & Row.

McClure, E. B. (2000) A meta-analytic review of sex differences in facial expression processing and their development in infants, children, and adolescents. *Psychological Bulletin, 126*(3), 424–453.

McCormick, K. M., Jolivette, K., & Ridgley, R. (2003). Choice making as an intervention strategy for young children. *Young Exceptional Children, 6*(2), 3–10.

McIntosh, K., Flannery, K. B., Sugai, G., Braun, D., & Cochrane, K. (2008). Relationships between academics and problem behavior in the transition from middle school to high school. *Journal of Positive Behavior Interventions, 10*(4), 243–255.

McLeod, B. D., Sutherland, K. S., Martinez, R. G., Conroy, M. A., Snyder, P. A., & Southam-Gerrow, M. A. (2017). Identifying common practice elements to improve social, emotional, and behavioral outcomes of young children in early childhood classrooms. *Prevention Science, 18*(2), 204–213.

McWayne, C., Fantuzzo, J., Cohen, H. L., & Sekino, Y. (2004). A multivariate examination of parent involvement and the social and academic competencies of urban kindergarten children. *Psychology in the Schools, 41*(3), 363–377.

McWilliam, R. A. (1996). *Rethinking pull-out services in early intervention: A professional resource.* Baltimore, MD: Paul H. Brookes Publishing Co.

McWilliam, R. A., & Scott, S. (2001). A support approach to early intervention: A three-part framework. *Infants & Young Children, 13*(4), 55–62.

Melville, J. D., Kellogg, N. D., Perez, N., & Lukefahr, J. L. (2014). Assessment for self-blame and trauma symptoms during the medical evaluation of suspected sexual abuse. *Child Abuse & Neglect, 38*(5), 851–857.

Merritt, E. G., Wanless, S. B., Rimm-Kaufman, S. E., Cameron, C., & Peugh, J. L. (2012). The contribution of teachers' emotional support to children's social behaviors and self-regulatory skills in first grade. *School Psychology Review, 41*(2), 141–159.

Miller, J. J., Fletcher, K., & Kabat-Zinn, J. (1995). Three-year follow-up and clinical implications of a mindfulness meditation-based stress reduction intervention in the treatment of anxiety disorders. *General Hospital Psychiatry, 17*(3), 192–200.

Miller, S. P. (1994). Peer coaching within an early childhood interdisciplinary setting. *Intervention in School and Clinic, 30*(2), 109–115.

Milunsky, A., Jick, H., Jick, S. S., Bruell, C. L., MacLaughlin, D. S., Rothman, K. J., & Willett, W. (1989). Multivitamin/folic acid supplementation in early pregnancy reduces the prevalence of neural tube defects. *JAMA: The Journal of* the American Medical Association, 262(20), 2847–2852.

Minke, K. M., & Anderson, K. J. (2005). Family-school collaboration and positive behavior support. *Journal of Positive Behavior Interventions, 7*(3), 181–185.

Moes, D. R. (1998). Integrating choice-making opportunities within teacher-assigned academic tasks to facilitate the performance of children with autism. *Research and Practice for Persons with Severe Disabilities, 23*(4), 319–328.

Moreno, G., & Gaytán, F. X. (2013). Focus on Latino learners: Developing a foundational understanding of Latino cultures to cultivate student success. *Preventing School Failure: Alternative Education for Children and Youth, 57*(1), 7–16.

Moreno, G., & Segura-Herrera, T. (2014). Special education referrals and disciplinary actions for Latino students in the United States. *Multicultural Learning and Teaching, 9*(1), 33–51.

Morrison, E. F., Rimm-Kauffman, S., & Pianta, R. C. (2003). A longitudinal study of mother–child interactions at school entry and social and academic outcomes in middle school. *Journal of School Psychology, 41*(3), 185–200.

Mulvaney, M. K., & Mebert, C. J. (2007). Parental corporal punishment predicts behavior problems in early childhood. *Journal of Family Psychology, 21*(3), 389–397.

Murray, F. B. (2007). Disposition: A superfluous construct in teacher education. *Journal of Teacher Education, 58*(5), 381–387.

Murray, M. M., & Mandell, C. J. (2006). On-the-job practices of early childhood special education providers trained in family-centered practices. *Journal of Early Intervention, 28*(2), 125–138.

Muscott, H. S., Pomerleau, T., & Szczesiul, S. (2009). Large-scale implementation of program-wide positive behavioral interventions and supports in early childhood education programs in New Hampshire. *National Head Start Association DIALOG, 12*(2), 148–169.

National Association for the Education of Young Children. (2017). *Principles of effective practice: Family engagement.* Retrieved from https://www.naeyc.org/familyengagement/principles

National Association of Child Care Resource and Referral Agencies (NACCRA). (2012). *Leaving children to chance: 2012 update.* Washington, DC: Author.

National Childhood Traumatic Stress Network. (2017). *Type of traumatic stress.* Retrieved from http://www.nctsn.org/trauma-types

National Council on Child Abuse and Family Violence. (2015). *Parental substance abuse a major factor in child abuse and neglect.* Retrieved from http://www.nccafv.org/parentalsubstanceabuse.htm

National Institute of Mental Health. (2017). *Major depression among adults.* Retrieved from https://www.nimh.nih.gov/health/statistics/prevalence/major-depression-among-adults.shtml

National Scientific Council on the Developing Child. (2008). *Mental health problems in early childhood can impair learning and behavior for life* (Working paper No. 6.). Retrieved from http://www.developingchild.net

Neal, J. W., & Neal, Z. P. (2013). Nested or networked? Future directions for ecological systems theory. *Social Development, 22*(4), 722–737.

Neitzel, J. (2011). Early indicators of developmental delays in infants and toddlers. *Perspectives on Language and Literacy, 37*(3), 25–26.

Neitzel, J., & Wolery, M. (2009). *Steps for implementation: Simultaneous prompting.* Chapel Hill, NC: National Professional Development Center on Autism Spectrum Disorders, Frank Porter Graham Child Development Institute, The University of North Carolina.

Nelson, J. R., Colvin, G., & Smith, D. J. (1996). The effects of setting clear standards on students' social behavior in common areas of the school. *The Journal of At-Risk Issues, 3*(1), 10–19.

Nese, R. N., & McIntosh, K. (2016). Do school-wide positive behavioral interventions and supports, not exclusionary discipline practices. In Bryan G. Cook, M. Tankersley, & T. J. Landrum (Eds.), *Instructional practices with and without empirical validity: Vol. 29. Advances in learning and behavioral disabilities* (pp. 175–196). Bingley, United Kingdom: Emerald Group Publishing Limited.

Neufeld, S. (2015). *Expelled in preschool.* Retrieved from http://hechingerreport.org/expelled-pre school/

Noguera, P. A. (2003). The trouble with black boys: The role and influence of environmental and cultural factors on the academic performance of African American males. *Urban Education, 38*(4), 431–459.

Norris, D. J. (2001). Quality of care offered by providers with differential patterns of workshop participation. *Child and Youth Care Forum, 30*(2), 111–121.

Nungesser, N. R., & Watkins, R. V. (2005). Preschool teachers' perceptions and reactions to challenging classroom behavior: Implications for speech-language pathologists. *Language, Speech, and Hearing Services in Schools, 36*(2), 139–151.

Odell, S. J. (1990). *Mentor teacher programs: What research says to the teacher.* Washington, DC: National Education Association (NEA).

Oden, S., & Asher, S. R. (1977). Coaching children in social skills for friendship making. *Child Development, 48*(2), 495–506.

OHS National Center on Parent, Family and Community Engagement. (2011). *Family Engagement and Ongoing Child Assessment series.* Retrieved from http://eclkc.ohs.acf.hhs.gov/hslc/tta-system/family/docs/family-engagement-and-ongoing-child-assessment-081111.pdf

Okado, Y., & Bierman, K. L. (2015). Differential risk for late adolescent conduct problems and mood dysregulation among children with early externalizing behavior problems. *Journal of Abnormal Child Psychology, 43*(4), 735–747.

Olsen, M., Astor, S., Booth-Miner, J., & Miner, S. (2007). Strengthening families: Community strategies that work. *Young Children, 62*(2), 26–32.

Orlando, R., & Bijou, S. W. (1960). Single and multiple schedules of reinforcement in developmentally retarded children. *Journal of the Experimental Analysis of Behavior, 3*(4), 339–348.

Palmer, S. B., Summers, J. A., Brotherson, M. J., Erwin, E. J., Maude, S. P., Stroup-Rentier, V., . . . & Chu, S. Y. (2012). Foundations for self-determination in early childhood: An inclusive model for children with disabilities. *Topics in Early Childhood Special Education, 33*(1), 38–47. doi:0271121412445288

Parry, P. A., & Douglas, V. I. (1983). Effects of reinforcement on concept identification in hyperactive children. *Journal of Abnormal Child Psychology, 11*(2), 327–340.

Patel, V., Flisher, A. J., Hetrick, S., & McGorry, P. (2007). Mental health of young people: A global public-health challenge. *The Lancet, 369*(9569), 1302–1313.

Patterson, G. R. (1982). *Coercive family process* (Vol. 3). Eugene, OR: Castalia Publishing Company.

Patterson, J. M. (2002). Integrating family resilience and family stress theory. *Journal of Marriage and Family, 64*(2), 349–360.

Peine, H. A. (n.d.). Utah Department of Health/CSHCN/ABLE Program, assessing positive and negative reinforcers in children (2–6). Retrieved from http://www.able-differently.org/wp-content/uploads/2012/01/Reinforcement_Survey_Ages_2-6.pdf

Pereira, J., Vickers, K., Atkinson, L., Gonzalez, A., Wekerle, C., & Levitan, R. (2012). Parenting stress mediates between maternal maltreatment history and maternal sensitivity in a community sample. *Child Abuse & Neglect, 36*(5), 433–437.

Perry, D. F. (2011). *Early Childhood Mental Health Consultation (ECMHC) Project: Standards for the State of Maryland.* Retrieved from http://earlychildhood.marylandpublicschools.org/system/files/filedepot/24/ecmhstand093009.pdf

Perry, D. F., Allen, M. D., Brennan, E. M., & Bradley, J. R. (2010). The evidence base for mental health consultation in early childhood settings: A research synthesis addressing children's behavioral outcomes. *Early Education and Development, 21*(6), 795–824.

Peth-Pierce, R. (2000). *A good beginning: Sending America's children to school with the social and emotional competence they need to succeed.* Bethesda, MD: National Institute of Mental Health.

Phillips, D. A., & Shonkoff, J. P. (Eds.). (2000). *From neurons to neighborhoods: The science of early childhood development.* Washington, D.C.: National Academies Press.

Pianta, R. C., Kraft-Sayre, M., Rimm-Kaufman, S., Gercke, N., & Higgins, T. (2001). Collaboration in building partnerships between families and schools: The national center for early development and learning's kindergarten transition intervention. *Early Childhood Research Quarterly, 16*(1), 117–132.

Pianta, R. C., Mashburn, A. J., Downer, J. T., Hamre, B. K., & Justice, L. (2008). Effects of web-mediated professional development resources on teacher-child interactions in pre-kindergarten classrooms. *Early Childhood Research Quarterly, 23*(4), 431–451.

Pica, R. (2006). Physical fitness and the early childhood curriculum. *Young Children, 61*(3), 12–19.

Plantin, L., & Daneback, K. (2009). Parenthood, information and support on the internet: A literature review of research on parents and professionals online. *BMC Family Practice, 10*(1), 34.

Positive Behavior Interventions and Supports. (2018). *PBIS and the law.* Retrieved from https://www.pbis.org/school/pbis-and-the-law

Poston, B. (2009). Maslow's hierarchy of needs. *Surgical Technologist, 41*(8), 347–353. Retrieved from http://www.ast.org/pdf/308.pdf

Poulou, M. (2005). Perceptions of students with emotional and behavioural difficulties: A study of prospective teachers in Greece. *Emotional and Behavioural Difficulties, 10*(2), 137–160.

Powell, D. S., Batsche, C. J., Ferro, J., Fox, L., & Dunlap, G. (1997). A strength-based approach in support of multi-risk families: Principles and issues. *Topics in Early Childhood Special Education, 17*(1), 1–26.

Powell, D., & Dunlap, G. (2009). *Evidence-based social-emotional curricula and intervention packages for children 0–5 years and their families (roadmap to effective intervention practices).* Tampa: University of South Florida, Technical Assistance Center on Social Emotional Intervention for Young Children. Retrieved from http://challengingbehavior.fmhi.usf.edu/do/resources/documents/roadmap_2.pdf

Powell, D. S., Fixsen, D. L., & Dunlap, G. (2003). *Pathways to service utilization: A synthesis of evidence relevant to young children with challenging behavior.* Tampa: University of South Florida, Center for Evidence-Based Practice: Young Children With Challenging Behavior.

Preston, D., & Carter, M. (2009). A review of the efficacy of the picture exchange communication system intervention. *Journal of Autism and Developmental Disorders, 39*(10), 1471–1486.

Ramsden, S. R., & Hubbard, J. A. (2002). Family expressiveness and parental emotion coaching: Their role in children's emotion regulation and aggression. *Journal of Abnormal Child Psychology, 30*(6), 657–667.

Raver, C. (2003). Young children's emotional development and school readiness. *Social Policy Report, 16*(3), 3–19.

Raver, C., & Spagnola, M. (2002). "When my mommy was angry, I was speechless": Children's perceptions of maternal emotional expressiveness within the context of economic hardship. *Marriage & Family Review, 34,* 63–88.

Raver, C. C., & Knitzer, J. (2002). *Ready to enter: What research tells policymakers about strategies to promote social and emotional school readiness among three- and four-year-old children.* Promoting the Emotional Well-Being of Children and Families (Policy Paper #3). New York, NY: National Center for Children in Poverty.

Raver, S. A., & Childress, D. C. (2014). *Collaboration and teamwork with families and professionals.*

Baltimore, MD: Paul H. Brookes Publishing Co. Retrieved from http://archive.brookespublishing.com/documents/collaboration-and-teamwork-with-families.pdf

Ray, R. A., & Street, A. F. (2005). Ecomapping: An innovative research tool for nurses. *Journal of Advanced Nursing, 50*(5), 545–552.

Reedy, C. K., & McGrath, W. H. (2010). Can you hear me now? Staff–parent communication in child care centres. *Early Child Development and Care, 180*(3), 347–357.

Reid, D. H., Everson, J. M., & Green, C. W. (1999). A systematic evaluation of preferences identified through person-centered planning for people with profound multiple disabilities. *Journal of Applied Behavior Analysis, 32*(4), 467–477.

Reinhartsen, D. B., Garfinkle, A. N., & Wolery, M. (2002). Engagement with toys in two-year-old children with autism: Teacher selection versus child choice. *Research and Practice for Persons with Severe Disabilities, 27*(3), 175–187.

Renk, K., Boris, N. W., Kolomeyer, E., Lowell, A., Puff, J., Cunningham, A., . . . & McSwiggan, M. (2016). The state of evidence-based parenting interventions for parents who are substance-involved. *Pediatric Research, 79*(1), 1–7.

Rimm-Kaufman, S. E., Larsen, R. A., Baroody, A. E., Curby, T. W., Ko, M., Thomas, J. B., . . . & DeCoster, J. (2014). Efficacy of the Responsive Classroom approach: Results from a 3-year, longitudinal randomized controlled trial. *American Educational Research Journal, 51*(3), 56–603.

Rispoli, M., Burke, M. D., Hatton, H., Ninci, J., Zaini, S., & Sanchez, L. (2015). Training Head Start teachers to conduct trial-based functional analysis of challenging behavior. *Journal of Positive Behavior Interventions.* doi:10.1177/1098300715577428.

Ritz, M., Noltemeyer, A., Davis, D., & Green, J. (2014). Behavior management in preschool classrooms: Insights revealed through systematic observation and interview. *Psychology in the Schools, 51*(2), 181–197.

Rodriguez, M., Ayduk, O., Aber, J., Mischel, W., Sethi, A., & Shoda, Y. (2005). A contextual approach to the development of self-regulatory competencies: The role of maternal unresponsivity and toddlers' negative affect in stressful situations. *Social Development, 14*(1), 136–157.

Rogers, S. J. (2000). Interventions that facilitate socialization in children with autism. *Journal of Autism and Developmental Disorders, 30*(5), 399–409.

Rogers, S. J., Hayden, D., Hepburn, S., Charlifue-Smith, R., Hall, T., & Hayes, A. (2006). Teaching young nonverbal children with autism useful speech: A pilot study of the Denver model and PROMPT interventions. *Journal of Autism and Developmental Disorders, 36*(8), 1007–1024.

Rogers, T. M. (2016). *The influence of caregiver mental health on parenting focused intervention service utilization and parenting behavior change* (Doctoral dissertation). Georgia State University, Atlanta.

Roskos, K. A., Christie, J. F., & Richgels, D. J. (2003). The essentials of early literacy instruction. *Young Children, 58*(2), 52–60.

Rowland, C. (2017). Communication Matrix [Web site]. *Design to learn projects at Oregon Health & Science University.* Retrieved from https://communicationmatrix.org/

Rubin, K. H. (1998). Social and emotional development from a cultural perspective. *Developmental Psychology, 34*(4), 611–615.

Ruef, M. B., Higgins, C., Glaeser, B. J., & Patnode, M. (1998). Positive behavioral support: Strategies for teachers. *Intervention in School and Clinic, 34*(1), 21–32.

Runswick-Cole, K. (2007). *Parents as advocates: The experiences of parents who register an appeal with the Special Educational Needs and Disability Tribunal (SENDisT)* (Doctoral thesis). The University of Sheffield, United Kingdom.

Rush, D. D., Shelden, M. L., & Hanft, B. E. (2003). Coaching families and colleagues: A process for collaboration in natural settings. *Infants and Young Children, 16*, 33–47.

Rush, D. D., & Shelden, M. L. L. (2011). *The early childhood coaching handbook.* Baltimore, MD: Paul H. Brookes Publishing Co.

Russell, J. A. (2012). Introduction to special section: On defining emotion. *Emotion Review, 4*(4), 337.

Ryan, J. B., Sanders, S., Katsiyannis, A., & Yell, M. L. (2007). Using time-out effectively in the classroom. *Teaching Exceptional Children, 39*(4), 60–67.

Ryan, S., & Cole, K. R. (2009). From advocate to activist? Mapping the experiences of mothers of children on the autism spectrum. *Journal of Applied Research in Intellectual Disabilities, 22*(1), 43–53.

Saarni, C. (1999). *The development of emotional competence.* New York, NY: Guilford Press.

Safran, S. P., & Oswald, K. (2003). Positive behavior supports: Can schools reshape disciplinary practices? *Exceptional Children, 69*(3), 361–373.

Salazar, M. J. (2012). Home–school collaboration for embedding individualized goals in daily routines. *Young Exceptional Children.* doi:1096250612446870. Retrieved from https://www.utoledo.edu/education/grants/partner-project/focus/docs/home-school%20collaboration.pdf

Salzinger, S., Feldman, R. S., Hammer, M., & Rosario, M. (1993). The effects of physical abuse on children's social relationships. *Child Development, 64*(1), 169–187.

Sameroff, A. (Ed). (2009). *The transactional model of development: How children and contexts shape each other* (pp. 3–21). Washington, DC: American Psychological Association.

Sameroff, A. J., & Chandler, M. J. (1975). Reproductive risk and the continuum of caretaking casualty. In F. D. Horowitz, M. Hetherington, S. Scarr-Salapatek, & G. Siegel (Eds.), *Review of child development research* (Vol. 4). Chicago, IL: University of Chicago Press.

Sandall, S. R., & Schwartz, I. S. (2008). *Building blocks for teaching preschoolers with special needs* (2nd ed.). Baltimore, MD: Paul H. Brookes Publishing Co.

Sansosti, F. J., Powell-Smith, K. A., & Kincaid, D. (2004). A research synthesis of social story interventions for children with autism spectrum disorders. *Focus on Autism and Other Developmental Disabilities, 19*(4), 194–204.

Scaramella, L. V., & Leve, L. D. (2004). Clarifying parent–child reciprocities during early childhood: The early childhood coercion model. *Clinical Child and Family Psychology Review, 7*(2), 89–107.

Schaefer, J. D., Caspi, A., Belsky, D. W., Harrington, H., Houts, R., Horwood, L. J., . . . & Moffitt, T. E. (2017). Enduring mental health: Prevalence and prediction. *Journal of Abnormal Psychology, 126*(2), 212–224.

Schickedanz, J. A. (2014). Rethinking story reading in U.S. preschools: Making story comprehension and social-emotional understanding the priority. *Asia-Pacific Journal of Research in Early Childhood Education, 8*(2), 5–25.

Schim, S. M., & Doorenbos, A. Z. (2010). A three-dimensional model of cultural congruence: Framework for intervention. *Journal of Social Work in End-of-Life & Palliative Care, 6*(3–4), 256–270.

Schneider, R., Yurovsky, D., & Frank, M. C. (2015). *Large-scale investigations of variability in children's first words*. Proceedings of the 37th Annual Conference of the Cognitive Science Society, Cognitive Science Society, Austin, TX.

Schofield, T. J., Conger, R. D., & Conger, K. J. (2016). Disrupting intergenerational continuity in harsh parenting: Self-control and a supportive partner. *Development and Psychopathology, 29*(4), 1–9.

Schore, A. N. (2015). *Affect regulation and the origin of the self: The neurobiology of emotional development*. New York, NY: Routledge.

Schwartz, I. S., & Baer, D. M. (1991). Social validity assessments: Is current practice state of the art? *Journal of Applied Behavior Analysis, 24*(2), 189–204.

Scott, T. M., Anderson, C. M., & Spaulding, S. A. (2008). Strategies for developing and carrying out functional assessment and behavior intervention planning. *Preventing School Failure: Alternative Education for Children and Youth, 52*(3), 39–50.

Sethna, V., Murray, L., Netsi, E., Psychogiou, L., & Ramchandani, P. G. (2015). Paternal depression in the postnatal period and early father–infant interactions. *Parenting, 15*(1), 1–8.

Sette, S., Spinrad, T. L., & Baumgartner, E. (2016). The relations of preschool children's emotion knowledge and socially appropriate behaviors to peer likability. *International Journal of Behavioral Development, 4*(41), 532–541. doi:10.1177/0165025416645667

Shackman, J. E., & Pollak, S. D. (2014). Impact of physical maltreatment on the regulation of negative affect and aggression. *Development and Psychopathology, 26*(4pt1), 1021–1033.

Shavelson, R., & Towne, L. (2002). *Scientific research in education*. Washington, DC: National Academy Press.

Shaw, D. S., Connell, A., Dishion, T. J., Wilson, M. N., & Gardner, F. (2009). Improvements in maternal depression as a mediator of intervention effects on early childhood problem behavior. *Development and Psychopathology, 21*(02), 417–439.

Shearer, M. S., & Shearer, D. E. (1972). The Portage project: A model for early childhood education. *Exceptional Children, 39*(3), 210–217.

Sheridan, S. M., Edwards, C. P., Marvin, C. A., & Knoche, L. L. (2009). Professional development in early childhood programs: Process issues and research needs. *Early Education and Development, 20*(3), 377–401.

Shevin, M., & Klein, N. K. (1984). The importance of choice-making skills for students with severe disabilities. *Research and Practice for Persons with Severe Disabilities, 9*(3), 159–166.

Shonkoff, J.P., Garner, A.S., Siegel, B.S., Dobbins, M.I., Earls, M. F., McGuinn, L., . . . & Wood, D. L. (2012). The lifelong effects of early childhood adversity and toxic stress. *Pediatrics, 129*(1), e232–e246.

Shonkoff, J. P., & Phillips, D. A. (Eds.). (2000). *From neurons to neighborhoods: The science of early childhood development*. Washington, DC: National Academies Press.

Shulman, C. (2016). Social and cultural contexts in infant and early childhood mental health. In A. Ben-Arieh (Series Ed.) & C. Shulman, *Research and practice in infant and early childhood mental health*: Vol. 13. *Children's well-being: Indicators and research* (pp. 43–65). New York, NY: Springer.

SIDRAN Institute for Traumatic Stress Education and Advocacy. (2016). *The post-traumatic stress disorder fact sheet*. Retrieved from https://www.sidran.org/resources/for-survivors-and-loved-ones/post-traumatic-stress-disorder-fact-sheet

Sigman, M. D., Kasari, C., Kwon, J. H., & Yirmiya, N. (1992). Responses to the negative emotions of others by autistic, mentally retarded, and normal children. *Child Development, 63*(4), 796–807.

Singh, N. N., Lancioni, G. E., Winton, A. S., Singh, J., Curtis, W. J., Wahler, R. G., & McAleavey, K. M. (2007). Mindful parenting decreases aggression and increases social behavior in children with developmental disabilities. *Behavior Modification, 31*(6), 749–771.

Siry, C., Ziegler, G., & Max, C. (2012). "Doing science" through discourse-in-interaction: Young children's science investigations at the early childhood level. *Science Education, 96*(2), 311–326.

Skaalvik, E. M., & Skaalvik, S. (2007). Dimensions of teacher self-efficacy and relations with strain factors, perceived collective teacher efficacy, and teacher burnout. *Journal of Educational Psychology, 99*(3), 611–625.

Skinner, B. F. (2014). *Contingencies of reinforcement: A theoretical analysis* (Vol. 3). Cambridge, MA: B.F. Skinner Foundation.

Smalls, K. J. (2013). A comparison of workshop training versus intensive, experiential training for improving behavior support skills in early educators. *Early Childhood Research Quarterly, 28*(2), 450–460.

Smith, A., & Bondy, E. (2007). "No! I won't!" Understanding and responding to student defiance. *Childhood Education, 83*(3), 151–157.

Smith, A. A., & Hubbard, P. M. (1988). The relationship between parent/staff communication and children's behaviour in early childhood settings. *Early Child Development and Care, 35*(1), 13–28.

Smith, C. L., Calkins, S. D., Keane, S. P., Anastopoulos, A. D., & Shelton, T. L. (2004). Predicting stability and change in toddler behavior problems: Contributions of maternal behavior and child gender. *Developmental Psychology, 40*(1), 29–42.

Smith, J. D., Dishion, T. J., Shaw, D. S., Wilson, M. N., Winter, C. C., & Patterson, G. R. (2014). Coercive family process and early-onset conduct problems from age 2 to school entry. *Development and Psychopathology, 26*(4Pt1), 917–932.

Smith, S. W., Lochman, J. E., & Daunic, A. P. (2005). Managing aggression using cognitive-behavioral interventions: State of the practice and future directions. *Behavioral Disorders,* 227–240.

Snyder, J., Edwards, P., McGraw, K., Kilgore, K., & Holten, A. (1993). *Escalation and reinforcement in family conflict: Development origins of physical aggression.* Wichita: Kansas State University.

Sobel, A. & Kugler, E. G. (2007). Building partnerships with immigrant parents. *Educational Leadership, 64*(6), 62–66. Retrieved from http://www.ritell.org/resources/Pictures/Fall%202016%20Conference%20Resources/Building-PartnershipsWImmigrantParents.Ed_Leadership.pdf

Son, H., & Sung, J. (2014). The effects of teacher's self-efficacy on children's sociality: The serial multiple mediating effects of job-satisfaction and the quality of teacher-child interaction. *Korean Journal of Child Studies, 35*(2), 191–209.

Soodak, L. C., & Erwin, E. J. (2000). Valued member or tolerated participant: Parents' experiences in inclusive early childhood settings. *Research and Practice for Persons with Severe Disabilities, 25*(1), 29–41.

Spiker, D., Hebbeler, K., Wagner, M., Cameto, R., & McKenna, P. (2000). A framework for describing variations in state early intervention systems. *Topics in Early Childhood Special Education, 20*(4), 195–207.

Spinrad, T. L., Eisenberg, N., Gaertner, B., Popp, T., Smith, C. L., Kupfer, A., . . . & Hofer, C. (2007). Relations of maternal socialization and toddlers' effortful control to children's adjustment and social competence. *Developmental Psychology, 43*(5), 1170–1186.

Spriggs, A. D., Gast, D. L., & Ayres, K. M. (2007). Using picture activity schedule books to increase on-schedule and on-task behaviors. *Education and Training in Developmental Disabilities,* 209–223.

Squires, J., Bricker, D., & Twombly, E. (2015). *ASQ-SE-2™ User's Guide.* Baltimore, MD: Paul H. Brookes Publishing Co.

Squires, J., Bricker, D., Waddell, M., Funk, K., Clifford, J., & Hoselton, R. (2014). *Social-Emotional Assessment/Evaluation Measure (SEAM™),* Research Edition. Baltimore, MD: Paul H. Brookes Publishing Co.

Stanulis, R. N., & Manning, B. H. (2002). The teacher's role in creating a positive verbal and nonverbal environment in the early childhood classroom. *Early Childhood Education Journal, 30*(1), 3–8.

Stayton, V. D. (2015). Preparation of early childhood special educators for inclusive and interdisciplinary settings. *Infants & Young Children, 28*(2), 113–122.

Steed, E. A., & Durand, V. M. (2013). Optimistic teaching: Improving the capacity for teachers to reduce young children's challenging behavior. *School Mental Health, 5*(1), 15–24.

Stefanidis, A., & Strogilos, V. (2015). Union gives strength: Mainstream and special education teachers' responsibilities in inclusive co-taught classrooms. *Educational Studies, 41*(4), 393–413.

Stein, N. L., Leventhal, B., & Trabasso, T. R. (Eds.). (2013). *Psychological and biological approaches to emotion.* New York, NY: Psychology Press.

Stockall, N. S., Dennis, L., & Miller, M. (2012). Right from the start: Universal design for preschool. *Teaching Exceptional Children, 45*(1), 10–17.

Stormont, M., Lewis, T. J., & Beckner, R. (2005). Positive behavior support systems: Applying key features in preschool settings. *Teaching Exceptional Children, 37*(6), 42–49.

Straus, M. A. (2000). Corporal punishment and primary prevention of physical abuse. *Child Abuse & Neglect, 24*(9), 1109–1114.

Straus, M. A. (2001). *Beating the devil out of them: Physical punishment in American families* (2nd ed.). New Brunswick, NJ: Transaction Publishers.

Stremmel, A. J., Benson, M. J., & Powell, D. R. (1993). Communication, satisfaction, and emotional exhaustion among child care center staff: Directors, teachers, and assistant teachers. *Early Childhood Research Quarterly, 8*(2), 221–233.

Substance Abuse and Mental Health Services Administration. (2016). *Mental and substance abuse disorders.* Retrieved from https://www.samhsa.gov/disorders

Sugai, G., & Horner, R. (2002). The evolution of discipline practices: School-wide positive behavior supports. *Child & Family Behavior Therapy, 24*(1–2), 23–50.

Summers, J. A., Hoffman, L., Marquis, J., Turnbull, A., Poston, D., & Nelson, L. L. (2005). Measuring the quality of family–professional partnerships in special education services. *Exceptional Children, 72*(1), 65–81.

Summers, J. A., Marquis, J., Mannan, H., Turnbull, A. P., Fleming, K., Poston, D. J., . . . & Kupzyk, K. (2007). Relationship of perceived adequacy of services, family–professional partnerships, and family quality of life in early childhood service programmes. *International Journal of Disability, Development, and Education, 54*(3), 319–338.

Sutton, R. E., & Wheatley, K. F. (2003). Teachers' emotions and teaching: A review of the literature and directions for future research. *Educational Psychology Review, 15*(4), 327–358.

Swaggart, B. L., Gagnon, E., Bock, S. J., Earles, T. L., Quinn, C., Myles, B. S., & Simpson, R. L. (1995). Using social stories to teach social and behavioral skills to children with autism. *Focus on Autistic Behavior, 10*(1), 1–16.

Swartz, M. I., & Easterbrooks, M. A. (2014). The role of parent, provider, and child characteristics in parent–provider relationships in infant and toddler classrooms. *Early Education and Development, 25*(4), 573–598.

Swartz, R. A., & McElwain, N. L. (2012). Preservice teachers' emotion-related regulation and cognition: Associations with teachers' responses to children's emotions in early childhood classrooms. *Early Education & Development, 23*(2), 202–226.

Swick, K. J., & Williams, R. D. (2006). An analysis of Bronfenbrenner's bio-ecological perspective for early childhood educators: Implications for working with families experiencing stress. *Early Childhood Education Journal, 33*(5), 371–378.

Symons, F. J., McDonald, L. M., & Wehby, J. H. (1998). Functional assessment and teacher collected data. *Education and Treatment of Children, 21*(2), 135–159.

Technical Assistance Center on Social Emotional Intervention for Young Children. (2011). *Home page.* Retrieved from http://challengingbehavior.fmhi.usf.edu

The Fred Rogers Company. (2017). *Dealing with death* [Online resource]. Retrieved from http://www.fredrogers.org/parents/special-challenges/death.php

Trivette, C. M., Dunst, C. J., & Hamby, D. W. (2010). Influences of family-systems intervention practices on parent-child interactions and child development. *Topics in Early Childhood Special Education, 30*(1), 3–19.

Troster, H., & Brambring, M. (1992). Early social-emotional development in blind infants. *Child: Care, Health and Development, 18*(4), 207–227.

Tschantz, J. M., & Vail, C. O. (2000). Effects of peer coaching on the rate of responsive teacher statements during a child-directed period in an inclusive preschool setting. *Teacher Education and Special Education: The Journal of the Teacher Education Division of the Council for Exceptional Children, 23*(3), 189–201.

Tullis, C. A., Cannella-Malone, H. I., Basbigill, A. R., Yeager, A., Fleming, C. V., Payne, D., & Wu, P. F. (2011). Review of the choice and preference assessment literature for individuals with severe to profound disabilities. *Education and Training in Autism and Developmental Disabilities, 46*(4), 576–595.

Tuominen, M. C. (2003). *We are not babysitters: Family childcare providers redefine work and care.* New Brunswick, NJ: Rutgers University Press.

Turnbull, A. A., Turnbull, H. R., Erwin, E. J., Soodak, L. C., & Shogren, K. A. (2015). *Families, professionals, and exceptionality: Positive outcomes through partnerships and trust.* Columbus, OH: Pearson.

Turnbull, A., Turnbull, H. R., Wehmeyer, M. L., & Shogren, K. A. (2013). *Exceptional lives: Special education in today's schools.* Columbus, OH: Pearson.

Ursache, A., Blair, C., Stifter, C., & Voegtline, K. (2013). Emotional reactivity and regulation in infancy interact to predict executive functioning in early childhood. *Developmental Psychology, 49*(1), 127–137.

Vail, C. O., Tschantz, J. M., & Bevill, A. (1997). Dyads and data in peer coaching: Early childhood educators in action. *Teaching Exceptional Children, 30*(2), 11–13.

Van Acker, R., Boreson, L., Gable, R. A., & Potterton, T. (2005). Are we on the right course? Lessons learned about current FBA/BIP practices in schools. *Journal of Behavioral Education, 14*(1), 35–56.

Vandell, D. L. (1996). Characteristics of infant child care: Factors contributing to positive caregiving: NICHD early child care research network. *Early Childhood Research Quarterly, 11*(3), 269–306.

van Randenborgh, A., Hüffmeier, J., Victor, D., Klocke, K., Borlinghaus, J., & Pawelzik, M. (2012). Contrasting chronic with episodic depression: An analysis of distorted socio-emotional information processing in chronic depression. *Journal of Affective Disorders, 141*(2), 177–184.

Van Ryzin, M. J., Kumpfer, K. L., Fosco, G. M., & Greenberg, M. T. (Eds.). (2015). *Family-based prevention programs for children and adolescents: Theory, research, and large-scale dissemination.* New York, NY: Psychology Press.

Vargo, K. K., Heal, N. A., Epperley, K., & Kooistra, E. (2014). The effects of a multiple schedule plus rules on hand raising during circle time in preschool classrooms. *Journal of Behavioral Education, 23*(3), 326–343.

Verdugo, R. R. (2002). Race-ethnicity, social class, and zero-tolerance policies: The cultural and structural wars. *Education and Urban Society, 35,* 50–75.

Vig, S., Chinitz, S., & Shulman, L. (2005). Young children in foster care: Multiple vulnerabilities and complex service needs. *Infants & Young Children, 18*(2), 147–160.

Vilardo, B. A., DuPaul, G. J., Kern, L., & Hojnoski, R. L. (2013). Cross-age peer coaching: Enhancing the peer interactions of children exhibiting symptoms of ADHD. *Child & Family Behavior Therapy, 35*(1), 63–81.

Vinh, M., Strain, P., Davidon, S., & Smith, B. J. (2016). One state's systems change efforts to reduce child care expulsion taking the Pyramid Model to scale. *Topics in Early Childhood Special Education, 36,* 159–164. doi:10.1177/0271121415626130.

Viola, T. W., Salum, G. A., Kluwe-Schiavon, B., Sanvicente-Vieira, B., Levandowski, M. L., & Grassi-Oliveira, R. (2016). The influence of geographical and economic factors in estimates of childhood abuse and neglect using the childhood trauma questionnaire: A worldwide meta-regression analysis. *Child Abuse & Neglect, 51,* 1–11.

Vismara, L. A., Colombi, C., & Rogers, S. J. (2009). Can one hour per week of therapy lead to lasting changes in young children with autism? *Autism, 13*(1), 93–115.

Vogel, D. L., Heimerdinger-Edwards, S. R., Hammer, J. H., & Hubbard, A. (2011). "Boys don't cry": Examination of the links between endorsement of masculine norms, self-stigma, and help-seeking attitudes for men from diverse backgrounds. *Journal of Counseling Psychology, 58*(3), 368–382.

Voorhees, M. D., Walker, V. L., Snell, M. E., & Smith, C. G. (2013). A demonstration of individualized positive behavior support interventions by Head Start staff to address children's challenging behavior. *Research and Practice for Persons with Severe Disabilities, 38*(3), 173–185.

Vygotsky, L. S., Luria, A. R., & Knox, J. E. (2013). *Studies on the history of behavior: Ape, primitive, and child.* New York, NY: Psychology Press.

Waanders, C., Mendez, J. L., & Downer, J. T. (2007). Parent characteristics, economic stress and neighborhood context as predictors of parent involvement in preschool children's education. *Journal of School Psychology, 45*(6), 619–636.

Wagner, M., & Davis, M. (2006). How are we preparing students with emotional disturbances for the transition to young adulthood? Findings from the National Longitudinal Transition Study—2. *Journal of Emotional and Behavioral Disorders, 14*(2), 86–98.

Watson, T. S., & Steege, M. W. (2003). *The Guilford practical intervention in the schools series. Conducting school-based functional behavioral assessments: A practitioner's guide.* New York, NY: Guilford Press.

Weaver, J., Filson Moses, J., & Snyder, M. (2016). Self-fulfilling prophecies in ability settings. *The Journal of Social Psychology, 156*(2), 179–189.

Weber, A., Fernald, A., & Diop, Y. (2016). When cultural norms discourage talking to babies: Effectiveness of a parenting program in rural Senegal. *Child Development,* doi:10.1111/cdev.12882

Webster-Stratton, C. (1990). Stress: A potential disruptor of parent perceptions and family interactions. *Journal of Clinical Child Psychology, 19*(4), 302–312.

Webster-Stratton, C. (2015). The Incredible Years series: A developmental approach. In M. Van Ryzin, K. Kumpfer, G. Fosco, & M. Greenberg (Eds.), *Family-based prevention programs for children and adolescents: Theory, research, and large-scale dissemination* (pp. 42–67). New York, NY: Psychology Press.

Webster-Stratton, C., & Reid, M. J. (2004). Strengthening social and emotional competence in young children—the foundation for early school readiness and success: Incredible years classroom social skills and problem-solving curriculum. *Infants & Young Children, 17*(2), 96–113.

Webster-Stratton, C., Reid, J. M., & Stoolmiller, M. (2008). Preventing conduct problems and improving school readiness: Evaluation of the incredible years teacher and child training programs in high-risk schools. *Journal of Child Psychology and Psychiatry, 49*(5), 471–488.

Wehmeyer, M., & Schwartz, M. (1997). Self-determination and positive adult outcomes: A follow-up study of youth with mental retardation or learning disabilities. *Exceptional Children, 63*(2), 245–255.

Weisz, J. R., Suwanlert, S., Chaiyasit, W., Weiss, B., Walter, B. R., & Anderson, W. W. (1988). Thai and American perspectives on over- and under-controlled child behavior problems: Exploring the threshold model among parents, teachers, and psychologists. *Journal of Consulting and Clinical Psychology, 56*(4), 601–609.

Weller, L., & Aminadav, C. (1989). Attitudes towards mild and severe mental handicap in Israel. *Psychology and Psychotherapy: Theory, Research and Practice, 62*(3), 273–280.

Wheeler, J. J., & Richey, D. D. (2010). *Behavior management: Principles and practices of positive behavior supports* (2nd ed.). Upper Saddle River, NJ: Pearson.

Wheeler, J. J., & Richey, D. D. (2014). *Behavior management: Principles and practices of positive behavior supports* (3rd ed.). Boston, MA: Pearson.

Whipple, W., et al. (2012). *Key principles of early intervention and effective practices: A crosswalk with statements from discipline-specific literature.* Retrieved from http://ecpcta.org/resources-eci/wp-content/uploads/sites/1337/2015/07/Wendy_Whipple-KeyPrinciplesEI_effectivepractices.pdf

Wiefferink, C. H., Rieffe, C., Ketelaar, L., De Raeve, L., & Frijns, J. H. (2013). Emotion understanding in deaf children with a cochlear implant. *Journal of Deaf Studies and Deaf Education, 18*(2), 175–186.

Wilks, T., Gerber, R. J., & Erdie-Lalena, C. (2010). Developmental milestones: Cognitive development. *Pediatrics in Review, 31*(9), 364–367.

Williams, J. M. G., & Kabat-Zinn, J. (2013). *Mindfulness: Diverse perspectives on its meaning, origins and applications.* New York, NY: Routledge.

Williford, A. P., & Shelton, T. L. (2014). Behavior management for preschool-aged children. *Child and Adolescent Psychiatric Clinics of North America, 23*(4), 717–730.

Willig, J. H., Krawitz, M., Panjamapirom, A., Ray, M. N., Nevin, C. R., English, T. M., . . . & Berner, E. S. (2013). Closing the feedback loop: An interactive voice response system to provide follow-up and feedback in primary care settings. *Journal of Medical Systems, 37*(2), 9905.

Wilson, B. J., Fernandes-Richards, S., Aarskog, C, Osborn, T, & Capetillo, D. (2007). The role of emotion regulation in the social problems of boys with developmental delays. *Early Education and Development, 18*(2), 201–222.

Wilson, K. R., Havighurst, S. S., & Harley, A. E. (2012). Tuning in to kids: An effectiveness trial of a parenting program targeting emotion socialization of preschoolers. *Journal of Family Psychology, 26*(1), 56–65.

Wong, C. (2013). A play and joint attention intervention for teachers of young children with autism: A randomized controlled pilot study. *Autism, 3*(17), 340–357. doi:10.1177/1362361312474723.

Wood, R. (2015). To be cared for and to care: Understanding theoretical conceptions of care as a framework for effective inclusion in early childhood education and care. *Child Care in Practice, 21*(3), 256–265.

World Health Organization. (2001). *The World Health Report 2001: Mental health: New understanding, new hope.* World Health Organization.

Wulczyn, F. (2004). Family reunification. *The Future of Children, 14,* 95–113.

Yoon, J. (2002). Teacher characteristics as predictors of teacher-student relationships: Stress, negative affect, and self-efficacy. *Social Behavior and Personality: An International Journal, 30*(5), 485–493.

Yost, D. S. (2006). Reflection and self-efficacy: Enhancing the retention of qualified teachers from a teacher education perspective. *Teacher Education Quarterly, 33*(4), 59–76.

Zaslow, M., Tout, K., Halle, T., Whittaker, J. V., & Lavelle, B. (2010). *Toward the identification of features of effective professional development for early childhood educators: Literature review.* Washington, DC: Office of Planning, Evaluation and Policy Development, U.S. Department of Education.

Zembylas, M. (2007). Emotional ecology: The intersection of emotional knowledge and pedagogical content knowledge in teaching. *Teaching and Teacher Education, 23*(4), 355–367.

ZERO TO THREE. (2016). National Caregiver Survey. *Tuning in: Parents of young children tell us what they think, know, and need.* Retrieved from https://www.zerotothree.org/resources/series/tuning-in-parents-of-young-children-tell-us-what-they-think-know-and-need

Zimmermann, P., & Iwanski, A. (2014). Emotion regulation from early adolescence to emerging adulthood and middle adulthood: Age differences, gender differences, and emotion-specific developmental variations. *International Journal of Behavioral Development, 38*(2), 182–194.

Zins, J. E., Weissberg, R. P., Wang, M. C., & Walberg, H. J. (Eds.). (2004). *Building academic success on social and emotional learning: What does the research say?* New York, NY: Teachers College Press.

Zinsser, K. M., Christensen, C. G., & Torres, L. (2016). She's supporting them; who's supporting her? Preschool center-level social-emotional supports and teacher well-being. *Journal of School Psychology, 59,* 55–66.

Index

Page numbers followed *f* and *t* indicate figures and tables, respectively.